n

S T S S
STAGE and SCREEN STUDIES

Volume 6

Edited by
Kenneth Richards

PETER LANG
Oxford · Bern · Berlin · Bruxelles · Frankfurt am Main · New York · Wien

Mark Taylor-Batty

Roger Blin

Collaborations and Methodologies

PETER LANG

Oxford • Bern • Berlin • Bruxelles • Frankfurt am Main • New York • Wien

Bibliographic information published by Die Deutsche Bibliothek
Die Deutsche Bibliothek lists this publication in the Deutsche National-
bibliografie; detailed bibliographic data is available on the Internet at
‹http:/dnb.ddb.de›.

British Library and Library of Congress Cataloguing-in-Publication Data:
A catalogue record for this book is available from *The British Library,*
Great Britain, and from *The Library of Congress,* USA

ISSN 1660-2560
ISBN 978-3-03-910502-1
US-ISBN 978-0-8204-7508-0

© Peter Lang AG, European Academic Publishers, Bern 2007
Hochfeldstrasse 32, Postfach 746, CH-3000 Bern 9, Switzerland
info@peterlang.com, www.peterlang.com, www.peterlang.net

Printed in Germany

Contents

Acknowledgements

I am extremely grateful to Donald Roy, my principal source of encouragement and motivation.

Thanks also to David Bradby, whose gentle encouragement and desire to see this volume produced has been a keen motivating factor.

For accepting to meet me and share with me their memories of Roger Blin, I should also like to thank André and Barbara Acquart, Jean Duvignaud, Isabelle Famchon, Hermine Karagheuz, Eduardo Manet, Jean Martin, Matias and Chantal Petit. Thanks too to Juliette Taylor-Batty for her invaluable advice on some details of translation. My gratitude also extends to Stephen Barber, Michel Bataillon, Noël Blin, Albert Dichy and the staff of the Institut Mémoires de l'édition contemporaine, Éléonore Hirt, James Knowlson, Mrs J. Ladds and Mrs E. Lancaster, Lois Overbeck, Roger Planchon, Mlle Pocheau and the staff of the Bibliothèque Nationale, Département des arts du spectacle. Thank you to Alexis Kirschbaum and Alan Mauro. For their direct or indirect help, my thanks also goes to Claudine Bitbol, Caroline Christie, Christina Dackéus, Louise Dadd, Eve Doe-Bruce, Catherine Greensmith, Gaynor Johnson, Ian Morgan, Niru Nityanandan, Terence Raghunath, Helen and Larry Seibenmann, Roger Whitehouse, Arianne, Emma, Gareth, Helen and Noreen.

Introduction

Roger Paul Jules Blin was born in his childhood home of 3 avenue de Madrid in the Parisian suburb of Neuilly-sur-Seine on 22 March 1907, the first of five children to enter the modest, comfortable household of Paul and Marthe Blin. In that opening decade of the last century, the very craft of stage directing as we know it today was still very much in its infancy. Just five miles from Neuilly and exactly twenty years before Blin's first breaths, the man held to be the first true modern director, André Antoine, had opened the doors to his experimental theatre project, the Théâtre Libre, in a small rented hall in the Passage de l'Elysée des Beaux-Arts, Montmartre. There, the first seeds of the then cutting-edge practices of stage Naturalism were sewn, initiating a chain of fringe theatre arts movements that would have a huge impact upon twentieth-century European stage practice. As Naturalism took root on Parisian stages, Symbolist poets sought to check its growth; by the 1890s men such as Paul Fort and Antoine's student Aurélien Lugné-Poë had established forums for experimental work and foreign innovations at the Théâtre d'Art and Théâtre de l'Œuvre. It was on the stage of l'Œuvre, a decade before Blin's birth, that Alfred Jarry's creation Ubu first roared his ignoble, blood-thirsty oaths, effectively raising the curtain on twentieth-century avant-garde drama. Independent theatre movements such as these sprung up like mushrooms in the darker side streets of Paris, mostly in the regions south of the Seine, and in these new rehearsal environments the figure of the director was slowly evolving. By the time Blin was to turn to the performance arts as a young man in the 1930s, various cultures of anti-commercial, avant-garde experimentation were very firmly established.

In the last decades of nineteenth-century Europe, the theatre was the mass entertainment environment of the age, much as television is today, and just as many might now bemoan the 'dumbing-down' of contemporary broadcasting in plot-thin soap operas or the easy appeal of 'reality TV', commentators in late nineteenth-century Paris sought out forums where fresh ideas and new writing could be exposed to new audiences, rejecting the structures and ethos of the commercial stage offerings of nightly distractions in the plush theatres of the Right Bank boulevards, or the equally lucrative vaudeville farces and operettas. There was a theatre led by commercially-driven actor-managers, with a repertoire dictated by the audience-pulling names of a few successful writers and the attraction of important star actors. The cult of celebrity reigned, and the value of a play script was considered secondary to the box-office potential of stars such as Aimée Desclée and Sarah Bernhardt. Successful playwrights were those that wrote to a formula known to appeal to the middle-class audiences who sought pre-supper distraction in easily digestible performances. Eugène Scribe, arguably the most popular French writer of the nineteenth century, wrote over a hundred plays of the 'well made' type. This was a theatre of immediate realism, by which was understood a credible representation of recognisable characters in credible situations. Victorien Sardou and Eugène Labiche did much to sculpt the French playwriting standard of the latter half of the nineteenth century, capitalising on Scribe's legacy to create what became a mainstream theatre of fluid, witty dialogue and complex plots in which action was constructed from intrigues and misunderstandings.

Whilst much of this writing did not preclude some social commentary, many decried the manner in which the commercial stage stifled the nobler artistic objectives of examining human truth. The Naturalist movement, inspired in part by Charles Darwin's recently published theories on how environment influences individual and group development, had already begun by the 1870s to have a significant influence on the disciplines of sociology and history, on the visual arts and, of course, on the novel in works by writers such as Gustave Flaubert, the Goncourt brothers and Émile Zola. In his 'Le Naturalisme au theatre' (1881) Zola appealed for a man of genius to apply his naturalistic premises to the art of drama, and consequently to awaken the theatre from its slumber of bourgeois comedy and light drama. It was not a playwright who answered this call, but in taking up the cause of Naturalism in the theatre, André Antoine made significant steps in defining the role of the modern director.

The recognised need for a director figure had evolved most certainly as a result of the fashions for greater verisimilitude in stage representations of life that had developed over the century, greatly assisted by the improvement of the technologies, such as gas lighting, that assisted in the creation of more and more realistic illusions. In order to oversee the various facets of theatrical illusion and ensure a unity of vision and purpose, a central controlling figure, was deemed necessary. Innovators such as Duke Georg II of Saxe-Meiningen exposed theatrical representation to the detail of precise historical research, took control of the proper integration of two and three-dimensional scenic elements and made significant organisational innovations in the choreography of crowd scenes. His popular and acclaimed European tours of Shakespeare and Classical works (1874–90) helped to establish the recognised benefits of an artistic overseer in theatrical production. Meiningen undermined the logic of the star-system, obliging his actors to take both lead and secondary roles and establishing a practice of ensemble acting that served, along with all his other innovations, to bring the artistic possibilities at his disposal to the service of the text.

The centrality of text was therefore also a key component in the development of the role of the director, and was certainly a key motivation for Antoine and other European innovators such as Otto Brahm in Berlin and Konstantin Stanislavsky in Moscow, all of whom were impressed by the work of the Meiningen troupe and each determined in their own way to provide some small antidote to the excesses of commercial stage practice. Encouraging new writing went hand in hand with the innovations in stage practice these men pursued, and the question of interpretation – of how the new texts should be transferred from ink to gesture, tone, image and choreography – became key to their individual achievements.

In France, the Naturalist movement in the theatre, and the Symbolist reaction that followed hard on its heels, did a great deal not only to promote new writing, to create forums for the presentation of innovative foreign writers such as Henrik Ibsen, Maurice Maeterlinck and August Strindberg, and forge new audiences and create credible new modes of approaching rehearsal and performance, but these movements also did a good deal to establish a set of agendas that were to form the basis of much of twentieth-century French and European stage practice. A tension was established between the safe commercialism of the boulevard theatres and the experiments and artistic risks taken at independent and arts theatres. Jacque Rouché's Théâtre des Arts (1910–13) and Jacques Copeau's influential Théâtre du Vieux-Colombier (1913–14 and 1919–24) furthered the exploration into modes of responding to dramatic literature and fully established the creative role of the stage director, and, significantly, the notion of fidelity to an author's text. Copeau's concerns with a theatre's relationship with its audience, with the constituency of a group of actors, with training methods and with interpretative responses to plays within given aesthetics had considerable reforming influence on the postwar generation of theatre artists. His lasting influence first established itself in the shape of the 'Cartel des Quatres' of Charles Dullin, Louis Jouvet, Georges Pitoëff and Gaston Baty, the first two having trained under Copeau. The Cartel, four directors running separate theatres who pooled energies and shared ideals, served to establish in the 1920s a notional solidarity in the objectives and aesthetics of the independent stage movement that earned the fringe theatres a mainstream credibility and audience.

Much of the work of men such as those listed here was concentrated on revitalising stage traditions and rediscovering audiences, and centred almost wholly on the presentation of repertoires of contemporary plays and 'the classics'. Other energies were in operation in the first decades of the last century which sought to reconsider the use of stage space, inspired not by the pursuit of service to a playwright's text, but by the very expressive potential of the stage itself: form, rhythm, light, structure, colour and the juxtaposition of such elements. The ideas of the Swiss Adolphe Appia and the English Gordon Craig permeated the Parisian artistic climate through publication by and collaborations with such artists. Though the Symbolists and practitioners such as Lugné-Poë had sought to embrace the visual potential of stage-craft and directors such as Jacques Rouché attempted to implement and laud the theories of Appia and Craig, the French reform of stage practice continued to focus primarily on the relationship between the playwright, the director and the public. It was not until Antonin Artaud's theoretical writings in the 1930s and 1940s, and the practice of innovators such as Jean-Louis Barrault, and Blin after him, that any lasting experiment in the search for a scenic language unique to the conditions of the stage was pursued.

Another facet of the development of early twentieth-century stage practice that contributed to the intellectual and cultural climate that Roger Blin was to enter, was the drive to create theatre that spoke to the social concerns of the large groups of people. The creation of a truly popular, socially responsible French theatre was an ongoing concern of much of the last century. Firmin Gémier, the melodrama actor who, in 1896, had first donned Jarry's distorted, pear-shaped Ubu costume, established France's first National stage at the Théâtre National Populaire in 1920 which, though broadly unsuccessful, helped to establish the concept of theatre as a public service, and access to theatre as a public right. Jean Vilar reignited the ambition for a Théâtre National Populaire after the Second World War, established the Avignon festival and was a key figure in promoting the works and practices of Bertolt Brecht on the French stage.

If one was to invent a character who might represent the ambitions of the French avant-garde, who embodied much of the aforementioned history of the twentieth-century Parisian stage, you would need to conceive a personality and biography not dissimilar to that of Roger Blin's. But to invent a character who befriended Surrealist artists, who wrote passionate reviews as a young journalist of iconic films such as Marcel L'Herbier's *L'Argent* (*Money*) or Robert Wiene's *The Cabinet of Dr Caligari*, who participated in Jean Cocteau, Jean Renoir and Marcel Carné's first steps in cinema, who trained under Charles Dullin, who acted alongside a youthful Jean-Louis Barrault, who became Antonin Artaud's assistant director and who went on to direct the world premières of Samuel Beckett's and Jean Genet's plays, such a fictional character would be perceived as bordering on the incredulous. Of course, such a life was in fact lived, and Roger Blin's name is remembered principally today through his attachment to some of these other names. As a director, he sought to efface his own work, convinced that his best contributions were such that they might not be determined by the paying public. Confounding the work of scholars who might wish to trace and define his rehearsal room strategies, he rarely made any notes prior to a rehearsal period and never did so during rehearsals. Modest to an extreme, his attitude to his skills as an actor or director was that he was simply 'a special-ised worker';[1] a revealingly old-fashioned socialist perspective on his input to the staging of plays, but one that perhaps contributed to his having no desire or motivation to capture in print his thoughts and theories on stage practice. Given this, it was tremendously pleasing that a lengthy series of interviews undertaken with him in what turned out to be the last years of his life were compiled, edited and collated by Lynda Bellity Peskine and published in 1986. These *Souvenirs et propos*[2] provide illuminating insight into Blin's attitudes, humour and opinions and offer crucial testimony to his numerous productions and activities. His recollections and anecdotes usefully pepper the follow-ing book, which hopes in some way to clarify the role Blin played in key historic performances, offer fresh perspectives on some of the material considered, and finally provide an attempt at a definition of the methodology of a director who sought for his work to remain invisible.

1   Blin to René Thevenet, in *Enfin-Film*, 12, 19.7.47. All translations are my own, unless indicated. Where standard translations of common texts exist, I have em-ployed those. Scholars wishing to be informed of original French texts that are not easily accessible are welcome to contact me.
2   Roger Blin, *Souvenirs et propos*, ed. Lynda Bellity Peskine (Paris: Gallimard, 1986).

A biographical background

Roger Blin's earliest exposure to the theatre would not have been dissimilar to that of other children of middle-class Parisian families growing up in the first quarter of the last century. As a child, he was taken to see the travelling circuses that visited Paris and the opening few ages of his published memoirs, *Souvenirs et propos*, contain recollections of slapstick scenes of clowning. He vaguely recalls seeing the clowns Grock and Charlie Chaplin before the First World War and, in a different theatrical tradition, the elderly Sarah Bernhardt in Jean Racine's *Athalie* after it.[1] His earliest recollections of theatrical material show how the deception at the heart of dramatic representation intrigued him. The first play proper that he remembered seeing was a propaganda piece, performed during the first few months of the 1914–18 War, in which his own uncle, Jacques Deguy, played the role of a foreign spy. Once discovered, this character was heroically roughed up by the French characters, thereby providing a suitably rousing, patriotic ending to the amateur drama. The eight year old boy screamed to see his uncle treated in this way, confused by what he later referred to as the 'theatrical deception that was yet to seem an art to me.'[2] Seeing this familiar uncle in make up, with whitened hair, and in a strange costume had alarmed the young spectator, creating a confused state of mind in which he recognised his uncle but saw clearly that the man he thought he knew had somehow been possessed by an unknown personality: 'It was him and it wasn't him. A theatrical mystery that was revealed to me for the first time.'[3]

He was to suffer a similar alienating experience when he took on his first acting role, at the age of fourteen, in a school production of

1 Blin remembered seeing Bernhardt after the accident which left her with a false leg. This was her 'come-back' production of *Athalie* in April 1920. It is not unlikely that Blin saw Chaplin in Fred Karno's slapstick troupe, which performed in Paris before the war.
2 Blin, *Souvenirs et propos*, p.22.
3 Ibid.

Molière's *Le Bourgeois gentilhomme* (*The Would-Be Gentleman*). Again, the young boy was disturbed by the pretence of theatre. 'My friends and I were wearing make-up for the show. They'd put wigs on us,' he recalled. 'With a powdered face and this wig, I felt like somebody different. This troubled me extremely.'[4] Discovering this capacity to leave behind his own personality and adopt another was an experience not just confined to his boyhood. He recalled a similar ordeal that occurred much later when he was still relatively new to professional acting. Playing the part of the author/narrator in Jules Laforgue's *Hamlet, ou Les Suites de la piété filiale* (*Hamlet or the consequences of Filial Piety*) he had to walk on stage in morning coat and top-hat each night in front of the curtain to read out the prologue. He recounts how, in an extremely nervous state on the night of the première, he sensed his own personality recede and the rehearsed role, the character, take over:

> There was me, there was a gentleman next to me whom I could barely hear. I wasn't there, I was standing beside myself, watching. After two or three minutes, I felt the sensation of joining the other; we came together again. I had not done much acting yet. It was an extraordinary feeling. I was absolutely in a panic and at the same time, not at all.[5]

Noël Blin recalls his brother's nerves on the occasion: 'Roger swore to me he'd been terrified, that he'd got through it by squeezing tightly on his walking cane.'[6]

These three anecdotes relate to three isolated encounters with the displacement of reality in the theatre, but it may not be too fanciful to see them as part of a psychological continuum: the confusing sight of seeing an uncle made up to be someone else, the disturbance felt at doing the same to oneself and the odd sensation of a quasi-independent nervous energy in the act of performance itself. These three accounts of coming face to face with the 'lie' of the theatre are so many links in a chain of experience which contributed to Blin's growing

4   Ibid.
5   Ibid., p.43.
6   Noël Blin, *Souvenirs sur Roger Blin*, 31.3.85, unpublished, forwarded in correspondence with the author, p.20.

understanding of the interface between actor and adopted character and of the power of drama to use this mysterious elision between reality and illusion to seize an audience's attention and play with their sensibilities. The very fact that he recounts all three in his *Souvenirs et propos*, revealing how they were fused together in his memory, testifies to their importance within his artistic formation. In a further reminiscence he explained how he first discovered and developed a taste for the skills of captivating and affecting an audience. In Clamart, on a Catholic retreat away from school after the baccalaureate, he and a group of classmates experienced a theatrically presented sermon:

> We were at prayer all day and, in the evening, there would be a sermon. Some fellow who spoke about sin on the last night gave his sermon in the dark with just a few candles lit in front of him... To mark each section of his talk, he would extinguish a candle... after having blown out the last one, he spoke of death and of hell... in the dark... This gave me a definitive aversion to religion... and a taste for *mise en scène*.[7]

These memories have all the qualities of core experiences, their contours magnified by the imagination of a young man and representing a source of inspiration to his own creative impulses.

During his teenage years Blin developed a taste for theatre-going. At first he went to the Comédie-Française for a diet of the classics and poetry recitals, or to the Olympia to enjoy the music-hall entertainers. Then one of his teachers recommended that he and his fellow students should see the productions mounted by the new experimental directors such as Charles Dullin and Georges Pitoëff. Seeing the work of the innovative Cartel practitioners came as an eye-opener to Blin, presenting him with a challenging new alternative to what he had become familiar with at the Comédie-Française. 'I was very struck by the total absence of realism in Dullin's *mises en scène*,' he later recalled, 'the décors were all very schematic, painted in *trompe l'oeil* or constructed from flats. This form of theatre opened me to new things, to stylisation.'[8]

7   Blin to Jean-Pierre Thibaudat, in *Libération*, 12.2.83.
8   Blin, *Souvenirs et propos*, p.23.

The theatre was nevertheless not the form of artistic expression that he first chose to pursue. After passing his Baccalauréat, he registered in 1925 at the Sorbonne to study for a licence-ès-lettres honours degree, only to abandon this two years later and enrol instead at the Grande-Chaumière art academy in Montparnasse. Here he was to cultivate an interest in drawing and painting which was to stay with him the rest of his life.

In the late 1920s, Blin began to take a serious interest in theatre and cinema as intellectual leisure activities, and the generous exposure to the artistic and intellectual environment of Paris during the early years of the Cartel and what was a productive era for the indigenous film industry no doubt generated in Blin a frame of mind that was eventually to take him in the direction of dramatic expression. Moreover, the places he frequented and the people with whom he associated were instrumental in exciting in him a desire to work in the performing arts. He became a subscribing member of Paris's first ciné-club, Charles Léger's 'La Tribune libre du cinéma', which had been established in 1925 to establish audiences for experimental cinema. At the Sorbonne he made the acquaintance of a group of students also interested in the cinema and these introduced him to his first gainful employment, as a writer of film criticism. He began submitting articles to a variety of magazines and had work printed in *L'Ami du peuple*, *L'Humanité*, *L'Action française* and *La Revue du Cinéma*. The appeal to him of the German impressionist cinema and Scandinavian films he lauded in print provides an early indication of his taste for the marginal and the experimental. He joined a group of young freelance critics who, between them, sought effectively to monopolise the independently written columns of the numerous Parisian newspapers and magazines, delighting in occasionally being able to get reviews that championed the fringe films of the avant-garde in the right-wing press. Blin recalled:

> There were a few people, such as myself, who had infiltrated the newspapers to pass on our ideas. Using pseudonyms, we wrote in *L'Action française*, *L'Ami du peuple* to contribute to the defence of a certain kind of cinema. We sought to give a liberal tinting to those unworthy rags. In this way, we could write about the films we liked and which people were obliged to discover, in almost clandestine conditions, in tiny theatres or basements: Buñuel films, Soviet films

and all the old American serials [...] Occasionally, we might write a big article about certain American comics, such as [Harry] Langdon, and then dismiss in two lines some rubbish for which Paramount were paying for large advertising space in the same issue.[9]

As his reputation grew, Blin found himself drawn actively into the film industry itself and closer to those who sought to bring images of the French working class onto French screens. 'I was writing the cinema chronicle in *L'Humanité*,' he remembered. 'This got me into the studios where I got walk-on parts to start with. A few years later I was initiated into *mise en scène* through acting as assistant to the directors [Jean] Renoir and [Pierre] Chenal.'[10]

It can be safely assumed that Blin's nascent political consciousness was aroused after his having rejected the comfortable suburbs for the grittier milieu of the Latin Quarter, and that it found expression, in word and deed, as a result of his immersion in the social activities of the young friends and acquaintances he made there. A renunciation of his middle-class upbringing had geared in him an intuitive appetite for left-wing politics, while his experience of a more Bohemian lifestyle as a student gave him some inkling of a world that was far less comfortable than the one he had grown up knowing, and, at the same time, gave him the vocabulary with which to articulate a sense of injustice. Speaking in 1947, he had this to say about his time at the Sorbonne:

I'm poor, but I'm free. The Montparnasse bedsit in which I live suits me fine. I should say that it is all the same more comfortable than the hovel that I lived in not long ago at Lilas. And yet it was at this hovel that I discovered the world. The world and all its misery, and the revolutionary will that this incites.[11]

As a young man, Blin embraced with enthusiasm the discovery that the standards associated with his background might be rejected on a number of ethical and political grounds. This early repudiation of bourgeois values was the origin of an element of anti-establishment

---

9   Blin to Michel Fauré, in Fauré, *Le Groupe Octobre* (Paris: Christian Bourgois, 1977), pp.288–9. For examples of Blin's criticism, see Odette Aslan, *Roger Blin*, trans. Ruby Cohn (Cambridge: Cambridge University Press, 1988), p.13.
10 Blin to René Thevenet, in *Enfin-Film*, 12, 19.7.47.
11 Ibid.

venom that was to become characteristic of his work and working attitude. Indeed, as far as he was concerned, his attainment of social awareness was the springboard to the rest of his life and to his professional career: 'I was brought up at Sainte-Croix de Neuilly,' he once said, speaking of his Catholic school education, 'I belonged to a family of right-wing, liberal Christians. I started by moving out.'[12]

Part of a middle-class (though never affluent) family, living in a comfortable home near the Bois de Boulogne in the pleasant west Paris suburb of Neuilly-sur-Seine, the son of the respected district doctor, Roger Blin took on the role of adolescent misfit with verve. As the eldest child, he typically dominated over his three brothers and one sister, teasing these as elder brothers do, but also earning their respect (Noël Blin remembers how his brother undertook to educate him by passing him the sketches of nude models he had made during life classes at the Grande-Chaumière). As a teenager he would take his brothers and sister to the theatre and the cinema, first in Neuilly to see the likes of Harold Lloyd in his silent comedies or Douglas Fairbanks as Robin Hood, but later introducing them to Parisian Cinemas to see less mainstream films, such as Georg W. Pabst's *Loulou* (adapted from the notorious play by Frank Wedekind) at the Courbevoie cinema, or the avant-garde films he was reviewing in Paris. Blin's taste in films did not always meet with the approval of his parents, just as his choice of reading material was hardly that which they had encouraged in him, to which his brother Noël Blin testifies:

> Roger gave me a Kafka, *The Castle* [...] I was eleven [...] Later on, it was Roger who brought home unknown, scandalous authors: Faulkner, James Cain, Erskine Caldwell, Lorca, and disturbing novels: *Of Mice and Men*, *Tobacco Road*, *The Postman Always Rings Twice* [...] When Roger brought *Le Canard enchaîné* into the house my father was provoked into a rage, and tore it up.[13]

Blin slowly cut away the ties that bound him to his background, starting with where he lived. On leaving home to become a student at the Sorbonne he initially took a 'chambre de bonne' close to home,

12   Blin, 'Hommage: Roger Blin', in *Acteurs*, 5 (May 1982), pp.64–6 (p.64).
13   Noël Blin, *Souvenirs sur Roger Blin*, p.8. The *Canard enchaîné,* which is still published, was a weekly satirical magazine, akin to *Private Eye*.

but soon insisted on his parents finding him an apartment in Paris proper. After living near the Pont de Neuilly (supervised by a neighbour at his mother's behest), then by the Porte Maillot he decided the only way to make a clean break was to find the means to pay his own rent. He consequently found himself drifting between a number of addresses, small sixth-floor rooms or artists' studios, the conditions of which depended very much on the state of his wallet. It was not until 1950, in fact, at the age of forty-three, that he finally settled and moved into his rented flat at 264 rue St. Honoré, down the road from Les Halles, where he was to reside until his death in 1984.

Throughout his youth, Blin's dress sense changed accordingly with his habitat. 'His manner of dressing,' recalled his brother, 'evolved towards a very sober elegance which never left him.' This evolution began by his moving away from youthful taste for affectation ('He was well-groomed, elegant, slicked-back hair, with a trilby, gloves, pocket handkerchief')[14] in favour of a less pronounced, classless, if somewhat eccentric, appearance ('He has a unique way of his own of wearing large peasant shirts beneath a straight-cut jacket for which he himself designed the cut').[15]

Blin was afflicted with a serious stammer. The impediment originated from an early childhood accident in which he had experimented with feeding a small plastic swan with the flame of a candle. The resultant unexpected explosion caused a complete but temporary loss of voice, followed by the stammer that he would struggle for the rest of his life to control.[16] When he eventually gravitated towards the stage, the stammer was an obvious disadvantage, but he considered teaching himself to control his diction to be a matter of resistance: he once stated 'If my hands had been cut off, I would have tried to become a sculptor!'[17] The discipline required, he reasoned, would serve as a sort of therapy: 'If I became an actor, it was primarily to

14   Ibid., p.16.
15   Jean Rougeul, 'Les Nouveaux talents', *Paris-Cinéma*, July 1947.
16   In the last few hours of his life, Blin did finally regain the ability to speak free from any impediment. Hermine Karagheuz to Mark Batty, 5.1.95.
17   Blin in Paul-Louis Mignon, *Le Théâtre d'aujourd'hui A-Z* (Paris: L'Avant-Scène/Michel Brieunt, 1966), p.57.

gain control over myself,' he asserted.[18] As a teenager, he was so impressed by the diction and breath control achieved by the actors and actresses of the Comédie-Française that he would try to imitate their sounds at home in front of the mirror. A decade later it was a similar attempt to control his impediment that spurred him on.

> From the onset, I had to overcome my shyness, my speech impediment. Having a stammer, and being left-handed to boot, it was necessary that every word that I managed to pronounce on stage carried significance, that it should be funny. I cultivated a sense of humour as a way of having my difficulties in getting words out overlooked. This struggle against myself put me on the side of those in revolt, it separated me from my class of birth, from the ideas that were put in my head, from religion.[19]

Here is a significant element of Blin's spirit. His hesitant speech and his introversion caused him to feel something of a social outsider. His efforts to overcome these afflictions were equally fundamental; this refusal to accept the apparently pre-ordained, was a piece with a tendency to rebelliousness which was never to leave him and perhaps goes some way towards explaining why he remained stubbornly anti-establishment to the end of his life. A revealing example of his casual but almost reflexive flippancy towards social convention was given by the English journalist Peter Lennon, who remembered meeting Blin in the Tuileries Gardens washing his feet in the fountains, 'a prohibited activity'.[20] Such a seemingly inconsequential detail is eloquent of Blin's whole outlook. In his first ever interview – on the occasion of his first (and, for the cinema, only) leading role – the spirit of youthful intransigence in a man of forty came across with some force:

> I don't want to be a 'star'. I don't want to become full of myself. I detest all this inflation of celebrity which the public encourages and which, for a capitalist society, is such a good mode of oppression and such a good instrument for profit, in the same way as are metaphysics and the morality of heroism and sainthood.[21]

18   Blin to Édith Moyal, in *Télé 7 jours*, 12.2.66.
19   Blin to Nella Bielski, in *Le Matin*, 1.4.77.
20   Peter Lennon, 'Heroes and Villains', *The Guardian*, 1.12.90.
21   Blin to René Thevenet, in *Enfin-Film*, 12, 19.7.47. Blin played Julien in Edward T. Gréville's *Pour un nuit d'amour* (*For a Night of Love*).

Today, so candidly a Marxist interpretation of the priorities of the film industry would seem hackneyed, but Blin's pronouncement was no mere affectation; for him at that time his stance was a fusion of the passion and the integrity with which he governed his life, a blend that was to become characteristic of his work as a director. Blin's personal code of ethics very much affected his manner of working with actors and designers, and most of all his relations with playwrights and their texts. His stubbornness became a trademark, but it was never the obdurate short-sightedness of arrogance; instead it resembled more the ardent integrity of uncorrupted youthful idealism. His friend Jean-Louis Barrault pithily summed up this aspect of his personality:

> Roger has two or three key facets. He is highly cultured, has a desire to get away from the rest of the world and a sort of stubbornness in wanting to be marginal. [...] It's a convenience, being marginal, like young men adhering to a political party. I still tease him.[22]

Although there is more than a grain of truth in Barrault's forthright assessment – and Barrault of course spoke with the warmth and affection of a close friend – it would be a disservice to his achievements to dismiss Blin's obstinacy as merely a character trait. That he was able to ensure, to his own satisfaction, that his actions met the demands of his conscience was a measure of the depth of his integrity. Behind his front of stubbornness lay valid, heartfelt convictions. Blin lived through two world wars, both of which had palpable effects on his life and on the lives of those close to him. During the first, which he experienced as a young child (he was eleven when armistice was declared), his father was arrested by the Germans and detained in a prisoner-of-war camp near Berlin, later to be returned to his family in exchange for a German prisoner held by the French, an arrangement of the Red cross. That war also took his uncle Jacques Deguy from the family. Though a child at the time, Blin was indelibly marked by his awareness of what was going on around him during the 1914–18

---

22   Jean-Louis Barrault to Pierre Chabert, 'Artaud, Blin, Beckett', in *Revue d'Esthétique*, ed. Chabert, no. hors série: 'Samuel Beckett' (Paris and Toulouse: Privat, 1986), pp.174–8 (p.176).

hostilities. In an interview with *Libération* in 1977 he recounted his still vivid memories:

> I wasn't very old, but I remember Poincaré's squealing voice at the inaugur-
> ation of the monument to the dead in Neuilly: it was terrifying, with all this
> patriotic patter. I was a kid and I knew it was false. My father took me to the
> gunpowder factory in Sevran and I saw the Algerian workers dying of hunger.
> Aged ten, I got a sudden awareness of a world that I hadn't known at all at
> Sainte-Croix de Neuilly, cosseted in a poor, but well-principled family. [...]
> When the armistice came in 1918 I wasn't at all excited: I refused to go and
> watch the victory parade, having those images in my head.
>   What struck me most of all was an article I read in *Le Matin* in 1917, the
> year of the mutinies, which were hardly mentioned in the newspapers. A soldier
> had refused to wear a uniform that was still heavily stained with the blood of a
> friend who'd just been killed. His Colonel put him to the firing squad, but
> because he was a good soldier, all the same, he was present at the execution,
> paying the soldier military honours, and saluting him. The newspaper cited this
> gesture as something sublime (in recalling this, Roger Blin is close to tears).
> That put me in a right bloody state. And so, afterwards, anything that had any-
> thing to do with the army, with war, all that, I never went along with it, never.
> Even as a kid, at school. The dates of battles in history revolted me. Revolted.[23]

Throughout his life Blin maintained a keen anti-military stance, the conviction for which perhaps stemmed from this early realisation of the potential for hypocrisy and inhumanity in those who control the destinies of ordinary people. With the coming of the Second World War and the German Occupation, Blin remained in Paris. He was not mobilised, due to his weak heart, but took on the responsibility of acting as a courier for the Resistance under the pseudonym Valentin and courted imprisonment, or worse, were he to be discovered. He once came very close to being convicted after an interrogation and search by the Gestapo, but his resistance pass was fortuitously still hidden in one of his trouser turn-ups upon release from their offices. Working for the Resistance from within the film industry, he secured links with the free south-west and assisted Jewish friends across the border to Switzerland. He was arrested on two occasions, once by the

---

23   Blin, 'Seule la poésie peut apporter la vérité aux gens', *Libération*, 15.6.77.
     pp.51–4 (p.54). Raymond Poincaré was President of the French Republic
     (1913–20).

militia in Valence in June 1943, and a year later during the insurrection in Paris, in which he participated.[24]

Such, then, were the personal qualities and experiences that Blin brought with him when he embarked on a career as theatre director in 1949, at the mature age of forty-two: a healthy contempt for authority, be it home-grown or alien, and a notorious intractability towards compromise in his work, counterbalanced by a private fund of humility; an engaged social awareness and an acquaintance with political activism at first hand; a thorough immersion in the literary and cultural life of Paris in the 1920s and 1930s which led to a lengthy apprenticeship as an actor, both on stage and in films. It was this experience of acting, undertaken initially as much as a means of financial survival as of artistic expression, and the stimulating encounters it afforded, that drew Blin into the theatre community. 'I never thought I'd become an actor,' he once stated, 'I was more attracted to literature or painting. Then, as it happened, I was lucky enough to meet Dullin, Artaud, Barrault who helped me to move very close to the intellectual problems of the theatre.'[25] In particular, Blin identified two of his friends from this period as 'both my godparents. Contradictory godparents, of course':[26]

> I was very close to Artaud, and to Prévert too. I got a great deal from both of them. And I never developed any cultural inclinations because of them. All of Artaud's work, as well as Prévert's, was anti-cultural [...] I veered between Artaud and Prévert who together scrubbed clean the stains of Neuilly-sur-Seine in me. Artaud opened the theatre up for me and Prévert gave me a certain type of humour; theatre and humour with provocation.[27]

The following chapter will consider in detail the period between Blin's formal education and his first productions as director at the Gaîté-Montparnasse theatre, with emphasis on the various practitioners who shaped his experience during that time, Artaud and Prévert especially. This period in which his reputation as a stage and screen

24   René Thevenet, *Enfin-Film*, 12, 19.7.47.
25   Blin in *Combat*, 3.5.66.
26   Blin in *Acteurs*, 5 (May 1982), p.64.
27   Blin, *Souvenirs et propos*, p.34.

actor developed might be considered the training ground for his subsequent career as a director. In considering that 'training', his interaction and collaboration with a variety of friends and practitioners identifies a series of possible influences.

First Stages – Friendships and associations

The Groupe Octobre

Blin made his living in the 1930s wherever he could, continuing his journalism and finding work in films. In 1933 he collaborated with Pierre Chenal on a social realist adaptation of a Marcel Aymé novel, *La rue sans nom* (*Street Without a Name*)[1] and casually took on his first professional acting engagements, accepting small roles in Marc Allégret's *Zouzou* (1934), Jean Vigo's *Atalante* (1934) and Albert Valentin's *Taxi de minuit* (*Midnight Taxi*, 1935). These growing connections in the film industry introduced him to a whole society of artists, actors and journalists of the Left Bank in Paris. Here he had found a community to which he felt he belonged and from which he could find steady employment and support. 'We helped each other as best we could; we'd eat at one person's then another's' he remembered, and joked of the benefit of his stutter; 'I made a bit of money in films. My employment was quite stable: everybody wanted me for the roles of village idiot or deaf-mute.'[2]

Perhaps through his acquaintance with Allégret, Blin became aware of the work of the agit-prop workers' theatre company, the Groupe Octobre, the most prominent and celebrated of the companies that comprised the Federation of French Workers' Theatre.[3] Octobre was founded in 1932 when Jacques Prévert came into contact with a party of young workers who had broken away from their amateur theatre company, the Groupe Prémices, to set up a more politically

---

1   Blin assisted Chenal both in the writing and the direction of the film, in which he also acted.
2   Blin to Nella Bielski, in *Le Matin*, 1.4.77.
3   La Fédération du théâtre ouvrier en France, an umbrella association which supported and represented political theatre companies. Other groups included the Groupe Mars, the Groupe Combat and the Groupe Regard.

aware association which might comment on the socio-economic issues of the day. Paul Vaillant-Couturier, the editor of the communist daily paper *Humanité*, had advised the group to approach Prévert to write a sketch critical of the use of propaganda in the popular press. The performance of the resulting piece, *Vive la presse* (*Long Live the Press*) at the 'Fête de l'Humanité' in April 1932 constituted the official birth of the Groupe Octobre (named after the month of the 1917 Soviet revolution). They followed up this initial success later the same year with an anti-military piece, *La Bataille de Fontenoy* (*The Battle of Fontenoy*), which subsequently won first prize at the 1933 International Workers' Theatre Olympiad in Moscow.

The group energetically produced a collection of short pieces incorporating a variety of styles, from vaudeville and pantomime to music-hall and drama. Often their work was written quickly, to respond to events. *L'Avènement d'Hitler* (*The Accession of Hitler*), for example, was performed the day after the Reichskanzler's coming to power in January 1933 (with Prévert in the title role) and *Citroën* was written, rehearsed and performed hours after the announcement of a strike at that manufacturer's factory. Their work was often 'rough and ready' in form, the driving force being to produce potent material rather than high performance standards, which were frequently constrained by the limitations imposed by each new venue, the availability of actors and the haste with which scripts were written or montages of scenes assembled. 'Technically, the result might appear weaker than with the Prémices group,' founder member Lazare Fuchsmann explained, 'but the impact was considerable. Notably of the more well-written texts and those that grabbed current affairs by the throat.'[4] The poet Marcel Duhamel, another Octobre member, put this more succinctly in a brief comment in his memoirs: 'We performed as we would have sold *L'Humanité*.'[5]

The popularity of the group grew steadily amongst a broad audience demographic, encompassing workers' groups and left-wing intellectuals, and in a short space of time they managed to collect a

4   Lazare Fuchsmann to Michel Fauré, in Fauré, *Le Groupe Octobre*, p.288–9.
5   Marcel Duhamel, *Raconte pas ta vie* (Paris: Mercure de France, 1972) *L'Humanité* was the organ of the French Communist Party.

crowd of admirers and followers, of which Roger Blin was one. What set the group apart from the numerous other such workers' theatre groups of the time was the breadth of their vision. Instead of concentrating for the most part on specific incidents of controversy and putting together a performance in response to it, in the manner of a politically-geared news broadcast, the Groupe Octobre were motivated by the world movement of socialist revolution and they brought this wider perspective to bear on everything they did. Moreover they used Prévert's poetry, with its seasoning of surrealism, to communicate their message rather than the chants, sloganeering, reciting of manifestos and documentary representation of incidents favoured by other groups.

Already acquainted with Prévert and many of his colleagues through his work in film, Blin followed the group with interest. 'From a political point of view,' he thought, 'the texts were always extremely significant, even with Jacques Prévert's puns, spoonerisms, hallucinatory delirium. Every performance had a specific significance.'[6] He felt comfortable in the company of the people surrounding Prévert. 'A number of them lived in adjoining rooms to Prévert's studio on the Rue Dauphine in a quasi-communal setup' Elizabeth Strebel tells us. 'They shared meals together, frequented the little bistros of neighboring St.Germain-des-Près, and often attended the midnight sessions of the local cinema houses.'[7] Blin thrived in this environment of committed, creative people, which offered camaraderie, emotional support and intellectual stimuli, consolidating his intuition that a micro-society could function communally. Here were others who lived marginally, making a living where they could, others who shared his political convictions and with whom he was given the opportunity to relax into the art of performing, through the serious desire to communicate a message of socialist solidarity.

The activities of groups such as the Octobre were symptomatic of the French political climate of the depression years. The instability

6   Blin in Fauré, *Le Groupe Octobre*, p.269.
7   Elizabeth Grottle Strebel, *French Social Cinema of the Nineteen-Thirties* (New York: Arno Press, 1980), pp.166–7. The midnight showings were at reduced prices.

of the French parliament of the early 1930s had led to the country having experienced five governments in less than two years by the end of 1934. Though the 1932 elections had shown a clear majority in favour of the left, shared between the Radical Socialist party and the Socialist party,[8] the two together would not agree on an economic policy capable of efficiently addressing the effects of the depression and world slump which, at the turn of the decade, were at their most severe. The Radicals' counter-voting repeatedly brought down the Socialists' proposed economic programmes, resulting in a rapid turn-over of governments in the eighteen months following the general election. A period of legislative paralysis and economic decline en-sued, and consequently an erosion of faith in the parliamentary system set in. All this was fuelled by major public scandals involving leading government figures and large sums of money. Extreme right-wing factions became increasingly vociferous, and this at a time when their policies were achieving footholds in Europe with Fascism ripening over the borders in Germany and Italy and threatening to rear its head in Spain. Pressure mounted and eventually erupted in violent and bloody clashes between the police and right-wing anti-parliamentarian demonstrators on 6 February 1934 in the Place de la Concorde, across the bridge from the lower house, the Palais Bourbon, where the new head of government, the Radical-Socialist Édouard Daladier, was being given the vote of confidence. Seventeen died during the incident and more than a thousand were reported wounded. The following day Daladier stood down. One interpretation of these events was that the demonstration had been no less than a frustrated Fascist putsch that would have brought an end to the Third French Republic. The French Left's traditional response to a threat of such magnitude had always been to rally together and unite. Accordingly, on 10 February, an 'Appel à la lutte' ('call to fight') was put together, emphasising the urgent need to undermine the Fascists' manoeuvres by a 'unity of action' on the part of all workers' organisations. Blin added his name to this petition alongside those of Paul Éluard, Fernand Léger, André Malraux and Jacques and Pierre Prévert. On 12 February the Socialists,

8   By the term 'Socialist Party' I am referring to the 'Section française de l'inter-
     nationale ouvrière' (SFIO).

along with the French Communist Party,[9] held demonstrations in re-action to the violence of the sixth, and in a show of solidarity the Con-fédération Générale du Travail declared a general strike for the same day.[10] These events were instrumental in the formation of the Front Populaire, a dominant French political force in the 1930s.

Against such a background it is unquestionable that left-wing sympathies would have sharpened, making people all the more willing to demonstrate, to become actively involved, to co-operate in holding back any perceived or actual threat from the Right. Protests were organ-ised against Pierre Laval's right-wing government, and the workers' theatre movements threw themselves into the demonstrating process. Blin remembered one particular episode in 1934:

> At one point an incident erupted: the police had killed an unemployed person who had entered a depot looking for work. There was an amazing burial: three to four hundred thousand people, incredible for the period. I took Barrault along. Prévert, Leduc, and Tchimoukow had written a spoken chorus. At every public protest, at the 1st of May demonstrations, we would place ourselves at certain places in the rally and, at the desired moment, we'd perform our spoken chorus.[11]

It was a year of much political agitation. On 24 April 1934 Blin associated himself with the Surrealists to join in their demonstrations against the French government's decision to deport the exiled Leon Trotsky. The movement towards the political union of the left acceler-ated throughout 1935; the Radical Socialists joining the other socialist groups in their condemnation of the Laval government despite their own participation in coalition with that government, while the Com-munists and the Socialists concluded a pact of unity. Both events pre-cipitated the signing by all parties of the left of the programme of the Front Populaire in January 1936. The Groupe Octobre, despite being more in line politically with the extreme left, were active in promoting this union of forces and in voicing its policies. They would take the poetry of Prévert, Paul Éluard and Louis Aragon onto the factory floor

---

9   Le Parti Communiste Français.
10   The French equivalent of the Trade Union Congress or the AFL–CIO.
11   Blin in Fauré, *Le Groupe Octobre*, p.273.

and perform their sketches wherever they were invited by the unions or the Communist party. 'We did all we could, early on, for the advent of the Front Populaire,' Blin recalled. 'Firstly by aligning ourselves, through our work, on the side of the class-struggle, and then by signing, from 1934 onwards, numerous manifestos in support of extended unity of action.'[12] Given his friendship with members of the group and his corresponding political sympathies, it was perhaps inevitable that Blin would join in the activities of the Groupe Octobre.

> For me, the Groupe Octobre, whilst being amateur and not taking itself seriously, performed highly incisive texts with an extremely good humour. We were *enfants terribles* saying witty things, and the best example of that the festival at Saint-Cyr.[13]

It was in the village of Saint-Cyr, in Brittany, in June 1935, that Blin made his first appearance with the group. The spectacle, organised by the local Communist municipality, was entitled 'La Grande Fête Bretonne'. This incorporated a procession through the streets by the costumed actors singing and carrying placards, all borne along on borrowed tractors, headed by Blin dressed as Henri III. The programme of events also included an anti-military display outside the officers' training school of Saint-Cyr which aroused indignation in various quarters and lead to complaints being written to the Minister of the Interior. The activities continued in the evening with a presentation of Prévert's *Suivez le Druide – revue bretonne en six tableaux* (*Follow the Druid: a Breton revue in six scenes*), in which Brittany was portrayed, contrary to its middle-class image of a tourist haven, as a place where poverty and hardship existed and where workers were ill-paid and exploited. The right-wing *Echo de Paris* dubbed the parade an 'odious communist masquerade' and gives us the best documented account of the event:

> This festival involved a procession through the streets of the town – home to the Ecole Spéciale Militaire – within which the army specifically was appallingly ridiculed. At the head was the municipality and... M. Cachin. Then his 'comrades', made up as officers and adopting grotesque poses and gestures,

12   Ibid., p.311.
13   Ibid., p.265.

preceded by placards with slogans on them. Of course, the clergy were not left out. A large banner carried by the 'Bretons emancipated from Paris' upon which were the words 'Down with religion – the opium of the people' went ahead of a man dressed in a cassock. A veritable orgy of placards cast slurs higgledy-piggledy upon war, the Croix-de-Feu, the French army, those who work in helmets or skullcaps.[14]

The summer of 1935 was a time in France when sympathies for the Left and appeals for a united popular front were at their highest and this spectacle at Saint-Cyr, which took place in the same month that the Laval government came to power, was a tour de force for the Groupe Octobre. *Suivez le Druide* had a repeat performance at Villejuif in July to coincide with an electoral meeting, after which the troupe suspended their activity until the new year, when it was to pick up again in the year of the Popular Front. Blin then involved himself as fully as possible in their work. He took part in a number of performances of Prévert's anti-family piece *La Famille Tuyau-de-Poêle* (*Keep it in the Family*), which had been in the group's repertoire since 1933, and joined the others in reciting spoken choruses to striking factory workers.

Consolidated by the conviction of his community of associates, Blin's politics became firmly fixed on the far Left. Up to the time when he joined the group, while he was keenly following their activities, their performances were anti-militaristic and expressed sympathy for the oppressed using a violent, humorous and powerful poetry. Summarising the atmosphere within the group, Blin must also be assessing his own political temperament of those years:

> In contrast with those of more militant groups [...] such as the Groupe Mars, for example, the shows that the Groupe Octobre gave were more globally oriented in the direction of revolution, in anarcho-communist directions. We were in liaison with the communists, but the internal tendencies of the Groupe Octobre, due to Prévert's personality, were anarchist and communist.[15]

---

14 *L'Echo de Paris*, 21.6.35. Marcel Cachin was head of the French Communist Party and then editor of *Humanité*. The Croix-de-Feu, later known as the Parti Social Français, was a French nationalist, Catholic, right-wing group involved in inciting the 6 February riot.

15 Blin, *Souvenirs et propos*, p.35.

Though independent of the Communist party, the Groupe Octobre in the early 1930s expressed views not dissimilar to the party's and frequently performed at its request. For the elections in 1936, the Communist party commissioned the making of a film, *La Vie est à nous* (*A Life for Us*, compiled by Jean Renoir) which was banned by Albert Sarrault's government commission for censorship, but was to become recognised as 'the first great militant film made in France'.[16] A number of the Octobre actors were recruited in the cast to act out documentary type sequences displaying poor working conditions. Blin featured in one section as a striking metal worker.

Ironically perhaps, it had been the political events of 1936 and the coming to power of the government of the Front Populaire that proved to be the catalyst to the break-up of the Groupe Octobre. For some, the aims of the struggle had been achieved and they had little motivation to continue. More specifically, however, it was a change in the policies of the Parti Communiste Français and of the new left-wing alliance that took the wind out of the group's sails: the move toward a more pro-military line was unacceptable to most of its members and rifts opened between them, as Blin recalled:

> Slogans of the order 'Pull up our sleeves!' 'Don't wave a fist at a priest!' 'Long live the Republican army!' 'The police are on our side!' could not suit us. We, whose existence and mission was entirely anti-colonialist, anti-police, anti-militarism, anti-church and, to a certain degree, anti-social-democracy, we had no further reason to exist. These words pulled the rug out from beneath our feet, but then there was also the beginnings of the war... For us at the knife-edge of the struggle against capitalist structures, no conversion was possible. We had no option but to break up.[17]

16   Strebel, *French Social Cinema of the Nineteen-Thirties*, p.168.
17   Blin in Fauré, *Le Groupe Octobre*, p.344.

Antonin Artaud

One of Blin's closest friends in the early 1930s outside of the Octobre group was the actor, poet and essayist Antonin Artaud. Like Prévert, Artaud had been expelled from the Surrealist movement by its leader André Breton. Blin had been fascinated as a teenager by the Surrealists and excited by the revolution through art they advocated. The noises they made – denouncing all established art forms and calling for an end to the reign of naturalism – stimulated Blin's interest as a young man, already consciously shedding his middle-class upbringing. Some of the drawings that he was producing in the late 1920s attest to this influence: one, *Le Cheval et l'humour humain*, is a surreal montage of metallic objects, and another, *La Chance de Rosalba*, is a sketched portrait of a large woman holding up three cards, all aces, her opened shirt revealing a split breast which appears to be melting into a pan of water held in the hand of a disembodied arm.[18] Having worked as a journalist for film review magazines, Blin certainly would have been aware of, and may even have admired, Artaud's work on screen, as well as on stage, and his curiosity would have been aroused further by some of the notoriety that inevitably attached to the young actor's name during the Théâtre Alfred Jarry projects in 1927 and 1928 (which specifically incurred the wrath of André Breton). Blin had consequently known of the Artaud long before the two men met in 1928 in the Salle Adyar, a cinema where Artaud, along with Breton, Louis Aragon, Paul Éluard, René Char and Benjamin Peret had turned up to disturb the showing of a naturalistic film – a common Surrealist activity. Having recently finished shooting scenes for Carl Dreyer's *La Passion de Jeanne d'Arc* (*The Passion of Joan of Arc*), Artaud was still sporting the tonsure he had adopted for his role as a monk and the bizarre haircut could only have added to the mystery surrounding him. After this first encounter Blin remembered feeling that he had been 'adopted' by Artaud, eight years his senior, and they subsequently spent much of their spare time together in cafés in

18   Both pencil drawings from 1928, reproduced in Blin, *Dessins – Festival D'Avignon* (Paris: A+A, 1985).

Montparnasse or Saint-Germain-des-Près. Their friendship and mutual respect grew from these frequent meetings and in the early 1930s they were seldom apart.

In March 1935, his friendship with Artaud came to artistic fruition in their collaboration on *Les Cenci*. Blin's job as assistant director on *Les Cenci* project involved systematically recording the movements Artaud accorded to each of the roles, charting on a plan of the stage the movements and moods of every actor, using a different coloured pencil for each character. In this way he constructed a sort of map of all the scenes as Artaud barked out his blocking, capturing in the one scene, for example, how 'patterns of aimless and ineffectual activity are established as the guests trace slow eddies about the stage and make stilted, pantomimic social gestures'.[19] Blin was asked to make a note of every such decision, and if Artaud did not tell him explicitly what he wanted, then Blin was instructed to read his mind.[20] The production incorporated Blin's first, brief stage appearance, in the role of a murderer, affording him his first stage notice.[21] Despite his given task as Artaud's assistant director, he had been persuaded to take on the role (to make up numbers in the cast), and was happy to have an opportunity to show his friend whether or not he could perform. He later recalled how his role simply required him to 'laugh out loud whilst beating [his] chest' and how Artaud, impressed with his performance, declared to him 'That's it, you're a medium.'[22]

This brief and difficult experience of theatrical production took place three months before Blin's baptism into the Octobre at Saint-Cyr. Together, these two events made for a curious training ground in the theatre, complementing the more disciplined, relatively sedate acting experience he had gained in walk-on roles for films. In both, there was the eagerness of dedication to a cause, of seeking subversive goals, of challenging audiences. In both, it was the enthusiasm of

19 Jane Goodall, *Artaud and the Gnostic Drama* (Oxford: Oxford University Press, 1994), p.129.
20 'Note down everything I say, but also that which I don't say, as you should be able to sense it.' Quoted by Blin in *Le Quotidien de Paris*, 19.5.81.
21 'Roger Blin and Henry Chauvet, in the mimed murder scene, are perfectly horrific and demonstrate a good deal of talent.' Armory in *Comoedia*, 8.3.35.
22 Blin, *Souvenirs et propos*, p.28.

commitment that ignited Blin's participation, not the appeal of theoretical models or intellectual argument or analysis.

In strictly practical terms, Blin was scarcely impressed by Artaud's approach. Having accepted the offer to work as assistant director during the rehearsal period of *Les Cenci* and having taken a small acting role in the production, he was in a position to watch Artaud put theory into action, and became critical of his friend's aptitude as a director:

> When we were rehearsing *Les Cenci*, Artaud would speak of the theatre naturally, but he knew absolutely nothing about how to talk to actors. It was rather funny because he would always use metaphysical examples or literary allusions that the actors could not understand. He never used the technical language of the theatre. Every time he said anything, he wanted it to be in relation to the whole meaning of the piece. Although he had worked with Dullin and Jouvet, he didn't know any professional jargon at all.[23]

Subsequently, as a director himself, Blin disliked note-taking and preferred to trust to intuition; he tended to play his *mises en scène* 'by ear' and scorned directors who put their ideas down onto paper before even casting a play. Comparing his working methods to those of Artaud he made one point quite categorically: 'I do not hold to the religion of *mise en scène*, as he did'.[24]

Blin was separated from his friend during Artaud's years in asylums before and during the war. The period of their separation began with Artaud's abortive journey to Ireland in 1937. This ended in his deportation, following which he was held for over a fortnight at the hospital in Le Havre and interned in the psychiatric hospital of Quatre-Mares outside Rouen in October. When he was eventually transferred to the Henri-Rousselle hospital at the Sainte-Anne asylum, closer to Paris, in April 1938, Blin managed to see him again for the first time since his disappearance. With the exception of his mother, he was the only visitor Artaud was prepared to entertain. After this, Blin started to receive letters again and was, in fact, the only person to receive correspondence from Artaud during this period. These letters,

23   Ibid., pp.32–3.
24   Blin in *Les Nouvelles littéraires*, 31.3.77.

in some of which Artaud asked to be supplied with drugs, were sent to him at the café du Dôme as Artaud had misplaced his address.[25] They culminated in a particularly curious and rather disturbing letter that arrived half-burned and smeared with blood. Stephen Barber suggests that this may have been one of the many 'spells' – pieces of paper covered with symbols and colours – that Artaud would send to curse or protect their recipients in 1939. It 'contained a ferocious warning to the people whom Artaud believed were preventing him from receiving heroin'[26] and impelled Blin to go out of his way to visit the asylum in the hope that somehow the contents of the letter might be of some use to those concerned with Artaud's treatment and detoxification. He was to be all the more disturbed by the reception accorded him by Jacques Lacan, the 'chef de service' at Sainte-Anne, who completely discounted the significance of the letter, having already declared Artaud incurable and unlikely ever to be capable of writing again. He was to be sent to the larger Ville-Evrard asylum with others whose cases were written off. Blin's outrage was unmistakable: 'They hadn't tried anything at all,' he complained. 'They'd just put him with the others, at Ville-Evrard. With those who were considered untreatable.'[27] To compound his distress, Artaud had been unwilling to receive Blin at this visit and he was able only to catch a glimpse of his old friend from a distance, unshaven, sitting with his back to a tree, watching other inmates playing football around him. Blin would not see Artaud until later, after his transfer in February 1939 to Ville-Evrard, where he was to be found in the section for drug addicts, garbed in the same grey uniform as all the others there. During their meetings, and in letters which he received, Blin, whose father Artaud knew to be a doctor, was often asked for laudanum to relieve pain. So tormented was Artaud by his pains that he would even resort to threats in his letters, or just straightforward emotional blackmail:

25   Blin was living at 5 cité Falguière in the fifteenth *arondissement*, an address which Artaud later scribbled in one of his notebooks. Antonin Artaud, *Œuvres Complètes,* XXIV (Paris: Gallimard, 1956–94), p.413, note no.2 to p.43.
26   Stephen Barber, *Antonin Artaud, Blows and Bombs* (London: Faber and Faber, 1993), pp.103–4.
27   Blin to Jean-Pierre Faye, 'Artaud vu par Blin' in Faye, *Le Récit hunique* (Paris: Seuil, 1967), p.311.

If you have, as I sensed the other day, any true affection for me, then make that extra effort for me and don't say 'I'll try' or 'if I get the chance I'll do it'; tell yourself 'I'm going to do this because he's suffering, because it's urgent and essential'.[28]

Artaud would often complain to him about his suffering, recounting his ordeals with succubae and incubi and telling tales of pain and hallucination, all with the specific aim of acquiring drugs to combat his visions and alleged persecution. Blin continued to supply him with cigarettes and money, and supported him with visits throughout his four-year stay at Ville-Evrard until his transfer in January 1943 to the asylum at Rodez, north-east of Toulouse.

Though Blin was never able to visit Rodez, the pair kept in touch through their exchange of letters, broken inevitably by Blin's touring and numerous changes of address. This correspondence offered Artaud a constant source of support and affection and within it we can find signposts indicating the strength and nature of the friendship between the two men. A short series of letters involving the journalist Anne Manson, for example, demonstrates their bond clearly. In the first, sent to Manson in December 1943, Artaud attempts to catch up with his friend after a lacuna in their correspondence. In second and third letters, which followed in the new year, he expressed his affection for Blin and Barrault, and asked after an address for Blin.[29] Once the message reached Blin that he was in Artaud's thoughts he wrote a letter of reassurance.

My very dear Artaud,
It is with great emotion that I learned from Anne Manson that you wish to see me. I unfortunately cannot travel to Rodez just now. I'm acting in a Norwegian play at the Vieux-Colombier... Believe that you are in my thoughts... Please forgive us what must seem to you like abandonment, though I call you in my heart incessantly.[30]

28 Letter from Artaud to Blin, dated November 1940, in Jean-Louis Brau, *Antonin Artaud* (Paris: Éditions de la table ronde, 1971), p.203.
29 Letters to Anne Manson, dated 4.1.44 and 27.12.43, Artaud, *Œuvres Complètes*, XXIV, p.172 and X, p.157, respecively.
30 Blin to Artaud, dated 24.1.44. Artaud, *Œuvres Complètes*, X, p.309 (note 4). Blin refers to Gunnar Heiberg's play *La Tragédie de l'amour* (see p.58).

To which Artaud promptly replied:

My very dear friend,
No, I know perfectly well that you have not all abandoned me, and I haven't
stopped feeling your thoughts and your hearts all around me.[31]

In addition to such letters, the relationship between Artaud and Blin is documented by other minor references which Artaud makes to his friend in letters to other acquaintances. Perhaps more revealing still are the two instances where Blin's name appears in the later writings collected under the title 'Cahiers de Rodez'; once where it is incorporated into a poem[32] and, more poignantly, where it is simply inscribed, like a thought transposed, in the margin of the opening page of one of the writer's workbooks.[33]

It is within the context of this close friendship that any attempt to assess the influence Artaud may have had on Blin's artistic career ought to be made. Enthusiasts of the work of Artaud, all too eager to find evidence of the influence supposedly exerted by their legendary subject, are often content to point the finger at those who, like Blin, knew and worked with the man early in their careers, and opt to see in stylistic choices in their subsequent work the indelible mark of his impact, thereby placing Artaud at the centre of Expressionism's last supper, surrounded by apostles of his writings. As a result of his own reticence to discuss his working methods, Blin often fell prey to such pigeonholing at the hands of journalists seeking neatly to sum up his approach. Such straightforward linking of Blin's work with Artaud's theories has also found its way into analytical criticism. David Whitton's excellent *Stage Directors in Modern France*, for example, references Roger Blin in just three instances; of these, two present him simply in relation to Artaud, firstly describing him as 'greatly influenced by Artaud', later implying that Blin found a 'central point of

---

31 Artaud to Blin, dated 29.1.44. Artaud, *Œuvres Complètes*, X, p.187.
32 'Roger Blin you are there, sir, little Germaine told me.' Artaud, *Œuvres Complètes*, XVI, p.178.
33 Artaud, *Œuvres Complètes*, XVI, p.196. The associated editorial note reads: 'Name written transversally in the margin of the first page of the notebook.' (p.362.)

reference in his [Artaud's] writings'.[34] Yet, simply to instance the Artaud/Blin association in respect of *Les Cenci* and then to conclude that Blin must have been a disciple of Artaud, integrating the master's theories into his developing practice, is far too crude an inference. It was nevertheless a commonplace critical shorthand that dogged much of Blin's career. Although the experience that Blin gained through collaborating with Artaud cannot be disregarded, particularly as *Les Cenci* represented his true theatrical initiation (as both actor and assistant director) – Blin certainly recognised that there 'was a certain convergence of certain aspirations and certain dispositions between Artaud and me.'[35] – one must, nevertheless, balance an understanding of the work done within the context of the bond between the two men. In identifying reasons which eventually drew Blin more closely into a life of professional acting and directing, one cannot neglect the significance of that particular rehearsal period, of living with Artaud's theories and determinations, trying to understand what his friend was endeavouring to achieve, and philosophically accepting the inevitable compromises and failures he had to withstand. 'I suffered with him over his impotence,' Blin remembered, 'his impotence in seeing his projects through to completion.'[36] Awareness of this element of person-al involvement allows us to posit a certain objectivity in the creative relationship between the two men and a knowledge of their friendship partially obviates any attempt to pinpoint exactly what baggage Blin took away from his time with Artaud.

The urge to see a positive connection between Artaud's visions and Blin's *oeuvre* inevitably asserts itself given the latter's attraction to the dramatic worlds of August Strindberg, Arthur Adamov, Jean Genet and Samuel Beckett, the first of whom was greatly admired by Artaud, the other three having been, in their turn, regarded by some critics as his literary heirs. A critical tendency has been to see in Blin's productions of the work of these playwrights evidence of an Artaudian influence upon him. This convenient generalisation belies

---

34   David Whitton, *Stage Directors in Modern France* (Manchester: Manchester University Press, 1987), pp.125 and 136.

35   Blin in *Libération*, 14.6.77.

36   Blin in Faye, 'Artaud vu par Blin', p.316.

the simple fact that Blin's practical involvement with the plays of such as Beckett and Genet was the outcome of his own personal interests, ethics and politics, those same factors that had drawn him close to Artaud in the first place. These are the sympathies and leanings that become emphasized and reinforced when shared with others of the same mind. Blin himself attempted to state this case in an interview for the Italian arts publication *Sipario* in 1965. When pressed to concede that writers such as Beckett, Ionesco and Genet owed a debt to the theories of Artaud, he was adamant in his refusal to do so:

> If all we do is focus on phrases, paragraphs and parts of Artaud's writing then we could make references to the work of these artists. Artaud talks of the petrifaction of language, of the influence of visible symbols, of the significance of gesture, of the pressure on man from the inanimate world and, certainly, all of this is in the works of the authors of the 1950s, but not thanks to Artaud and not because of Artaud. I don't believe there is a single work of any of these authors which has a single link with what Artaud meant by 'theatre of cruelty'. If Artaud's ideas are reflected in the works of these authors it is by pure coincidence, justified by the fact that Artaud had a liberating vision of global theatre, including all these things but intending to go far beyond them in search for a mythical, improbable theatre.[37]

When confronted in 1949 with the manuscript of Samuel Beckett's *En attendant Godot* (*Waiting for Godot*) Blin was strongly attracted to the text by its poetic beauty and by its overt theatricality, but this could not simply have been because Artaud had awakened or implanted in him some notion of a theatre of images over and above the plane of dialogue. He felt sure that the essentially optimistic Artaud would have hated the play on the grounds that it was 'a work of tragic resignation'.[38] Clearly, Blin had developed his own theatrical preferences from a multitude of other sources. His taste for stylistic experimentation, for instance, predated his acquaintance with Artaud, as witnessed by his work as a film critic in the late 1920s, denouncing the popularity of crude realism in favour of the films of F.W. Murnau or Nikolai Okhlopkov. Moreover, one cannot easily overlook his decidedly Trotskyite political attitudes which set him significantly apart

37 Blin to Guido Boursier, in *Sipario*, June 1965, 20.1, p.28.
38 Blin in Marowitz, *Artaud at Rodez*, p.81.

from the apolitical Artaud. It was these beliefs that fuelled his repugnance for corruption or oppression and which were the governing factors in his attraction to the work of Genet, for example, as opposed to the reputedly Artaudian structures of that author's plays. If an analysis of Blin's productions reveals a catalogue of techniques which might demonstrate an affinity with Artaud's attitudes, then at the same time it is evident that Blin also strove to accomplish on stage something to which Artaud never aspired; to present in a theatrical context questions of social or political import. Politics and poetry were two sides of a single coin minted in Blin's career. Speaking of his most politically contentious productions of Jean Genet's *Les Paravents* (*The Screens*) and *Les Nègres* (*The Blacks*), he recalled: 'I was very happy to direct these plays, at those times specifically, because they had extraordinary reverberations and because theatre, for me, is about that too.'[39] These 'extraordinary reverberations', the social impact that theatre might effect, is supplementary to and of a different order from, the resounding effects of sound, light and gesture that Artaud wrote of in his essays. Artaud used the same word (in French, 'retentissement') in a different sense in his essay 'En finir avec les chefs-d'œuvre' ('No More Masterpieces'), speaking of the way drama can charm its audience like music may charm a snake.[40] More than the 'cruel' plunge into the viscera of an audience to revive their vitality and awaken their metaphysical senses, Blin is clearly talking of other kinds of noises left behind when a play is over; the controversy, the rubble after the demolition of received values, the echo of shock that may hopefully lead to a constructive re-appraisal of human attitudes and social relationships. As an engaged humanist and socialist, Blin's ambitions were often to arouse debate and stimulate thought. To trace some of the roots of this attitude, one needs to recall the climate of the 1930s French political landscape, the war which followed, and to consider his dedication to and participation in the work of Jacques Prévert's Groupe Octobre.

39 Blin, *Souvenirs et Propos*, p.202.
40 Antonin Artaud, *The Theatre and its Double*, trans. Victor Corti (London: Calder, 1993), p.61.

Blin did, of course, make some connections between Artaud's objectives and the directing he later undertook. 'Of course, I never forgot certain things we used to talk about,' he recalled in 1977, 'and, when I mounted *Les Paravents* or *Les Nègres* then, of course, that search for a density, an affective density comes from that which fascinated me in him.'[41] Although he recognised that he had gained a thirst for what he termed a 'densité affective' (see p.227) from his friendship with Artaud, and more specifically from his understanding of his friend's desire to mediate the substance of human experience by physical poetic means, his search for this 'density' within a textual format essentially separates him from Artaud's pursuit of gestural and sensual expression divorced from literary textual structures. Rather than corroborating direct influence, Blin's recognition of their common ground demonstrates how certain beliefs and concepts were fully understood and concretised through his friendship with Artaud.

One area where we may legitimately try to ascertain what inspiration Blin derived from his experiences with Artaud is in his personal understanding of the much abused term 'Theatre of Cruelty'. Blin saw Artaud's chief objective as revolt, the evocation of a higher state of awareness of that particular cruelty that is embodied in the contradictory experiences of living. He wished to show that a human being alive is a being in a state of revolt; revolt against life and against death which is not only its cruelly irrevocable conclusion, but the mocking determinant of life. The result of this, to Blin's mind, would be to bring about greater moral awareness in an audience, and he insisted that 'what [Artaud] wanted was a moral insurrection'.[42]

Any utterance by Blin on the subject of Artaud was coloured by a desire to protect and to defend his late friend's intentions and achievements, unpicking popular misconceptions and condemning the distortions of Artaud's vision that swept the theatres of Europe in the 1960s and 1970s. Take, for instance, this outspoken comment:

> Every time some guy rolls around on the ground screaming, they call him the son of Artaud. He looks at himself in the mirror, and tells himself 'I am pale. I am the son of Artaud', add a bit of dry ice to that and we're off! I've always

41   Blin in *Libération*, 15.6.77.
42   Blin in *Le Quotidien de Paris*, 19.5.81.

44

been against that kind of thing [...] without Artaud's terrible experience, it cannot be anything other than apery.[43]

At the heart of this kind of defence was the stark memory of Artaud's personal torments and sufferings, of psychological anguish and physical agony witnessed at first-hand. Blin knew that Artaud was very much that which he wrote, knew that he had expressed, not only in his letters and poetry but also woven into his theorising, how humanity appeared to him in all its harshness, and how he believed himself to have suffered directly at the hands of Western society. Having known Artaud and seen his distress, or watched him trying hard in the face of adversity to execute his most precise wishes through performance, it was impossible for Blin to divorce that knowledge of the man from his acquaintance with the writings. For Blin the suffering, and its residue in the written works of Artaud, was to be respected for its own sake, not mined eagerly for clues as to how to approach certain aspects of production, not imitated for effect, not indulged in for the spectacle it could provide. 'When Artaud spoke of a "Théâtre de la Cruauté"', he explained, 'he wasn't thinking of recreating the Grand-Guignol. Cruelty, for him, was a state of revolt that had nothing to do with scenes of blood or with anything that had anything to do with fascism.'[44] Admittedly, we are dealing here with a subjective response, and one that revealingly articulates Blin's own rejection of mere 'theatricality' or show.

To seek evidence of any 'Artaudian' approach in the work of Roger Blin is to neglect, belittle even, the simple fact that Artaud had a profound impact on Blin's life first and foremost as a tormented, often distant, misunderstood friend and colleague. Artaud had said to Barrault; 'Tragedy on the stage is not enough for me, I am going to bring it into my life',[45] and intentionally or not, he succeeded. Here lay the seeds of Blin's understanding of 'Cruauté'. He could never have

43   Blin in *Libération*, 15.6.77.
44   Ibid. Le Théâtre du Grand-Guignol, situated in Pigalle, was notorious in the late nineteenth century for its naturalistically grisly horror shows, making use of real meat, offal and animals' organs such as eye-balls for its effects.
45   Jean-Louis Barrault, *Memories for Tomorrow*, trans. Jonathan Griffin (London: Thames and Hudson, 1974), p.82

been expected to disclose all the details to a reporter or interviewer, but the signs are clear enough to dissuade us from viewing his work as that of a disciple. 'That which he gave me goes well beyond that which one might see in what I have done',[46] he emphasised, later stating that:

> It is more in terms of morality, ethics, of the conduct of one's life, a kind of research into life within poetry, in a fundamental, permanent revolt, that Artaud was able to give me anything, more than in terms of theatrical technique.[47]

To chart the origins of Blin's involvement in the theatre is no straightforward task. He was not a man of the stage in the same way as were Barrault, Dullin or Antoine. If these three names might be evoked as representing something of the solid core of the evolution of twentieth-century French stage practice, then Blin's work has to be considered as tangential to theirs. He did not dedicate his life to the theatre in the same way as such innovators. Though his reasons for choosing to express himself through acting and directing were sincerely and strictly observed, with no room for compromise, it was the circumstances of his life, not an innate urge to be a performer, that determined his choice of career, and his methods and attitudes to his work were forged more by the effect of his personal relationships than by admiration for the technical or intellectual ingenuity of others working in the field. By persuading him to perform in *Les Cenci*, and asking him to assist in mounting that production, Artaud opened a door to a career in the theatre for Blin, but once *Les Cenci* was over with, Blin's immediate dramatic development was in political street-theatre and his career progressed over the ten years of his friend's internment, removed from his sphere of influence and in directions not always in keeping with it. By the time Artaud was released from Rodez, Blin had become an established, if minor, film actor and had begun to be sought after for roles on stage. Through Artaud, Blin may have developed a more acute appreciation of poetry, not simply of language, but of image and mood – the poetry of space and motion that one ascribes to theatrical potential. More importantly, though, he

46   Blin in *Les Nouvelles littéraires*, 31.3.77.
47   Blin in *Libération*, 15.6.77.

seems to have taken from Artaud a particular orientation and a belief, amounting almost to a conviction, in theatre as a powerful forum for addressing issues of human experience.

The significance of Blin's activities in the mid-1930s lies in its diversity. That Blin could take part in political demonstrations and performances of straightforward propaganda pieces within months of having worked with Antonin Artaud, struggling with new, experimental concepts of staging and theatrical action, suggests not only a keen interest and committed belief in both, but also a certain degree of open-mindedness and distance from the postures of either side. Knowledge of Blin's immersion in political theatre is important in that it gives us a clear indication of his persuasion before the strongly modifying factors of war and occupation. Again, as with our account of his friendship with Artaud, we can observe the strengthening of previously held convictions: that Blin held anti-establishment views had been clear since the 1920s and his period of collaboration with other reviewers to publicise avant-garde cinema, but his introduction to Prévert and the latter's circle of friends brought a reinforcement and politicisation of such attitudes, culminating in the desire for direct action within the framework of the Groupe Octobre.

If, with Artaud, Blin was able to discuss, explore and experiment with surrealist ideas and to intellectualise on theatre, through Prévert and political performances he arrived at a firm, clearly defined world-view. He spoke of having had a 'duel godparent Artaud-Prévert',[48] two complementary gravitational pulls attracting the orbit of his developing aesthetic and moral sensibility. It would be too simple to consider these two influences as polar opposites; Blin's engagement with both shared common root impulses. Like Artaud, Prévert had been expelled from the Surrealist movement by André Breton, and both men were fascinated by the auditory capacities of language. The experiments of the Group Octobre, specifically with choral material or with narrative shock techniques, were not totally at odds with Artaud's developing vision for a new theatre in the mid-thirties, and Artaud even lauded their work in an article written for *El Nacional* in Mexico, whilst there in 1936. Comparing the Octobre's achievements

48   Blin to Jean-Pierre Thibaudat, in *Libération*, 12.2.83.

to those of Barrault's early experiments, he identified these productions as the antidote to Copeau's obsession with text and praised how 'Jacques Prévert's buffoonery is both psychological and objective' and the manner in which his 'humour signals the disease of the times.'[49] Blin said of Prévert: 'He gave me intellectual and moral liberation, and also the discovery of corrosive laughter.'[50] An alchemy of sorts seems to have occurred in Blin of the elements derived from Artaud and Prévert and what they stood for in the 1930s, a process that forged the raw material of the young Roger Blin's spirit into the metal from which the mature director was made. It was a delicately balanced fusion of artistic integrity with political commitment which complemented each other well whilst holding in check any temptation to indulge in either.

Jean-Louis Barrault and Sylvain Itkine

During the rehearsals for Artaud's *Les Cenci*, Blin made the acquaintance of an ambitious young actor, Jean-Louis Barrault, who later bowed out of the project over misunderstandings between him and the 'star' of the show, Lady Abdy. Barrault, of course, was to become unarguably one of the most significant twentieth-century French theatre practitioners. His dexterity as a performer and ingenuity as adaptor and director earned him an outstanding and extraordinarily busy career: he gained a reputation for experimentation in the 1930s and went on to produce work of national and international significance over a period of five decades. Barrault's involvement in theatre began at Charles Dullin's stage school at the Théâtre de l'Atelier, making his first appearance as a servant to Dullin's Volpone in 1931. Having an insatiable creative curiosity, he soaked up instruction and experiment from whatever source he experienced. From Dullin he learnt the

---

49   Artaud, 'Le Théâtre Francais cherche un mythe', *Œuvres Complètes*, VIII, pp.254–6. (pp.255–6.)
50   Blin in Fauré, *Le Groupe Octobre*, p.265.

discipline of acting and the gravity of an actor's work. At the Atelier, he was taught the skill of improvisation and shown how to examine the emotions in order better to understand and manipulate them in performance. He complemented this training through his friendship with Étienne Decroux, from whom he learned mime and movement, and the two men undertook autodidactic research into the possibilities of bodily movement and gesture. It was a leaning towards this kind of work and a desire to find a potent non-realistic form of dramatic expression that finally came to fruition in Barrault's breakthrough production – a two-hour dramatic adaptation of William Faulkner's *As I Lay Dying*, performed at Dullin's Atelier in June 1935, three months after having left the *Les Cenci* project. The performance was Barrault's attempt to convey a whole story through mime, to stretch and optimise the expressive potential of face and body; for him it was 'theatre trying to purify itself',[51] a personal manifesto and an exposition of his theories on physicality.

Autour d'une mère (*Around a Mother*), as the production was named, received four public performances. Blin remembered seeing it two or three times, and enthusing about it to groups of his friends, whom he took along. His admiration for the work was extreme and he remembered how '*Autour d'une mère* was an event, a whole load of people went to see the show and many were very affected by it.'[52] One of the people Blin had accompanied to the performance was Artaud, and his appraisal of the performance became one of the most notable reviews Barrault ever received, being included in the compilation of essays that became *The Theatre and its Double*.[53]

Later that same month, Blin joined his Groupe Octobre friends and participated in an agit-prop street theatre protest event in Brittany (see pp.32–3). He introduced Barrault to the Octobre community and the young actor opened his living quarters, the Grenier des Augustins, to this society, and his rooms became a centre of artistic and intellect-

---

51   Blin, *Souvenirs et propos*, p.66.
52   Ibid., pp.40–1.
53   Artaud, *Théâtre et son double* (Paris: Gallimard, 1964), p.217. The passage was not included in the English edition, but can be found in Claude Schumacher and Brian Singleton (eds.), *Artaud on Theatre* (London: Methuen, 1989), pp.169–70.

ual activity, a hive of experimentation, a meeting room and rehearsal space for the community of artists and activists to which he and Blin belonged. The society supported its own and very often those involved in the Groupe Octobre were employed by the new independent group of French film makers that included Marcel Carné, Jean Renoir and, of course, the brothers Jacques and Pierre Prévert. Strebel points out how '[m]any of those who were involved with the Groupe Octobre would figure prominently as members of the Renoir team, the Carné team and the co-operative teams sponsored by the C.G.T. and Ciné-liberté.'[54] Prévert and Allégret were both later to offer Barrault substantial film work, including his celebrated role as the love-struck mime Baptiste Debureau in *Les Enfants du paradis* (*Children of Paradise*, 1945). In 1936, Blin himself was given work in four films and was offered a significant supporting role in 1937, alongside Louis Jouvet and Erich von Stroheim, in Pierre Chenal's film *L'Alibi*. In 1936 he took the part of Don Juan in the Octobre's adaptation of Miguel de Cervantes' farce *Le Tableau des merveilles* (*The Wonder Show*), translated by Prévert at Barrault's request. They performed first at the Salle Adyar in March 1936, and took the show with them to perform before an audience of protestors and strikers during the strike months of May, June and July. If the realities of touring and the difficulties of organisation scared many off, a handful, including Blin and Barrault who had enjoyed the experience of acting in and sharing the direction of the work, had developed a taste to go still further and transform the company into something more like a professional troupe. Blin had joined the group at the peak of its powers, at a time when its decline and dissolution were inevitable, but continued working with them, despite falling membership and receding support, until their aborted final production, *Bonne nuit capitaine* (*Good Night, Captain*), which failed to survive a long and turbulent rehearsal period in 1938. By this time most of the group had departed, either to pursue careers or simply because of shifts in political thinking as the pre-war climate augmented and polarised particular ideological stances. Those who remained, tried to hold onto a clear ideological line of approach to subject matter and hoped to forge what was left of the troupe into a

54 Strebel, *French Social Cinema of the Nineteen-Thirties*, p.168.

semi-professional theatre company. The short-lived Groupe Spartacus, taking militant material around youth hostels, was one such attempt. Barrault's interests, however, eventually focused elsewhere and neither Blin, nor any other remaining member of the original group, had the desire to take on the full organisational responsibility for holding the company together. *Le Tableau des merveilles* was to be their swan song.

Immediately upon the dissolution of Groupe Octobre, Barrault asked Blin to perform in another Cervantes project, *Numance* (*Numantia*) to be performed in April 1937. Barrault chose this story of a Spanish village collectively refusing to submit to the invading Roman army and preferring to die under siege in recognition of the plight of the Spanish caught up in the civil war that had erupted over the border. He remembered wanting to apply ideas he'd had in adapting Faulkner 'using a baroque classic, in which the real and the fantastic come together, in order to verify and bolster all those ideas.'[55] Blin is noted in the play's programme as having taken three roles: 'a numantin, the corpse, and fury (a supernatural character)' and the nature of the performance combined with the different requirements of his three roles presented Blin with perhaps his most demanding and fulfilling acting work to date. Here he was exposed to Barrault's thoughts and ideas on movement, gesture and the choreography of whole groups of actors. To his advantage, he was not totally untrained in movement work, having at one stage taken dance classes with the German dancer Jean Weidt, a student of Mary Wigman.

The originality of Barrault's ideas stimulated an atmosphere of collective creation in the company and produced some remarkable stage images. At one point, a heavily-made up Blin in the role of a corpse, 'with dark eye-sockets and rotting jowls', was slowly summoned from the grave by Barrault as a druid to prophesise the destiny of the village. Barrault, at this time, was on a trajectory to becoming the darling of the Paris theatre press, and his innovations in theatre practice were recognised and admired almost universally. One critic described his concept of drama as one which 'is anchored in the

---

55   Barrault, 'Retours à Numance', *Entretiens sur le theatre*, 18 (September/October 1966), p.2.

human body through its movements, gestures, cries, breathing.'[56] Assessing Barrault's work up to and including the production of *Numance*, Sylvain Itkine wrote that he believed the young director had 'restored the natural complementary component to the verbal magic of the theatre, and that is gesture.'[57]

In 1938 and 1939 Blin appeared in seven films, working most notably for Abel Gance in *Louise* and Marc Allégret in *Entrée des artistes* (*The Curtain Raises*). His stage apprenticeship continued with further exposure to Barrault's ingenuity throughout 1938, first joining him and Madeleine Renaud on tour with Fernand Crommelynck's *Le Cocu magnifique* (*The Magnificent Cuckold*) and then in Barrault's next dramatisation, that of Knut Hamsun's *Hunger*. This production had actually been suggested to Barrault by Blin, who had read the novel, had been overwhelmed by it, and passed his copy to his friend. He had recognised its potential for adaptation and believed that Barrault 'could make a little one-man mime and dance show of forty minutes or so out of it.'[58] Barrault expanded Blin's concept and offered him the part of his double in the production, a mark of the deepening trust and admiration between the two men, and one which gave Blin his most prestigious role to date. For its run of seventy nights, alongside *La Faim* (which was considered too short for a full evening's entertainment), Blin played the Laforgue role in Laforgue's *Hamlet, ou la suite de la piété filiale*, directed by Charles Granval.

In the production of *La Faim*, the central character Tangen walked the streets of Oslo soliloquising, but when engaged in conversation with his double the two spoke a strange gobbledegook of semi-comprehensible invented vocabulary, improvised on stage each night, an innovative device introduced by Barrault to represent the closed-in and paranoiac quality of Tangen's character. Integrating movement and voice, Barrault's powerful adaptation of Hamsun's novel was succinctly described by one critic as 'a Chatterton night-

56 Robert Kemp, *Feuilleton du Temps*, 26.4.37.
57 Sylvain Itkine, *L'Intransigeant*, 13.4.37.
58 Blin, *Souvenirs et propos*, p.41.

mare, overseen by Meyerhold'.[59] Barrault had written his *La Faim* as a text of rhythm and counterpoint, juggling with still new ideas:

> In it I was experimenting with many new resources: the play between actor and lighting (going up a staircase), simultaneous scenes, nonsense scenes – words that have no sense but whose sound plastically reproduces conversation and situation. Spoken text answered by a tune hummed with the mouth closed. Heartbeats, buzzings in the ear, 'physiological' (if I may use the term) musical effects and, above all, a man and his double. Roger Blin was the double. I played the man, Tangen. It was really a duet between us.[60]

The critic of *La Lumière* was impressed by what he described as a 'series of mimed, almost danced, tableaux, intercut with splendid fixed images which were often reminiscent of surrealist compositions, and by long monologues spoken either by the ravenous hero, Tangen […] or by his double, his unconscious self who follows him like a shadow.'[61] If Blin's earlier stage appearances in minor roles had been noticeable enough to deserve a line or two of commendation in some reviews, now his talent was being fully recognised.

As mature directors, Blin and Barrault demonstrated divergent characteristics. Blin's unassertive directing had nothing of the extravagance and visually ambitious nature of Barrault's touch. Though their temperaments were essentially different – Blin disapproved of some of the directions Barrault's enthusiasm led him; his decision to become a sociétaire of the Comédie-Française being one example – they shared enough of the same drive and a respect for one another's talents for their friendship to bond, and their rapport and respect led to a number of significant collaborations in the 1960s. Blin may have acquired a theatrical vocabulary that was undeniably to serve him well from his experience of participating in some of Barrault's earliest experiments. This craftsmanship, informed by the humanism of Prévert and the experience of Artaud, was to become characteristic of much of Blin's own work. Most significantly, it was thanks to Barrault that Blin gained a good deal of exposure.

59   Henri Bidou, *Marianne*, No.340, 26.3.39, p.16.
60   Barrault, *Memories for Tomorrow*, p.99.
61   *La Lumière*, 5.5.39.

The other significant influence on Blin's 'training' in the 1930s was provided by his friend Syvain Itkine, whom Blin had first met in 1930, at the screening of Jean Renoir's film *La Chienne* (*The Bitch*) in which Itkine played a lawyer. Whilst working as 'directeur de scène' at the Théâtre des Ambassadeurs in 1937, Itkine helped get Blin some stop-gap work. He appeared there as the simple peasant Ruprecht in Heinrich von Kleist's *La Cruche cassée* (*The Broken Jug*), directed by Georges Douking, and took part in the amateurish yet commercially successful production of Lenormand's *Pacifique*, in which he played a ghoulish Haïtian leper. Their friendship was consolidated by this assistance, and their frequent meeting, and Blin was inevitably drawn into Itkine's own theatrical ambitions.

Mirroring Blin's activity, Itkine was a member of the avant-garde and political theatre movements in Paris, founding himself the Octobre's sister company, the Groupe Mars. The son of a Jewish immigrant from Lithuania, Itkine had been an enthusiastic theatre-goer throughout his teenage years. At the age of fourteen he would often spend evenings at the Comédie-Française with groups of friends, even after his daily ten-hour shifts as an apprentice crimper in the tailoring industry. It was from these friends that he formed his first small amateur dramatic company, and he learnt the fundamentals of acting from tutor and friend René Simon. By the age of twenty the development of his stage work was secure enough to enable him to leave his job and become a professional actor. Tours of Europe and Northern Africa in the early 1930s helped to reinforce his reputation whilst consolidating his talents and in 1933 he joined Michel Saint-Denis's 'Compagnie des Quinze', within which he developed an interest in the craft of directing.

In 1936, based at Barrault's Grenier des Augustins, Itkine set up a co-operative of actors named the 'Théâtre des Cinq' which united the energies of Raymond Rouleau, Jean Servais and Julien Bertheau with those of Barrault and himself. He proposed Alfred Jarry's *Ubu enchaîné* (*Ubu in Chains*) for the end of their first season and set to work putting together a detailed set of proposals for the staging, organisation, and financing of the project. He enlisted the help of Max Ernst to design the decors and hoped to put together a programme 'with the maximum number of surrealist collaborators.'[62] In a similar spirit, he named his company of actors 'le diable écarlate' (the scarlet devil), a phrase lifted from Synge's *Playboy of the Western World*. The group enjoyed a generous budget of a million old francs and there followed eighteen months of preparation and rehearsal for four days of performance within the 'Théâtre d'essai de l'Exposition Internationale' held at the Comédie des Champs-Élysées. The 'Théâtre d'essai' (experimental theatre) was set up to culturally enrich the 'Exposition Internationale des Arts et Techniques' which took place in Paris in 1937. Itkine invited Blin to participate in the performance of *Ubu enchaîné*, offering him the role of the 'first free man'.

Itkine's enthusiasm for the Jarry play and his method of producing and directing it very much reflect the sort of attitudes Blin later showed in his work after the war: an emphasis on the importance of fidelity to the author and his text, coupled with an uncompromising disdain for commercial values. If Artaud had served as an inspiration to Blin intellectually and emotionally, and Prévert ethically, then Itkine may well have done so practically. Here was a successful young actor and director, advocating and practicing views and methods that excited Blin and that were still not accepted by the theatrical mainstream. Itkine firmly believed in a theatre of integrity and aspired not only to match the moral and artistic achievements of the Cartel but also to join Barrault on the avant-garde front line. He spoke in 1937 of his distaste for contemporary French theatre, bemoaning 'the financial dependence, both artistic and social, of the entire theatrical movement'.[63] He craved a revolutionary theatre, one which would question old values and formulae. *Ubu enchaîné* came as a natural choice; it appealed both to his politics and to his intellect. In his 'Notes à propos de Jarry', part of which was reproduced (as 'Intervention à propos de Jarry') in the brochure-cum-programme put together for the production, Itkine outlined his reasons for choosing this particular Ubu play as a declaration of war upon existing theatre: 'I lay great stress upon the fact that *Ubu enchaîné* – which does not offer a single

---

62   Itkine, 'Notes à propos d'Ubu enchaîné', in Henri Béhar, 'Une mise en scène surréaliste', *Revue d'histoire du théâtre*, 1.24 (1972), p.8.

63   Itkine, 'Lettre à X...', in *Revue théâtrale*, 8.23 (1953), p.15.

conclusion or concrete solution, and in which base powers triumph unilaterally [...] should serve as a point of departure for our scepticism.'[64] More to the point, Itkine wished to use the play as commentary by analogy upon the political climate of the times, just as a year later he chose to perform Roger Vitrac's *Le Coup de Trafalgar* (*Trafalgar's Trick*) in order to challenge pre-war bravado with a tale of the danger of blind patriotism. Jarry's grotesque humour emphasised the appalling potential of unleashed human ambition and the character of Ubu, a single face to the numerous contemporary aspects of the fascist threat, was a potent symbol on the stage in the late 1930s: 'At this particularly crucial era in human destiny,' Itkine justified, 'it is necessary to have all the nauseating glory, stuffed in Ubu's *gidouille*, right in front of our eyes. One day we will need to exterminate it in broad daylight.'[65] There is a resolute spirit here; a conviction over the significance that might be attached to a piece of drama, and an enthusiasm inspired of that conviction.

Itkine believed that the director should be the central controlling figure in any production and stated that '[w]ishing to put on a play he likes in the dramatic format which he prefers, it is legitimate that the director should enjoy an undisputed authority during the rehearsal period.'[66] Unlike Artaud, who, unskilled in man-management in the rehearsal room, took the same belief to authoritarian extremes, Itkine demonstrated a closeness to and a respect for the work and opinions of his actors. His instructions were not over-intellectualised and he was able to communicate his theories to his company in simple and realistic terms. 'That which was most striking in Sylvain's working method,' Blin remembered, 'was the serious approach, the consistent professionalism, without doctrine, without urgency – as he himself was discovering things by making us explore – he was sensitive to objections, to the chance discoveries to which he alone understood the

---

64   Itkine, 'Intervention à propos de Jarry', in *Revue d'histoire du théâtre*, 24 (1972), p.13.
65   Ibid., p.10. The word 'gidouille' is a made-up word Jarry applied to Ubu's swollen belly.
66   Itkine, 'Propos sur la mise en scène', in *Revue d'histoire du théâtre*, 16 (1964), p.237.

secret and which were our payment.'[67] Compared with the self-absorption of Artaud's enthusiasm and the political provocation of Prévert's dramatic verses, Itkine's active yet self-effacing involvement in theatre, his concern to serve the authors of the works he chose and his disciplined dedication to his practice seem to constitute a blueprint of what was to become Blin's approach to his own career as a director. In his 'Propos sur la mise en scène', in response to being questioned on the role of the director, Itkine emphasises the service a director owes to the playwright and an application of 'love and conviction' that could produce theatre of quality and integrity:

> Can one define theoretically the parameters within which the authority of the director is exerted in the service of the work, the precise moment when the interests of the work are no longer in accord with the director's demands? I have tried to express the most ideal objective. I am on the side of those who efface themselves whilst serving the text.[68]

The practice of 'invisible directing', of allowing a performance to grow almost organically out of the moods, rhythms and emotions woven into his text by the playwright, is an approach adopted by Blin throughout his career. It seems eminently possible that close collaboration with and respect for his friend may have influenced Blin in some way that became manifest when he himself came to have full directorial control over his own chosen productions ten years later. 'His objective, if I recall the numerous chats and discussions we had together,' Blin later recounted, 'was to bring together his creative work and his revolutionary faith, each magnified of course by humour.'[69] The assessment is one that could equally accurately be applied to Blin's work, and in some measure his friendship with Itkine was perhaps one of the more significant of those that were to 'shape' his interest and involvement in the theatre.

---

67 Blin, 'Qui était Sylvain Itkine?', in *Revue d'histoire du théâtre*, 16 (1964), p.232.
68 Itkine, 'Propos sur la mise en scène', from the document's footnotes, p. 238.
69 Blin, 'Qui était Sylvain Itkine?', p.232.

The War and after – Artaud's return

By 1939, Roger Blin had begun to gain recognition as a significant talent. He was described in an article in *Marianne*, the first ever on his subject, as a 'born actor, vagabond, odd, without steady employment' and his stage presence was keenly admired: 'His incomplete, naïve, broken gestures always bring to the text a touching youthfulness and an indefinable quality which makes one want to soothe him, to assure him that there's no need to be afraid, no need to be sad.'[70] In 1940 he was given work by Charles Dullin, some of whose courses he had once attended at the Atelier. Dullin had appreciated Blin's performance in Barrault's *La Faim* and offered him the part of Buckingham in a revival of *Richard III*. In the same year, Blin took a part in Maurice Tourneur's film version of Ben Jonson's *Volpone*. In 1941 he appeared in a double bill of Synge plays, directed by Raymond Raynal, performed at the Théâtre Monceau. Acting in *L'Ombre de la ravine* (*In the Shadow of the Glen*) and in *Le Baladin du monde occidental* (*Playboy of the Western World*), Blin was able to indulge in his taste for this particular playwright, and for Irish literature in general. 'As soon as I had *The Playboy of the Western World* in my hands,' he recalled, 'I adored all Irish drama.'[71] Being a friend of Raynal, Blin lent a hand with the directing and the two exercised their imagination trying to fit the two plays onto the small stage of the Monceau.

With the exception of a double-bill of Synge plays, a role in Gunnar Heiberg's expressionist drama *La Tragédie de l'amour* (*The Tragedy of Love*), directed by Fernand Ledoux, and an appearance in Roland Petit's production of Prévert's *Rendezvous* in 1945, Blin did little theatre or radio work during the Occupation. Instead he chose to lead drama classes in schools for the Theatre-in-Education movement the E.P.J.D. (Éducation par le jeu dramatique), accepting meal tickets in lieu of payment, and took a number of insignificant roles in films to help meet his other financial needs. The mission of the E.P.J.D, which had been established by Jean-Louis Barrault, Jean-Marie Conty, and

---

70   Lisane Garel, 'Ceux de chez Chéramy', in *Marianne*, No.349, 28.6.39, p.18.
71   Blin, *Souvenirs et propos*, p.67.

Marie-Hélène Dasté, was to ensure that school children were imaginatively stimulated within the new educational menu of the Vichy government. An incidental ambition of the movement was, as Barrault recalled, 'on occasion, [to] have an anti-governmental effect. To create a sort of resistance spirit among the young. In a very modest way, of course, but one which might lead somewhere.'[72]

At one point during the war, Blin's forthright integrity caused him to have to leave Paris altogether. He was called to re-shoot scenes of the film *Entrée des artistes*, which he had originally made under the direction of Marc Allégret in 1938. The scenes in which he had played opposite the Jewish actor (and friend) Marcel Dalio, were to be replaced, using a non-Jewish actor in Dalio's place. In order to re-release his film in wartime, Allégret was required to re-shoot such scenes in accordance with the newly imposed regulations of the Nazi Filmprüfstelle. These prescribed that, in order for a film to be deemed worthy of public exhibition, all Jewish film workers' names were to be erased from the credits of all films and that Jewish actors were to be edited from films and their scenes re-shot.[73] Blin declined to collude in this scheme and was highly critical of Allégret for conceding to the new demands. Failure to comply with the regulations meant losing his work permit and thereby his means of livelihood, but he did so nonetheless, in disgust at the anti-Semitic edict, and was obliged to leave Paris until the end of the war.

Early in March 1946 Artaud learned that he was to be released from the asylum at Rodez and told the publisher Jean Paulhan as much in a letter dated 11 March.[74] He was subsequently permitted an eight-day trial period of freedom in a hotel in Espalion, a little further north, in the department of Lot, from where he wrote an inspired letter to Roger Blin outlining at length his ambition finally to realise a

72   Barrault, *Memories for Tomorrow*, p.124.
73   Proscribed personnel were either non-arian or those otherwise considered 'enemies of the Reich'. The Filmprüfstelle provided two lists of such artists in September 1941; the first of non-Jewish workers whose films were not authorised for exhibition, the second of French Jews in the film industry.
74   Artaud, *Œuvres Complètes*, XI p.202.

'Théâtre de Cruauté'.[75] It is also in this letter that Artaud thanked Blin for his organising of the fund-raising performance being planned for his benefit at the Théâtre Sarah Bernhardt.[76] Blin had earlier received the news of his friend's imminent discharge from Arthur Adamov, who had visited Artaud at Rodez with Marthe Robert and had discussed the issue of Artaud's release with Dr Gaston Ferdière. Two stipulations governing Artaud's return to life in liberated Paris were laid down: firstly that he should reside in a clinic, and secondly that he should be financially independent. It was Adamov who set about to fulfil these conditions. The 'Association des amis d'Antonin Artaud' was formed, an organisation which, through its treasurer Jean Dubuffet, was concerned primarily in handling Artaud's funds. Adamov began collecting together a number of donated canvases and manuscripts to be auctioned off in conjunction with a benefit performance. For this fund-raising evening of readings from Artaud's works, he sought the co-operation of other friends of the artist such as Alain Cuny, André Breton, Jean-Louis Barrault (who subsequently denied being involved), and, of course, Roger Blin, all of whom were instrumental in the ensuring the success of the soirée. The aim was to raise enough money for Artaud to achieve the financial independence required to regain his freedom. Blin, however, was initially unable to confirm that he could participate in these readings as the shooting schedule in Nice for Gréville's film *Pour une nuit d'amour*, in which he had his first lead role, clashed with Adamov's proposed date. With as few as six days left, Adamov earnestly attempted to persuade Blin to return to Paris and contribute to the evening's readings:

> I am relying substantially upon your participation. You alone can and should recite the text from *Nouvelles révélations de l'être*. This is not flattery, it is the truth. You alone. I beg of you (I am asking it of you as a personal favour) come on Thursday [...] Artaud is here, free to go out and to come and go as he pleases, though still in a clinic, with Delmas in Ivry. He is magnificent. And it would please him a great deal if you were to come [...] If you knew of all the

75   Ibid., pp.215–8. An English translation can be found in *Artaud on Theatre*, pp.186–7.
76   Blin had previously informed Artaud of this venture in a note which Adamov forwarded in a letter dated 21.3.46 (unpublished, Blin Archive, IMEC).

difficulties I have had with this meeting. Rushed, pressure from all sides, I'm at the end of my tether, ill emotionally. Be here.[77]

Adamov's reasons for approaching Blin where threefold: firstly, he was fairly well acquainted with Blin and expected to be able to rely on his support to aid Artaud, whom they both held in esteem; secondly, Blin's reputation was becoming such that Adamov felt that adding his name to an already impressive list of contributors could only serve to promote the cause; thirdly, Adamov had great respect for Blin's ability as a speaker and actor, a point which emerges clearly from his letter of invitation:

> I hope that the text that we've chosen for you is to your liking. It's the first and last parts of the *Nouvelles révélations de l'être*. There is in those passages, more than in the rest of Artaud's work, something that goes singularly beyond literature, something terrible that you alone, of all the actors in Paris, could utter.[78]

Notwithstanding the need for a touch of flattery in his appeal, the core of Adamov's sentiment seems perfectly sincere. This admiration for Blin's artistic capabilities formed the basis of the bond of hope he later entertained in him as interpreter of his first full-length play *La Parodie* (*The Parody*). With the help of Barrault, who arranged with the film producers for him to be relieved long enough to return to Paris, Blin was able to attend and deliver the piece of Artaud's writing which Adamov had chosen for him. Paule Thévenin's eye-witness account of the performance demonstrates the deeply emotional quality of his recital:

> I was able to see Roger Blin appear on the stage and hear him recite the first pages of *Nouvelles révélations de l'être* in a staggering manner. He held that heart-rending text in his quivering hands, shaking more and more through emotion as he read it, and it seemed to me that he communicated it to the whole audience.[79]

77 Letter from Adamov to Blin, dated 1.6.46, Archives Roger Blin, Bibliothèque Nationale, département des arts du spectacle (Arsenal), Paris.
78 Ibid. The underlining is Adamov's.
79 Paule Thévenin, *Antonin Artaud, ce Désespéré qui vous parle* (Paris: Seuil, 1993), p.7.

The performance took place on 7 June 1946, the list of contributors reading like a directory of French theatre of the era: alongside the above names were those of Charles Dullin and Louis Jouvet, Jean Vilar, Madeleine Renaud and Maria Casarès. In addition to Blin's contribution, Barrault gave a reading from *Les Cenci*, and Breton offered an introductory 'avant-propos' to open the evening. The previous day the auction had been held at which canvases donated by Giacometti, Picasso, Bracque, Chagall, Duchamp, Léger and Dubuffet were sold together with autographed material offered by Gide, Sartre, Simone de Beauvoir, Éluard, Joyce, Mauriac and Audiberti. The two events together raised in excess of a million old francs. This sum, coupled with royalties that had started to accumulate from the recently reissued *Théâtre et son double* (1944) and from his latest publication *Au pays des Tarahumaras* (*In the Land of the Tarahumaras*, 1945), helped Artaud onto his feet financially, and gave him, for the first time, a stable and not insubstantial source of income on which he could live without hardship during what were to prove the final two years of his life.

Not only was Blin partly responsible for this new-found financial independence but also for the physical freedom enjoyed by Artaud at the Ivry clinic. Blin was at the head of a group of friends who had talked the clinic's director Dr Delmas into allowing Artaud his own key. Thus, during this final phase of Artaud's life he and Blin were able to frequent the cafés and bistros of the Left Bank together, as they had done a decade earlier, meeting up with other old friends, and a collection of newer ones such as Jacques Prevel and Jean Dubuffet.

When Artaud felt the need once more to confront an audience after more than a decade of silence, Blin supported him. Others among Artaud's pre-war acquaintances sought to discourage him or simply disassociated themselves from any such enterprise. Barrault, for example, felt that Artaud was too mentally ill and would benefit more from treatment than exhibition. Breton, too, was highly critical of his former associate's attempts to re-establish himself as a public speaker. Artaud's insanity was confirmed for these men, but Blin refused to acknowledge Artaud's supposed madness, and continued to do so throughout his life. 'It's not that he didn't believe it was so,' explains Jean Martin, 'but that he found it shouldn't be believed. He didn't think it was the only explanation for Artaud's behaviour.'[80] Blin encouraged Artaud in the project, *Histoire vécu par A-Mômo*, which took place on 13 January 1947 at the Vieux-Colombier theatre and which is often recorded as a final public humiliation for him. Blin's memory of the occasion was coloured with sadness:

> He was seated, a black table in front of him, with a pile of papers on it, as he had written a text especially for the evening. The whole room was in an extraordinarily emotional state... And then, little by little, at a given moment, he made some clumsy gesture, I don't know what... his papers went flying... he lost his glasses... he went down on his knees to pick up his papers... but of course not one sound of laughter in the house... We were all in a very anxious state, after all [...] and suddenly he took fright... he had sensed it... he told us afterwards, that the emptiness of the house had frightened him [...] He had not even been able to sense the emotion... he had not been able to feel the extraordinary love that we all had for him... he had found himself alone... and he left.[81]

Two months after that event, Artaud's gratitude for Blin's continued, unconditional support was expressed in a most surreal manner:

> The more I see of my friend Roger Blin, the more I recall, with a wondrous and maddening certainty,
> that he was the man two thousand years ago,
> attached to a cross
> a sort of stake
> as a TAU
> ON GOLGOTHA
> and who said to me,
> me, also attached and nailed even to a cross
> I vomit god, society and its lackeys, and wherever you go I shall follow.
> Yes, it was Roger Blin, not the good thief, but the bad thief who offered to me, Antonin Artaud, unknown, these words.[82]

80   Jean Martin to Mark Batty, 11.1.95.
81   Blin, quoted in Jacques Baratier, *Le Désordre à vingt ans*, in *L'Avant-Scène Cinéma*, 75 (November 1967), p.51.
82   Antonin Artaud, 'Un mot à propos de quelque chose', *Théâtre en Europe*, 2 (April 1984), p.17.

This is praise indeed, if somewhat unorthodox. Artaud's words here go far beyond what one might normally expect from a piece of dramatic criticism, which is what it purported to be. The review was hurriedly written on the night of Blin's performance in John Millington Synge's *L'Ombre de la ravine* (*In the Shadow of the Glen*) at the Vieux-Colombier theatre in March 1947,[83] exactly a year after Artaud had been released from the Rodez Asylum. So keen had Artaud been to see his friend on stage, despite Blin's discreet discouragement, that he interrupted the evening meal he was sharing with Paule Thévenin at the Vieux Paris restaurant, insisting on taking the remainder of his dinner with him in a paper napkin, rather than be late for the play's opening. That he was anxious not to miss Blin's performance is perhaps unsurprising. His exile from Paris in the numerous mental asylums in which he had been interned between 1937 and 1946 meant that he had never been able to witness any of his close friend's work since the minor role he himself had offered him in his *Les Cenci* over a decade earlier. Following that curious initiation to the stage, Blin had succeeded in building for himself a solid reputation as an actor of talent and integrity. It is perfectly natural, therefore, that Artaud was curious to see how Blin had developed over the years of their separation, having only ever heard of his accomplishments through their correspondence or on the very rare occasions when they had met. That very curiosity must have fuelled the zeal with which Artaud wrote 'Un mot à propos de quelque chose' which, although ostensibly a compliment to Roger Blin's skill as an actor, reads as a testimony to the bond between the two men; a declaration of respect and love which culminates in this expression of gratitude:

> And Roger Blin has indeed kept his word; he has followed me, for he is the one who, during my nine years of incarceration, made the most appearances at the asylums where I found myself, distressed and breathless, carrying cigarettes and money for me.[84]

---

83   This was a revival by Raymond Raynal of his *mise en scène* which had been mounted originally at the Théâtre Monceau in 1941 (see p.58).

84   Artaud, 'Un mot à propos de quelque chose', p.17.

Blin continued to encourage Artaud's creativity and offer his own skills in support, collaborating on some of his final projects; he agreed to read 'La Culture indienne'[85] ('Indian Culture') at an evening of readings organised at the Galerie Pierre during an exhibition of Artaud's drawings there in July 1947 and also worked on Artaud's final dramatic experiment, the powerful performance poem *Pour en finir avec le jugement de Dieu* (*To Have Done with the Judgement of God*), recorded for broadcast on Radiodiffusion Française. Blin read the section entitled 'La recherche de la fécalité' ('The Pursuit of Fecality') recorded between 22 and 29 November 1947, along with the other texts performed by Artaud, Paule Thévenin and Maria Casarès. An additional recording session held on 18 January 1948 involved Blin and Artaud screaming out a 'conversation' in Artaud's invented language to an accompaniment of kettledrums.

The work was scheduled to air at quarter to eleven on 2 February 1948, and was billed as a show that 'without doubt risked coming across as obscure or shocking for some.'[86] However, having previewed the recording on the day before its scheduled broadcast, the head of the radio station, Wladimir Porché, refused to sanction its transmission on grounds of its obscenity and blasphemy. This rejection was perhaps the last straw of frustration to his artistic ambitions and served to drain Artaud's remaining energies. Succumbing to cancer, Artaud died on 4 March 1948 following a self-administered overdose of chloral hydrate. Blin last met him only two days previously to discuss the outcome of a board meeting concerning the decision not to broadcast the radio project. He took part in the three-day 'relay' vigil over his friend's corpse, at night to keep the rats away, and during the day to keep the priests out.[87]

If, subsequent to Artaud's death, Blin remained stubbornly reticent on the subject of their relationship it must principally be due to the profound respect he held for the memory of someone to whom he

---

85   'Roger Blin spoke "La Culture indienne" in an incredible manner and got the crowd to their feet. Roger Blin was like a devil, Artaud said.' Jacques Prevel, *En compagnie d'Antonin Artaud* (Paris: Flammarion, 1974), p.155.

86   *Radio-Revue*, 1–7.2.48.

87   Blin in Marowitz, *Artaud at Rodez*, pp.81–2.

had been extremely close. If he was protective of the details of his friend's life his attitude can be attributed to an awareness of and a cynicism over the zeal of journalists and biographers to distort anything that might be said of Artaud to tally with their own suppositions and arguments. Whenever Blin did give brief accounts of his friendship it was usually with restraint, sprinkling his words with ambiguity, exuding discomfort at being asked to give an opinion or analysis of his friend's achievements, and qualifying any such comment with an element of vagueness, as in the following two examples:

> I have never wanted to formulate fixed opinions about Artaud. I could recount anecdotes, but I couldn't say if he was this or that, because he was both this and that. To understand better, I remind myself of how he was towards the end, that is to say at the peak of his lucidity.

> I simply cannot pass judgement on Artaud: as for his so-called madness, that was something else, a form of revolt. It was not a kind of escape for him, it was an experiment that he had pushed too far perhaps, sometimes he would pass over to the other side, as Breton would say. I don't know.[88]

A consolidated reputation

Shortly after the recording sessions for Artaud's radio play, Blin began rehearsals for a production that must have appealed to him greatly, not simply because it was to arouse some controversy but also because of the highly physical nature of the performance, the beauty and freshness of the text and the enthusiasm of his partners in the project. The director Georges Vitaly had asked the poet Henri Pichette to write a play in verse. The result, *Les Épiphanies*, was a particularly unconventional and surreal composition of poetic drama in five acts, set to backdrops by Roberto Matta, and focused around the character of the poet who is joined at various points by other characters, the poet's beloved and the devil (played by Blin). The play was premièred

---

88   Blin, *Souvenirs et propos*, p.33 and *Libération*, 14.6.77.

in December 1947 at the Théâtre des Noctambules, after a dispute over the text during late rehearsals at the Théâtre Edward VII, where it had originally been commissioned to show. That theatre's director, M. Bétaille, after having witnessed one rehearsal of the play, was so alarmed by what he saw and heard that he feared scandal and, refusing to allow the play to go on at the standard evening time, offered the company a trial matinée slot for their performances. This meant a slot at 6 o'clock in the early evening, and even that was on condition the play did not offend some 'normal' people Bétaille would bring to a rehearsal. In response to this insult, Vitaly simply rented the Noctambules on the Left Bank. That Blin had managed by this time to accrue a considerable reputation as an actor is attested in Henri Pichette's indignant letter to Bétaille, openly published in *Combat*:

> Whoever [...] now sees Roger Blin, once more working outside the more privileged theatrical and film worlds, will be able to imagine how passionately he feels in accepting this, in the extent of his of desire to participate [...] I salute the way he burns on stage.[89]

As things turned out no real scandal was provoked by the performance. The big box office names of Gérard Philipe and Maria Casarès had ensured the full booking of all 30 performances prior to opening night, and the critics focused their attention on the performance of Philipe (who had come to their and the public's attention in the lead role of Camus's *Caligula* in 1945), simply dismissing the text as incomprehensible if it was not to their taste. In spite of the full houses, and perhaps irritated by some of these reviews, Vitaly felt the play needed defending against the charge of being little more than an allegorical poem, as opposed to a legitimate piece of theatre:

> *Les Épiphanies* belongs, more than any other similar work of the same era, to that theatre of 'rupture' that we have been trying to create. Rupture in form, from normal dialogue, from the usual flow of scenes, rupture too from the contact with the public, because we are no longer appealing to the audience's reason and their critical faculties, but instead to their sensibilities, to their

89   Pichette in *Combat*, 22.11.47.

emotional receptiveness, their impressionability. Rupture, too, in décor, abstract décors, synthesising the atmosphere of each act.[90]

André Breton, in the audience for the première, applauded the work heartily and André Gide thought Blin 'excellent'.[91] His performance was also lauded by many critics, one recounting how '[h]e sculpted his role with all the boldness and intensity of the gargoyles of Notre-Dame. At the end, when he transformed himself into a dog in a kind of horrible trance, he showed himself to be a tragic actor of the greatest kind' and claimed that 'we all very much admire this artist who [...] is no ordinary actor, but often the equal of the poets he is representing.'[92] Clearly, by the end of the 1940s, Blin had made a strong name for himself as a supporting actor on both stage and screen. As a performer of the avant-garde he was recognised as being a 'silent, bitter poet whose gloomy style touches more than just the text which inspires him.'[93] His appeal was in the power and tone of his voice and in his physical appearance. Once it became known that he was capable of controlling his stammer when delivering rehearsed speech this first obstacle to his career was removed (he never stuttered on stage nor, curiously, during live radio or TV interviews – 'not when I'm being paid' he once quipped)[94] and his rich voice, 'vague, deep, captivating',[95] was sought after by producers of radio, film and theatre. With his tall, almost clumsy gait, and his thin face with high cheek bones (Artaud described him as having 'a head which looks like an enlargement of the shrunken heads of the Vivarois Indians'),[96] Blin had neither the physique nor features for standard lead or even major supporting roles, but his appearance did suit some of the more mar-

90   Vitaly in Anne Philipe and Claude Roy, *Gérard Philipe* (Paris: Gallimard, 1960).
91   Adrienne Monnier, *Mercure de France*, 9.12.48.
92   Ibid.
93   F.Charles Bauer, review of Heiberg's *La Tragédie de l'amour*, *L'Echo de la France*, 13.12.43.
94   Hermine Karagheuz, *Roger Blin: Une dette d'amour* (Paris: Séguier, 2002), p.18.
95   Lisane Garel, 'Ceux de chez Chéramy', *Marianne*, No.349, 28.6.39, p.18.
96   Quoted by Blin to Eric Neuhoff, in *Le Quotidien de Paris*, 19.5.81.

ginal, eerie, or plainly odd characters he came to play, such as lepers, beggars and assassins:

> Since 1936, in fifty or so films, he has created subtly tortured and vaguely disturbing characters, for which his singular physique and feverish gaze seem to have condemned him to play: Fagotin in *Capitaine Fracasse* (Gance), the suicidal tuberculosis sufferer in *Corbeau* (Clouzot), the bear trainer in *Visiteurs du soir* (Carné).[97]

Described here by his friend Jean Rougeul, one gets a further impression of the sorts of characters for which Blin was suited:

> A rather strange-looking person, a long silhouette, thin, with a swaying gait, his face handsome, bony, tormented, with piercing, heavy-lidded eyes, beneath a shaggy tuft of black hair. He is not averse to caping himself in a certain mystery and seems generally to have walked out of an Edgar Allen Poe novel in order to seek out, on a bench, at the invitation of an autumn rain, the shadow of Jules Laforgue. Drifting around in a stony raincoat, wearing a battered trilby which casts a shadow over his forehead, a large brightly coloured scarf around his neck, he sets off for this secret rendezvous with the swinging gait of an old seadog, a misleading gangster look and a poetic air that lingers in the fog for some time in his wake.[98]

Beyond his physical suitability for many of the roles he was offered, he was capable of gesture and movement which lent to his work a strong and attractive force of stage presence, described by one critic as 'something more than skill: a delicate touch which, sometimes, makes him capable of bringing forth, of making palpable, that which is invisible.'[99] By the late 1940s, Blin's reputation had reached such a level of respectability within the experimental theatre community that it is not surprising that there should have been a degree of interest among press reviewers favourable to the avant-garde for any work he might undertake as a director.

---

97   Marcel Martin, *La Revue du cinéma*, 392 (March 1984), p.19.

98   Jean Rougeul, 'Les Nouveaux talents', *Paris-Cinéma*, July 1947.

99   Georges Pelorson, review of Heiberg's *La Tragédie de l'amour*, in *La Révolution Matérielle*, 8.1.44.

The Gaîté-Montparnasse

As with his introduction to acting, Blin entered the world of professional directing through a chance set of circumstances involving his acquaintances. It was thanks to his Greek friend Christine Tsingos that he had his first, and last, experience as the owner of a theatre. Tsingos, another alumnus of Dullin's Atelier, had inherited a sum of money and wanted to acquire the Gaîté-Montparnasse theatre, which had become available in 1948. However, as foreign nationals, neither she nor her husband could legally manage the theatre under French law. She asked Blin to put his name to the contract as a sleeping partner in financial terms, but one who would be involved artistically in the running of the theatre. Situated on the rue de la Gaîté out in the fourteenth arrondissement amid music hall theatres and nightclubs, the Gaîté-Montparnasse, with an old reputation for simple comedies, was an odd venue for the type of drama to which Blin hoped to draw a public. Here, though, he would be able to indulge himself in a personal agenda of realising a theatre of integrity. His efforts were appreciated by some:

> It's a destitute theatre with worn-out seating, a rickety stage and tiny wings. It's cold in there and, as the actors perform, you can make out blasts of jazz music from a neighbouring nightclub, which the slenderness of the partition walls are unable to stifle. But, on stage, within a fragile painted cardboard décor, there are actors who – against all hope – still believe in the theatre.[100]

It was the Irish playwright Denis Johnston's *Moon in the Yellow River* that Blin first chose to direct. This play, though scarcely symptomatic of his inclination and taste for avant-garde drama, intrigued him as soon as he received the manuscript from his friend and its translator Jean-René Chauffard, It engaged him instantly, appealing primarily to his disposition towards Irish literature and culture. A portrait of Ireland during the political growing pains of the 1920s, the play, with its subtle black comedy and juxtaposition of absurdities and harsh reality, possessed a quality that charmed Blin. It may have been

100   Michel Déon, *Aspects de la France et du Monde*, 24.11.49.

the impulse to do justice to the play that compelled Blin to direct this piece; with it he wanted to combat the stereotypical view of Ireland that was common in the Boulevard theatres: 'OK, it's an Irish play, but not a folklore tale. Get that down', he told the journalist sent to enquire about the production.[101]

Set in a converted fort at the mouth of the Liffey in the formative years of the new republic, the play begins with the arrival of an optimistic and idealistic German engineer, Tausch, to work on the turbines of the adjacent powerhouse. The introduction of I.R.A. terrorists, intent on blowing up the powerhouse involves him in a debate over the power-struggle followed by a cycle of crime and retribution and his entanglement in the accompanying justifications and explanations. The play is capable of winning over an audience with a charming presentation of the contradictions stated as inherent in the nature of the Irish before then confronting them with substantial questions about the futility of acts of revenge. The drama trivialises its own tragedy, reaching thereby a potent level of poignancy with its blend of the comic and the serious. Dogma and its justifications are questioned, belittled or ridiculed, and the consequences of inflexible convictions are demonstrated plainly, stripped of any glory or significance. Although not a profoundly political play, the manner in which Johnston presents political action on a personal level by contrasting militant elements with more humanist ones, and by setting the action in a domestic environment, effectively creates a drama within which questions of importance can be dealt with in depth without being overly specific. *La Lune dans le fleuve jaune* opened on 25 May 1949 and, although it was not altogether successful commercially, the production received a collection of positive reviews which commended the ensemble nature of the acting and the subtlety of the *mise en scène*. 'How pleasant it is to see and listen to a troupe who, without stars, all serve the text in good faith,' stated one critic.[102]

The following year, Blin directed a short play by his friend, the journalist Jean Silvant, *Le Bourreau s'impatiente* (*The Executioner is Waiting*). This was mounted as the second half of a double bill with a

101   Blin to Jean-François Delay in *Combat*, 23.5.49.
102   Francis Ambrière, *Opéra*, 8.6.49.

production of Jean Cocteau's *L'Épouse injustement soupçonnée* (*Unfounded Suspicions about his Wife*) directed by Sacha Pitoëff, which attracted greater critical interest. Although Silvant's play was of no great literary merit, Blin liked the atmosphere it conjured and unusual nature of its construction: made up of a succession of tableaux, all set in a Dickensian England, it is a drama of persecution. Moreover, having made use of the play free of charge for his work with the students of the E.P.J.D.,[103] Blin was anxious that the author should at last receive some financial reward. There may also have been a desire to experiment, to try out new theatrical ideas as a risk, throwing to the wind all box-office concerns. Such an independent spirit, though it bemused some, earned Blin the admiration of others:

> Far be it for them now to stage a guaranteed success that might fill the cashbox. They continue with plays that I fear will come across to their audiences as a kind of provocation [...] You can see what might have attracted Blin to *Le Bourreau s'impatiente*, [the play] demands of its director an ability and a choreography no less skilful than that required by a Cocteau playlet. With a few touches, with a few characters, he knows how to create the atmosphere, set fantasies in motion, extract dream from reality and reality from dream.[104]

Artistically, however, the production made little impact and the best of reviews were little more than polite and for many critics the performance was merely 'Torture by boredom'.[105] To compound Blin's difficulties, it was during the run of this play that disaster struck and a fire caused serious damage to the theatre. Being the named manager, he was left with a debt that blighted him financially for three decades, having to repay contributions to the U.R.S.S.A.F.[106] for over ten years until President de Gaulle finally granted him an amnesty.

---

103 The 'Ecole pédagogique pour le jeu dramatique', for which Blin taught young adults between 1950 and 1953, was an organisation that had evolved from the wartime 'Éducation par le jeu dramatique' for which he had worked with schoolchildren (see pp.58–9). Both E.P.J.D organisations had been the work of Jean-Marie Conty, Jean-Louis Barrault, and Marie-Hélène Dasté.

104 Michel Déon, *Aspects de la France et du monde*, 9.3.50.

105 Gabriel Marcel, *Les Nouvelles Littéraires*, 30.3.50.

106 'L'Union de Recouvrement des cotisations de Sécurité sociale et d'allocations familiales', France's Social Security organisation.

Blin's major achievement at the Gaîté-Montparnasse, and perhaps the first significant milestone in his career as a director, was his production of August Strindberg's *The Ghost Sonata*. This was mounted in October 1949 in a double bill with Georg Büchner's *Woyzeck*, between Johnston's and Silvant's plays. Having admired the work for many years he convinced Christine Tsingos and her husband to entertain a production at the theatre and was finally able to take on the role of the student Arkenholz, one that he had long wanted to play. Blin himself directed Strindberg's play and the direction of *Woyzeck* was left to his colleague, Pierre Vernier. Unfortunately Büchner's play had to be dropped after only one performance. On the press night, the arrangements for changing from each tableau of *Woyzeck* to the next proved so complicated that the raising of the curtain was delayed by more than an hour and the performance of *La Sonate des spectres*, which was to play second, consequently suffered from this lack of organisation. The critic present from *Le Parisien libéré* recorded how the performance of Büchner's play was interrupted by an 'technical incident', how Blin was heard to shout 'rideau' to call the curtain down and how the full evening's programme did not finish until twenty past one in the morning.[107]

The decision to mount a play by Strindberg may have been initially prompted by Blin's receiving a proposal from Henri Membré, the then representative of Strindberg's inheritors in France, to perform *The Bond*. This Blin declined, explaining in a letter to Membré that he considered the play outdated and that he would prefer to leave it unperformed 'so as not to prejudice the memory of Strindberg'.[108] His own choice of *La Sonate des spectres*, he felt, was a play unlikely to compromise the playwright's reputation. It is worth noting that Strindberg at this time had yet to be accepted into the theatrical mainstream of mid-century France, though his literary influence was already widespread. On the French stage, the Swedish playwright had not managed to gain much recognition beyond his being the author of the

---

107   *Le Parisien libéré*, 25.10.49.
108   Letter from Blin to Membré, dated 6.3.49, quoted in Anthony Swerling, *Strindberg's Impact in France 1920–1960* (Cambridge: Trinity Lane Press, 1971), p.180.

naturalistic plays, *Miss Julie* and *The Father*. Of the post-Inferno plays, only *The Dance of Death* had received any serious exposure. It was Jean Vilar's production of this play in 1943 at the Théâtre Vaneau (revived in 1945 at the Théâtre des Noctambules and at the Studio des Champs-Elysées in 1948) that created an awareness of Strindberg to the French public and press during the 1940s, and it was during that decade that performances of his plays became more frequent.

In choosing to produce *La Sonate des spectres*, then, Blin was acting in the same spirit as Jean Vilar who, when giving his reasons for mounting *La Dance de mort* said 'I felt like I was performing an act of justice.'[109] Blin recognised the play's stature and wanted to communicate it to a public still unacquainted with this chamber piece, which had remained unperformed in the country since its French première at the Théâtre de l'Avenue in 1933:

> I think it's good theatre and not enough of that is done. *The Sonata* does of course have its bizarre, almost monstrous aspects, which is a characteristic of masterpieces, and certain moments are on the verge of comedy, as in all tragedies.[110]

Undaunted by critical pressure from within the theatrical community or from the press, Blin directed according to his instincts, not following any strict notions of how to approach a *mise en scène*. He recognised the limitations of the stage at the Gaîté-Montparnasse and seemed to have succeeded by ignoring the frustration he felt at the technical complexities of realising Strindberg's text:

> The décor was terrible at the Gaîté. We didn't have a lot of money and the designer was very nice, well-meaning, but knew nothing about Strindberg. What's more, on a stage as narrow and as shallow as the one at the Gaîté, to create a sense of mystery... Changes in décor took a terribly long time as there were no wings, no free room. The lighting was appalling too. Because of the poor financial and technical conditions, I wasn't able to do any of what I had envisioned, but I think I respected the spirit of the play.[111]

109   Ibid., p.176.
110   Blin to Frédéric O'Brady, in *Combat*, 4.10.49.
111   Blin, *Souvenirs et propos*, p.69.

Not only did the production enjoy a degree of commercial success – the play ran on its own for approximately 100 performances – but Blin also achieved most of his artistic goals and the majority of the press coverage was favourable. Jacques Lemarchand, distrusting the tiring experience of the disastrous press night, went to see the play a second time and assessed Blin's production as a triumph for Strindberg:

> By allowing us to see and hear *The Sonata* [...] Roger Blin and Christine Tsingos have broken further than ever before through the barriers that separate the public from the author of *Inferno*. And it is not just their intention that deserves to be praised here, it is their achievement [...] I believe that people who did not see *The Ghost Sonata* will say in five years time that they were there.[112]

The accomplishment was all the more marked by a favourable review of the performance which carried as far as Strindberg's homeland. Stellan Ahlström wrote praise of Blin's work in Sweden's *Samtid och Framtid*:

> The director is remarkably faithful to Strindberg's work. In the two interior scenes he makes use of drapes in the way that Strindberg himself recommended in the open letters to the Intimate theatre [...] Roger Blin's interpretation of *The Ghost Sonata* is the best representation of Strindberg offered in France for many years.[113]

Success and recognition of this order must have been gratifying for a man who had risked a good reputation by staging such a difficult play with extremely limited resources. It certainly vindicated the choices Blin and the Tsingos couple had made in deciding upon the tone of the repertoire they wanted to adopt for their theatre, all partners sharing the same drive to produce works of integrity and significance. Their enthusiasm did not go unrecognised. André Ransan wrote of the Gaîté-Montparnasse management in *Ce Matin-Le Pays* in November 1949:

---

112   Jacques Lemarchand, *Combat*, 8.11.49.
113   Stellan Ahlström, *Samtid och Framtid*, January 1950, pp.117–18.

It could be said that by taking on the management of the Gaîté-Montparnasse Roger Blin and Christine Tsingos have not taken the easy route. All the more so as they seem resolved to become the defenders and propagators of a choice repertoire, distinctive, somewhat austere, maybe even impenetrable at times, and consequently anti-commercial *par excellence*. None of the so-called boulevard drama at their theatre.[114]

This 'choice repertoire' was, on the occasion in question, the double bill of Strindberg and Büchner, a programme which in itself was demonstrative of the ambition that drove Blin at the outset of a career in directing. His exemplary choice of these writers of highly subjective drama, recognised as forefathers of the modernist avant-garde, reveal where Blin's artistic preoccupations lay at the end of the 1940s. His choice of *La Lune dans le fleuve jaune* confirms the impression that he sought to expose the work of neglected playwrights to a public and that of *Le Bourreau s'impatiente* demonstrated his interest in providing an outlet for the work of new dramatists otherwise spurned by the priorities of the commercial stage, an attitude reminiscent of the ambitions of the ciné-clubs he used to frequent a decade previously.

114 *Ce Matin- Le Pays*, 27.10.49.

Arthur Adamov

Roger Blin's first significant, creative collaboration with an author was with his friend Arthur Adamov. The two men had first met during the late 1920s in the various bars of the Saint-Germain-des-Près quarter on the Left Bank and had also found themselves together occasionally in the company of Antonin Artaud. In the 1930s, Adamov was frequently to be found with the poet Roger Gilbert-Lecomte and the Swedish painter Gustav Bolin, and Blin would often bump into these three 'tramp-princes', as he described them, along the boulevard Montparnasse. Their first actual encounter was when Adamov, probably having been told that Blin's father was a doctor, approached Blin for advice on where he could procure heroin for his partner Irène. Artistically and politically there was already the seed of an affinity between the two men: both hovered on the fringes of the Surrealist movement without being formal members of the group, both developed a fascination for the poet Artaud and were amongst the few who witnessed his production of Strindberg's *Le Songe* (*A Dream Play*). Both identified with the working class struggle, supported the formation of the Front Populaire and actively participated together in the demonstrations that accompanied the Communist party's strike in favour of Sacco and Vanzetti on 23 August 1927.[1]

Born only a year apart, belonging to the same social group of friends, sharing the same political convictions and frequenting the same social circles, the two men naturally enjoyed an acquaintance during the 1930s which served as a basis for the solid friendship that was to flourish after the separation caused by the Occupation. In the early years of their acquaintance, Blin found Adamov's company exhilarating, later describing him as having 'the presence of a Kafka

---

1   The execution of the Italian anarchists Nicola Sacco and Bartolomeo Vanzetti in the U.S.A. in 1927, following an apparent perversion of justice, caused outrage throughout the Left in Europe and demonstrations and riots took place in France, Germany and the UK.

who knocks the wind out of you',[2] with an engaging manner and appearance: 'He spoke in an interesting way. Even his physical build was out of the ordinary: a peculiar face, dark-skinned, faded clothes.'[3]

Adamov had called on Blin to read at the fund-raising revue he had organised for Artaud in 1946. Blin's reputation at this time was securely established and was to be further consolidated in 1947 with his appearance as Monsieur Diable in Henri Pichette's *Les Épiphanies*. When Adamov invited him to a reading of *La Parodie* in that same year he must have been hoping to interest Blin in the play actively rather than simply seeking endorsement of its worth.

Although he had heard much from his friend about the play during its genesis and was acquainted with his writing through the occasional fragments of the novel *L'Aveu* (*The Confession*) that Adamov would read to him, Blin's initial reaction to *La Parodie* was not wildly enthusiastic. Recognising the influences of Kafka and Strindberg, he nevertheless found himself seduced by the play's irony, humour and the obsessive nature of the characters. Perhaps more than anything else it was the honest quality of the writing that appealed to Blin, writing that had arisen directly from his friend's manias, pre-occupations and personal distresses:

> At the time of *La Parodie*, *L'Invasion*, *La Grande et la Petite Manœuvre*, Adamov had not yet become an 'author'; he was a man simply trying to escape his obsessions by making them tangible in some way within characters who were nevertheless always him.[4]

Blin quickly resolved to mount Adamov's play and the two set about the task of finding a theatre that would give it a home and sponsors to provide the necessary financial backing. Preliminary rehearsals began in 1948 for a projected production at the Théâtre de l'Œuvre, but Adamov was let down by the manager who, having originally undertaken to back a run of the play later withdrew his offer. This

2 Blin to Bettina Knapp, in *Tulane Drama Review*, 7.3 (1962), p.124.
3 Blin to Emmanuel C. Jacquart, 'Adamov était le roi des trois points', in *French Review*, 48.6 (May 1975), pp.996–1004 (p.997).
4 Blin, 'Témoignage', in Pierre Mélèse, *Adamov* (Paris: Seghers, 1972), pp.156–8 (p.157).

early disappointment was the first of a string of unfortunate setbacks that were to plague the play's production. For two whole years after its conception the play was the object of intense frustration. As he was to find with Beckett's *En attendant Godot*, Blin had great difficulty in finding a theatre manager who would even contemplate a performance and he and Adamov even considered the possibility of giving the French première outside France,[5] as he was later obliged to do with Beckett's *Fin de partie* (*Endgame*). A glimmer of hope appeared when Blin was approached in 1949 by Thanos and Christine Tsingos to act as 'gérant' to the Gaîté-Montparnasse theatre and both author and director envisaged the possibility of having *La Parodie* performed there during the first season of the new management. Clearly, the possibility of a production did come under discussion,[6] but in the end the Tsingos couple proved unwilling to handle the play, preferring instead to take on Blin's alternative suggestion of mounting a double bill of *La Sonate des spectres* and *Woyzeck*. Being an enthusiast of both Strindberg and Büchner, Adamov received the news with mixed emotions:

> I heard from Marthe and from the word on the street that you're putting on *La Sonate* and *Woyzeck*. I was both very happy and a little sad to hear it, I must admit. It's quite possible that I'll have access to 300,000 francs for *La Parodie*. If this proves so, I'd like to be certain that you will handle it, as soon as your production is finished.[7]

The potential subsidy Adamov referred to was from the Secrétaire d'état à l'Education Nationale, to whom he had applied for funding. In order to be eligible for it Adamov and Blin had to form a company, as individuals could not apply, and the fictitious Théâtre d'aujourd'hui was created, with Roger Blin as the named 'animateur'. In order to attract further sponsorship, a brochure was printed in the company's name in which numerous artists stated the case for Adamov's

5   Adamov wrote to Blin from Germany on a visit there in August 1951, when the prospect of ever seeing *La Parodie* performed was at its bleakest, to point out that there were options for performance there. (Letter dated 5.8.51)

6   A letter dated 13.8.49 written to Blin by Adamov from Nice, in which he queries Blin over Tsingos's decision, testifies to this.

7   Letter from Adamov to Blin, dated 14.9.49.

play. Jacques Prévert offered the most flattering reason for backing it: 'It is because I love theatre that I hardly ever go to the theatre, but if Roger Blin were to mount *La Parodie*, I'd be very happy.'[8] The most powerful argument in favour of a production was offered by Blin himself:

> I'd be tempted to speak of *La Parodie* as a notorious play. Those close to me already speak of it thus, in all seriousness. It is however a play that is yet to be staged. [...] So well-known to me is this play that it will need all its continually renewing freshness and its unending urgency for me not to get the impression, when we do finally stage it, that we are dealing with a revival, albeit a brilliant one. I come, therefore, to ask a few friends to help us remove *La Parodie*'s notoriety, to return it to its proper destiny, which is not to be the object of condolences, but to be brought to life by actors of flesh and blood, by lighting and a few bits of canvas, exactly as it came out of Arthur Adamov's little pencils.[9]

Blin endeavoured to gain further support for the unperformed work by securing a broadcast of three scenes from the play on O.R.T.F. (L'Office de Radiodiffusion Télévision Française) at the end of May 1951. The net product of this fund-raising campaign was a modest sum sufficient to serve as a production budget. On a 'carte pneumatique' postmarked Boxing Day 1951, Adamov announced to Blin that he had collected 13,500 francs for the production, presumably the result of the subscription appeal for *Théâtre d'aujourd'hui*. He also mentioned that he had received 10,000 francs from Armand Salacrou, that he expected 10,000 from Francis Garnung and anticipated a further 35,000 from other sources. André Gide and Jean Paulhan are also known to have contributed. Adamov even tried to extract funding from his estranged friend André Malraux, who had recently been minister for information under de Gaulle. Having received a letter of rejection, Adamov wrote a sarcastic and witty retort: 'I see, Monsieur Malraux, that the General has caused you to forget the particular.'[10] Armed, nevertheless, with the 300,000 old francs from their various sources, Blin and Adamov were finally able

---

8   Jacques Prévert, in *Théâtre d'aujourd'hui*, bulletin de souscription, 1949.
9   Blin, ibid.
10   Quoted by Blin in *Souvenirs et propos*, p.79.

to acquire the stage at the Théâtre Lancry for a run in June and July 1952, renting it for the minimum hire period of thirty days.

At that time, the Lancry was a recently converted salle des fêtes which had just accommodated the première of Eugène Ionesco's *Les Chaises* (*The Chairs*). Here, finally, Blin was able to produce Adamov's play as he had undertaken and had waited to do for what had amounted to five years, coupling it in a double bill with a short piece by Francis Garnung, *Le Service des pompes* (*The Petrol Pump Attendant*), which he also directed using the same cast. Playwright and director had shared so much frustration and shown such perseverance in getting *La Parodie* onto the boards that the play had come to represent a symbol of their friendship.

In the five years which had elapsed since *La Parodie*'s completion, Adamov had written two other plays, *L'Invasion* (*The Invasion*) and *La Grande et la Petite Manœuvre* (*The Greater and the Lesser Manoeuvre*). These had been mounted in the meantime by Jean Vilar and Jean-Marie Serreau respectively, opening within three nights of each other in November 1950.[11] The latter production is of specific interest as Blin assisted Serreau with his *mise en scène*, although he was never formally credited with having done so. Originally he was simply invited by Adamov and Serreau to join in the play's cast, and, having failed to convince his colleagues at the Gaîté-Montparnasse to consider *La Parodie* for the second season there, Blin left them to their own devices and took up the offer, first proposed in a letter from Adamov as early as July 1950:

> If Thanos stands in the way of a production of *La Parodie* when you open, Serreau and I would be very happy if you would accept the part of the mutilated man. I know that you like the play, and we really think that you would suit this part. Of course, there is no question of sacrificing *La Parodie*.[12]

---

11   Vilar was enthralled by Adamov's writings and contributed words of support in the the authors first published plays, offering the (then) provocative 'Adamov or Claudel? I choose Adamov!' Adamov, *La Parodie, L'Invasion* (Paris: Charlot, 1950), p.15.

12   Letter to Blin, dated 24.7.50.

La Parodie and *La Grande et la Petite Manœuvre* are similar works in that they share the typical confessional elements of Adamov's early writings, *La Parodie* itself being virtually a dramatisation of his highly personal and autobiographical novel *L'Aveu*. Adamov recognised that thematically *La Parodie* and *La Grande et la Petite Manœuvre* were very similar, admitting as much in a letter to Blin during the latter's composition: 'I would have preferred to have shown you *La Grande et la Petite Manœuvre* in which I recognise *La Parodie* to a certain degree. But I've only just started it.'[13] In his struggle to find an appropriate artistic form for his neuroses, Adamov developed an innovative dramatic structure which rejected both plot and psychology and presented no coherence, breaking the logic of cause and effect and the rational sequence of dialogue. Both plays follow their protagonists to their inevitable destruction. In *La Parodie* both the optimistic Employé and the masochistic N are led to their fates by the beautiful Lily. In *La Grande et la Petite Manœuvre* it is the Erna who causes the slow deterioration of Le Mutilé, who successively loses his hands and legs at each of her verbal and mental assaults. Blin, in these two productions, took the parallel parts of the Employé and the Mutilé, the eternal optimists who carry on unrelentingly in the face of the impossible, constantly finding reasons to cope and never stopping to assess the true nature of their condition. The role of the Mutilé was a physical ordeal for Blin, who suffered considerable pain to bring Adamov's masochist to life:

> I started by losing my hands – and to do that I had these wooden cone-like things which had hooks on the end – after which I attacked my legs. I folded the left leg, which I put inside a corset, the foot coming up to the top of my right leg. I put my trousers over the top, moving around on my knees, which, of course, caused me to fall over; I had to haul myself along, without arms or legs, to find the crutches. I don't know how I did it, but I managed. With my teeth, I think. I have to say that I was falling over so much then that one day it was my knee, another my hip or my spine.[14]

13   Letter to Blin, dated 3.12.49.
14   Blin in Élisabeth Auclaire-Tamaroff (ed.), *Jean-Marie Serreau – Découvreur de theatres* (Paris: L'Arbre Verdoyant, 1986), pp.36–7.

Blin's physical commitment to a production that was not likely to bring him any reward is in itself eloquent of his pioneering spirit and dedication to a new, revolutionary kind of theatre. Here was a new drama antedating the arrival of both Ionesco and Beckett, alongside whom Adamov was to be considered one of the mainstays of the new French avant-garde. He later summed up the period in his autobiography, *L'Homme et l'enfant* (*Man and Child*):

> What a glorious time the 1950s were! We had to beg, we spoke of putting on a play without even knowing which theatre would host it [...] But we created, Serreau, Roche, Blin, others certainly, and I, an idea more or less resembling what theatre should be. We were the authors, the actors, the directors of the operative avant-garde, face to face with the old, condemned theatre of dialogue.[15]

Along with Vilar and Serreau, Blin was among the first to recognise the worth of this emerging form of expression. Already familiar with non-naturalistic stage work and appreciative of the honesty inherent in Adamov's work, a man of Blin's character and experience was the ideal person to direct it. The fact that, despite his enthusiasm for Adamov's plays, Serreau should have chosen to involve Blin in the direction of *La Grande et la Petite Manœuvre*, is a clear acknowledgement of the understanding that the latter could bring to its production.[16]

La Grande et la Petite Manœuvre was performed at the Théâtre des Noctambules in November 1950, and managed to hold a run of twenty-five nights. The production was an impoverished one, financed by the theatre's manager and playing at the early hour of six-thirty, in the shadow of a 'safer', more audience-friendly offering later in the evening. The company also had to accept payment from a percentage of box-office takings and hope for good audiences. As for scenery, Jacques Noël put together a décor of sorts, filling the grey space with appropriate furniture and relying on the intelligent use of lighting to

---

15   Arthur Adamov, *L'Homme et l'Enfant* (Paris: Gallimard, 1968), p.97.
16   'It was Serreau himself who asked my friend Roger Blin to help out with the direction, Blin being the man in Paris who best knows my theatre.' Adamov, *Combat*, 1.11.50.

suggest particular locations, such as a city street, for example, evoked simply by dimming the lights and a background of recorded sounds.

Adamov threw himself into the realisation of his work with an unprecedented zeal. While Serreau concerned himself mainly with the blocking of the ten scenes of Adamov's play in rehearsal, he relied on Blin to deal with the actors' performances and the challenging task of making stage-sense of this powerfully original piece of playwrighting. The principal problem it posed was that, like the plays Ionesco was writing at the same time, it embodied a manipulation of everyday reality, the evocation of neuroses by means of magnifying and distorting aspects of the real world and underlying its themes through the use of grotesque concrete images, such as in a scene where a group of fingerless workers take a typing lesson. As such, the play demanded a style of acting that was certainly not naturalistic but which at the same time did not break too far away from recognisable reality. The same requirements were to confront Blin again two years later with his production of *La Parodie*. In an interview given in 1970 he discussed the difficulty peculiar to that evolving style of theatre which was subsequently to be labelled 'Absurd' and which he had been one of the first to confront:

> It was difficult to find the right degree of immediate realism and still maintain the dreamlike ambiguity that Adamov wanted. Real gestures, sudden, but anti-naturalistic, not the kind of gestures of the realistic boulevard theatre. I'd worked with Artaud, Dullin even, but I wasn't capable.[17]

Nevertheless Blin managed to build a suitably austere performance for himself as the Mutilé and to engender the necessary juxtaposition of humour and pathos for the piece to achieve its full potential in performance. Adamov, for one, was satisfied:

> Roger Blin, admirable in the role of the Mutilated man, cut short the laughter on each of his entrances, inspired fear, demanded respect. The desired dryness.[18]

17   Blin in René Gaudy, *Arthur Adamov* (Paris: Stock, 1971), p.50.
18   Adamov, *L'Homme et l'Enfant*, p.99.

84

Blin also received a good deal of favourable critical response in the press, both for his acting and for his collaborative work with Serreau on the *mise en scène*, consolidating his position as a major force in the avant-garde of the 1950s:

> Roger Blin plays the part of the mutilated man. I knew he was an excellent actor; I now know that he is a great actor. That imprecise word 'presence', too often used when one can't be bothered to analyse an actor's qualities, in this case makes complete sense [...] [F]ar from taking all the focus off those around him, far from taking advantage of that attention, he knows how to spread and distribute it, on each appearance, to all around him.[19]

At the same time, some critics also reacted favourably to the new kind of drama, welcoming its appearance and acknowledging its significance:

> I think *Manœuvre* has to be considered an important dramatic event. It is often said that there are two forms of theatre; that of the word and that of the gesture. A. Adamov demonstrates that there is a third, in which expression and communication arise neither from word nor from movement, but from a physical sensation. This is more or less precisely what A. Artaud demanded.[20]

Although, arguably, the name of Artaud is here invoked inappropriately, there is the recognition that Adamov, like Artaud, was working outside the traditional parameters of theatre art and striving to widen those parameters still further. Blin's growing interest in this writing is consistent with his developing taste for drama that expresses itself through poetry of image. Indeed his exposure to the work of Adamov may have been central to his subsequent alignment with and support for artists who pursued similar theatrical goals, and was certainly important in his growing reputation for being a central figure in the new avant-garde. His attraction to Pichette's *Les Épiphanies* half a decade earlier had been due to its complete junking of the workings of the naturalistic stage and psychological dialogue, but with Adamov Blin was admiring how a poetry *of* the stage, as opposed to Pichette's poetry *on* the stage, and as espoused by his friend and colleague

19   Jacques Lemarchand, *Le Figaro Littéraire*, 18.11.50.
20   Marc Beigbeder, *Parisien Libéré*, 17.11.50.

Artaud was truly available, amplifying the discoveries of Strindberg's brand of expressionism.

With *La Parodie* in 1952, Blin would again take a leading role as well as direct. The play traces the paths of four loosely linked individuals, none of whom succeeds in connecting successfully with any of the others. Trapped in an inhospitable world of police sirens, street cleaners, deafening noises and dazzling searchlights, their respective paths all lead eventually to solitude or death. The masochistic N (played in the première by Jean Martin) stalks death and waits to be run over by a car; the permanently unemployed but ever-optimistic Employee (played by Blin), a tireless character reminiscent of Ionesco's representative Bérenger, goes blind and is imprisoned; the ruthless journalist tires of his work whilst Lili, the object of all three men's desires, impossible to pin down, ends up destitute and finally flees into the night.

Once more the budget was restrictive, though not quite as meagre as it had been at the Noctambules. Adamov had requested a complex décor that would simultaneously represent internal and external locations, and would shift in perspective between scenes. Blin's friend, the artist Helena Vieira da Silva, offered to paint a backcloth for the production, devising a cityscape which captured the intimidating nature of a modern metropolis that the author had woven into his text and was perfectly matched to Blin's reading of it as 'a tragi-comic play of separation in a city which becomes more hostile the more it modernises.'[21] To create a non-naturalistic, alienating effect he designed a lighting plot which broke with the traditional, straightforward placing of lights to illuminate stage and actors. A fierce upward beam was achieved by situating five small lights at ground level, downstage front, and, instead of using battens, a number of vertical overhead spots helped to generate the desired eerie effect by casting distorting shadows over the actors' faces.[22] To show the isolation of each

21 Blin in *Combat*, 4.6.52.
22 The three notes Blin made regarding these decisions were, respectively: 'footlights not to be used as footlights nor battens as battens' '5 projectors, 250 [Watts] or less, instead of floods' 'use batten circuits for overhead spots.' From three unpublished pages of notes, concerned solely with lighting for the production of *La Parodie*, 1952. Fond Blin, IMEC, Paris.

character as they moved about on stage, Blin made use of a makeshift follow-spot, operated manually: 'One of my friends, who was on the balcony with a pocket torch, had to follow the movement of the actors. The poor fellow had to do that throughout the play for the whole of the run!'[23] Experimenting with everything he had to hand, he put together a 'rhesotatically controlled light without rheostat',[24] using increasing layers of gels to create the effect of dimming lights. To intensify atmosphere he recorded a soundtrack of screams, moans and chants simulating non-realistically the sound of a crowd. With the exception of machine-gun fire, for which he borrowed a radio recording, all sound effects were made using the human voice, producing a disturbing, alienating and potent impression on the audience.

Although Adamov was impressed by Blin's performance as the Employee ('Blin, alone, magnificent. He is the Employee as I had wanted; self-confident, touching, ridiculous'),[25] he was not satisfied with the overall production, finding fault with some of the other actors and with the Lancry stage. It is true, however, that he was already losing some interest in his earliest play and did not take as much interest in its rehearsal as he had done with the first productions staged two years earlier. Nonetheless, in the press that was sympathetic to the new avant-garde, Blin found that his own work as a director was being recognised. Marc Beigbeder stressed how 'in Roger Blin, Arthur Adamov has found a director and actor both strict and human at the same time',[26] to which Jacques Lemarchand added that 'he has triumphed in an astonishing performance which broadens, for me, his possibilities as an actor' and commended his directing as 'patient, discreet and remarkably intelligent, which are the signs of all he does.'[27]

The year 1952 and his production of *La Parodie* left Blin with a robust professional pedigree. At the Gaîté-Montparnasse, in the space of a couple of years, he had demonstrated an ability to tackle quite

23   Blin to Emmanuel C. Jacquart, 'Adamov etait le roi des trois points: Interview avec Roger Blin', *French Review*, 48.6 (May 1975), pp.996–1004 (p.998).
24   Blin, *Souvenirs et propos*, p.78.
25   Adamov, *L'Homme et l'Enfant*, p.104.
26   Marc Beigbeder, *Le Parisien libéré*, 7–8.6.52.
27   Jacques Lemarchand, *Le Figaro Littéraire*, 14.6.52.

disparate forms of drama, from Strindberg's *La Sonate de spectres* to obscure plays worthy of performance, such as Jean Silvant's *Le Bourreau s'impatiente*. He had shown himself to be a director not unduly influenced by any one mentor, free from the restrictions of theatrical dogma and unafraid of experiment. He had acquired a reputation for being indifferent to financial restrictions and dismissive of any moneymaking venture that did not carry the prospect of artistic fulfilment. After the fire which damaged the Gaîté-Montparnasse theatre he abandoned management in favour of continuing freelance as a director and actor, having now established himself in both fields. At this stage he probably did not anticipate that directing would become a career for life, though he had already proven himself sufficiently in that capacity for his name to be firmly identified with the values of the emergent non-commercial, avant-garde theatrical community. Nothing could have confirmed that identification more thoroughly or more enduringly than his next production, of a script that had been speculatively offered him during the run of *La Sonate des spectres* in 1949.

Samuel Beckett

En attendant Godot

The story of how *En attendant Godot* ended up in the Roger Blin's hands has become one of the many legends attached to the history of Samuel Beckett's work. A standard version of events has it that Beckett, having first seen Blin's production of *La Sonate des spectres* and being impressed – not only by its respectful interpretation but also by the half-empty auditorium – consequently handed over his script in the hope that it might receive the same treatment, on both counts. This is the sequence that Blin remembers, permitting himself the indulgence of believing that Beckett's trust had been won over by another of his productions:

> The show wasn't going well – very few spectators made the effort to see it. But amongst them one day was Beckett, who then came again a second time. Some time later, his wife Suzanne came to see me, and brought me the manuscript of *En attendant Godot*. Beckett had no doubt thought that what I'd done for Strindberg meant I was able to understand and mount his work.[1]

This is the order of events that James Knowlson gives in his authorised Beckett biography and, as an anecdote, is attractively robust. Odette Aslan, Deirdre Bair, Ruby Cohn and Anthony Cronin, however, situate the events in a different order: Tristan Tzara, being a mutual friend, had spoken enthusiastically to Blin about Beckett's play and had also recommended the director to the author. The scripts of Beckett's first dramas had already been sent to numerous theatre managers in Paris and had been rejected without compunction by them all. Suzanne Dumesnil, knowing at that point that there was nothing to lose by sounding out one more theatre director, took the

---

1   Blin, 'Témoignage', in Pierre Mélèse, *Samuel Beckett* (Paris: Seghers, 1966), pp.145–50 (p.145).

two manuscripts down to the Gaîté-Montparnasse, not far from their apartment in the fifteenth arrondissement. It was at this point that Beckett, an admirer of Strindberg, went to see Blin's production of *La Sonate des spectres* and appreciated what he saw so much that he decided to return later to watch it once more, impressed by the due diligence and respect with which Strindberg's work had been treated. That the auditorium had been less than half full may or may not have appealed to the author; perhaps he found the thought of his play being sought out by the more discerning playgoer at one of these small pocket theatres an attractive and soothing prospect. He may also have been further reassured by Blin's reputation (though Knowlson implies that he had some initial reservations).[2] His close fiend, Georges Pelorson, had warmly rated Blin in Heiberg's *La Tragédie de l'amour* in 1944 (see p.69) and it is unlikely that Beckett would have not heard talk of Blin's production of his fellow Dubliner (and former love rival) Denis Johnston's *Moon in the Yellow River* earlier in 1949.[3]

When Blin received the two manuscripts that year he knew little of their expatriate Irish author who had so far only gained a modicum of general recognition with his first novel, *Murphy*, published in French in 1947. Beckett had already earned for himself a certain amount of notoriety among the intellectual and surrealist circles which Blin frequented, and in addition to *Murphy*, some of his poetry and short stories had appeared in a number of Parisian literary reviews. Blin had even once recited a French translation of Beckett's poem *Alba*, originally published in the Communist review *Soutes*, on Max-Pol Fouchet's radio programme. Both of Beckett's manuscripts interested him greatly, and though he initially preferred the more complex, three-act *Eleuthéria*, he knew that its scenic demands for a simultaneous split set of 'two very different décors juxtaposed'[4] along with its cast of seventeen would require funding that would be simply impossible to raise. *En attendant Godot* would prove simpler, he

2   James Knowlson, *Damned to Fame: The Life of Samuel Beckett* (London: Bloomsbury, 1996), p.385.
3   Ibid., p.384.
4   Samuel Beckett, *Eleutheria*, trans Barbara Wright (London: Faber and Faber, 1996), p.5.

reasoned, requiring no scenery beyond a single frail tree and having a cast of just four actors and boy. Blin genuinely felt he had stumbled across a work of unusual quality; he recounted how on starting to read the manuscript he knew he would want to read it through again straight away, and how he immediately started to visualise it on stage – for him a sure sign of a play's worth. He was taken by the comic banter of Beckett's two protagonists as well as by the poignancy of their situation. Most of all, perhaps, he was struck and excited by the audacity of a play that had no plot, no straightforward development, and which offered no direct message or moral for its audience to digest. Blin read this form as confrontational, remarking that 'Beckett is a provocateur, like all extremely shy people'[5] and 'Godot without its provocation would be a play about the inability to communicate, and good deal of it too. I got the feeling on reading Godot that this play was really going to throw the cat amongst the pigeons on the theatrical scene.'[6] David Bradby qualifies Blin's vocabulary here, emphasising that 'the French word "provocation" has a stronger meaning than its English homonym, conveying challenge or even incitement.'[7] Clearly, Blin's initial response was that, in its structure and form, the play not only satisfied his desire to experiment within and further stretch the boundaries of what can be done with theatre, but also corresponded to his own desire to shock or disturb people into thought or self-awareness. Indeed, the great dramatic force of the play's metaphysical anguish seems, at first, to have gone straight over his head: 'When I read Godot,' he recalled, 'I was immediately seduced by the humour and provocation in the text. But I didn't get it all on first reading, notably the repetition in the second act'.[8] What gripped him on his first reading was the slick, rolling dialogue, the ease and sharpness of the humour, the laconic ridiculing of human aspirations and optimism within a wholesale, daring rejection of theatrical convention.

5   Blin to Maria Craipeau in *France observateur*, 17.10.63.
6   Blin, *Souvenirs et propos*, p.87.
7   David Bradby, *Beckett: Waiting for Godot (Plays in Production)* (Cambridge: Cambridge University Press, 2001), p.46.
8   Blin, *Souvenirs et propos*, p.81.

The attitudes and experience of life that had gone into the making of *En attendant Godot* were instantly accessible to a man of Blin's background and he was instinctively drawn to the work; here was the writing of an author who shared the same spirit of revolt, the same matter-of-fact atheism, the same sense of cynicism in the face of society and of the world. Author and director were eventually to meet the following year through the intermediary of Jérôme Lindon, Beckett's publisher at the Éditions de Minuit. In the summer of 1950, at Beckett's apartment in the rue des Favorites, the two men sat and discussed *En attendant Godot*, concentrating on pragmatic aspects of production and the apparently remote possibilities of mounting the play. In passing, Blin raised the inevitable question of the identity of Godot, more out of curiosity than necessity, but the gaffe was quickly circumnavigated to return to more congenial conversational waters:

> We spoke about this and that, about Ireland, about our dear Synge, stories of teeth and farts, about *Godot* very little, and mostly from a technical point of view. Things almost went wrong at one point. I must have looked rather dubious and suspicious when I asked the obvious question about Godot.[9]

At the Gaîté-Montparnasse the productions of *La Sonate des spectres* and Jean Silvant's *Le Bourreau s'impatiente* were both finished and Blin proposed Beckett's play for the following season. Christine Tsingos, however, vetoed any production on the grounds that the text offered no female role for her. Blin set about looking for other theatres that might accept the play, and this at the same time as he and Adamov were seeking funding and a home for *La Parodie*. He had a few copies of *En attendant Godot* typed and tried his luck with some of the theatre directors he thought might prove open to a short run, including Jean-Marie Serreau, who turned the play down as he could not afford to take any risks financially. For a while the Théâtre des Noctambules became a potential venue for a late 1950 production, having a dark period after the run of Adamov's *La Grande et la Petite Manœuvre* in which Blin was performing (see pp.82–6). This prospect fell through, however, and there were precious few other sources left to tap.

9   Blin, 'Une solidarité entre maigres', in *Arts*, 418, 3–9.7.53, p.5.

The shared frustrations of Blin and Beckett brought the two men closer together; in Beckett's desire to see one of his plays performed, the reassurance of Blin's persistence could only serve to fuel their growing mutual respect. In a letter to Blin, dated 15 January 1951, Beckett voiced formally his feeling that they could now address each other informally: 'Now that we are embarked on a dirty business together, I think we can say tu to each other.'[10]

In an attempt to arouse more interest in the play, Blin arranged for a recording of some of Vladimir and Estragon's banter to be broadcast over O.R.T.F.'s airwaves in February 1952, as this had proved a useful strategy for publicising *La Parodie* a year previously. Good fortune then arrived in the shape of a new government subsidy, established to provide financial aid for the production of original French plays. Having been written in French, *En attendant Godot* was eligible for this subsidy, despite the nationality of its author. Though he had a distinct distaste for government hand-outs of this sort, Blin nevertheless applied and was successful. The Minister for Arts and Letters, Georges Neveux, a screenplay writer and former surrealist poet, was a member of the selection committee, and proved so receptive to Beckett's play that he wrote a personal letter to Blin expressing his admiration for it and encouraging the director in his efforts to mount it.[11] The subsidy amounted to five hundred thousand old French francs. This, along with other sums of money which Blin had been able to collect from various sources, was enough to hire the Théâtre de Poche for a month. The manager France Guy agreed to offer a slot in late 1952, once the audiences for the successful run of Chekhov's *Uncle Vanya* (directed by Sacha Pitoëff) had been exhausted. Beckett was both daunted and delighted by the prospect of seeing his work finally produced. When in August 1952 he was led to believe that audiences for the Chekhov play were finally waning, he wrote to his director, then holidaying in Brittany, to let him know that

10   Deidre Bair, *Samuel Beckett: A Biography* (London: Jonathan Cape, 1978), p.411.
11   'You are absolutely right in wanting to mount *En attendant Godot*. It's an astonishing play. Needless to say, I am passionately in favour.' Letter from Georges Neveux to Blin, dated 22.1.52, reproduced in *Le Nouvel Observateur*, 26.10.81.

work could resume and to warn him of the trials now ahead: 'what awaits you is terrible' he prophesised.[12] The Poche continued to attract audiences, however, and the contract was reneged upon, much to the consternation of Beckett, Blin and Lindon. The paperwork had seemed so watertight that Lindon had even arranged for publication of *En attendant Godot* to coincide with the première, and the first edition subsequently appeared on 17 October 1952.

Later that same year, when the directrice of the Théâtre de Porte Chasseur was approached, she proved willing to have Beckett's play mounted there immediately, but she saw no need for Beckett's tree and refused Blin this sole element of décor as, she reasoned insistently, there would be little room for it on the tiny stage.[13] Blin then returned to Jean-Marie Serreau, taking his subsidy as bait. Serreau's Théâtre de Babylone was in dire straights after the disappointingly small houses attracted to a run of Strindberg's *Miss Julie* and Brecht's *The Exception and the Rule*. Though giving a home to Beckett's play must have seemed like adding ballast to a sinking ship, Serreau's short term financial needs were satisfied by the rental Blin could offer and contracts were signed by all three parties on 2 November 1952, scheduling performances for January of 1953.

Blin had begun rehearsing the play ahead of any contract being signed and preparations had intensified once a run at the Poche had been on the cards. Once that venue slipped through his fingers, he had decided to continue rehearsals, simply for the joy of working on the text if nothing else. The first rehearsals had involved working on the verbal volleys between the two protagonists, with Blin originally taking the role of Vladimir himself with another actor as Estragon, but gradually he came to the view that he would prefer to direct others in the two main roles. Actors came and went, either refusing to work

---

12   Letter from Beckett to Blin, dated 2.8.52. Quoted in Anthony Cronin, *Samuel Beckett: The Last Modernist* (London: Flamingo, 1997), p.413.

13   In his *Souvenirs et propos* (p.81) Blin recalls how it was at the Théâtre de Poche that his tree was refused. When Deirdre Bair interviewed Blin he on this occasion remembered the argument as having occurred at the Théâtre de Porte Chasseur (Bair, *Samuel Beckett*, p.420), which is supported by Anthony Cronin (*Samuel Beckett*, p.413), though the source of this may lie somewhere between Blin's two reminiscences.

further on a text that eluded them or, as no venue was found, leaving to take on more secure employment. Eventually, Blin enlisted a couple of friends who were prepared to commit themselves to the play despite the lack of a theatre and performance dates (contrary to the acting union policy). Both these were colleagues from the first season at the Gaîté-Montparnasse. Lucien Raimbourg, an actor versed in music hall, had been engaged by Blin in a series of café-concert type sketches named *Quatre pas dans le cirage* that had been programmed to fill a dark period whilst Denis Johnston's play had been in rehearsal.[14] For the other half of the couple Blin approached his old friend Pierre Latour, who he had directed in Silvant's *Le Bourreau s'impatiente.*[15] Raimbourg, with his diminutive frame and large inquisitive blue eyes, had come to Blin's mind in the role of Vladimir as he first read the script of *En attendant Godot*. Latour's large frame, he reasoned, would contrast effectively with the diminutive Raimbourg on stage. Rehearsals continued in earnest at the Maison pour tous in the rue Mouffetard, or at Blin's own home.

Arguably, this long gestation period contributed to the severe performance that came of it, as Blin's view of the play shifted away from his original emphasis upon comedy. It is likely that an earlier performance date would have led to a different, almost certainly lighter, interpretation. In fact, he originally envisaged placing the action more or less overtly within a circus ring; the dialogue having struck him as reminiscent of the rapid repartee of clowns or of the American comics for whom he shared a passion with Beckett:

> From 1949 to 1953, over four years, I had time to think, to experiment. What struck me first was the circus aspect. I thought for a while I could have the actors come on as though they were clowns, have them coming on stage in dressing gowns. At the back, there'd be a kind of portal; they would bring a canvas down on which the word sky would be written, or at least something that suggested a sky. They'd rub their feet in resin; they'd bring on a tree in a

14   This revue title, which translates as *Completely Without a Clue* (to be 'dans le cirage' means to be unable to see, understand or find one's way) offers a fitting irony, being perfectly suited to Beckett's first stage characters.

15   Renée Saurel reviewed Latour in Silvant's play, commending 'his cold, immobile acting, which gives his character an astonishing quality.' (Combat, 27.3.50)

box, in a pot. They'd throw their gowns into the wings and the play would have started at that point, with just the tree for decor and a little red bench along the back of the stage.[16]

Blin's thoughts were certainly not completely at variance with the feel of *En attendant Godot*; he was alert to the comic dimension of Beckett's play and had realised its worth as an integral part of this demanding vision of humanity. Indeed, to invest the comedy with an overtly conscious sense of performance is a temptation to which many subsequent directors have succumbed. The oblique references in the text to the theatre and to the presence of an audience certainly justify the portrayal of the two leading roles as performers and entertainers, and such a presentation, if handled with subtlety, can add a sharper and more grim edge to some of the play's darker moments. Beckett's own production of the play at the Schiller-Theater in Berlin in 1975 certainly veered towards such a style.

Blin came to consider that the great strength of the play lies in the ambiguity of identity and situation embodied in all the characters, and that this ambiguity of form is essential to the communication of the play's thematic material. The need for a delicate balance between the tragic endurance and the comic futility of the characters is paramount in order not to upset the force of the play's intended effect. Too heavy a weighting of the comedy, Blin realised, would undermine and detract too much from the pathos of the characters' situation, and this had been so starkly written and with such poetry that it must not be lost to the audience through a weakening or dilution of the dramatic fabric. In more practical terms, dressing a stage up to represent a circus ring would have stretched still further the small budget to which he would have been expected to work for the production.

On the other hand, Blin realised that too tragic an emphasis could also swamp a performance, and that what was required of him was a balancing act, juggling with the disparate elements the text offered, finding the most appropriate and powerful blend. Many years later he recalled the nature of the problem very clearly:

16   Andrée Waintrop, *Les mises en scène de Samuel Beckett par Roger Blin*, mémoire de maîtrise de l'I.E.T., Paris III, p.11.

For all its alleged meaninglessness, the play is not innocent. I mean, innocent in its structure. The traps, red herrings, allusions, the marked domination of the grammatical breathing rhythm were all concerns during the three years of rehearsal. First the lure of the circus [...] later the lure of farce, the lure of sentimentality, particularly as regards Vladimir. [...] I know that there are different levels in Godot, but you can't attain the desired magic without concentrating first and foremost on the most directly human level. For each character, I started quite simply with their physical impairments, either real or imagined. Beckett had heard their voices clearly, but couldn't describe these characters to me: 'All I can be sure of is that they are wearing bowler hats.'[17]

Blin directed with Beckett close at hand in 1952, and the author chose to attend rehearsals more or less regularly in the final weeks of the play's preparation, ready to nod approval at certain devices or movements that were felt to enhance the text, or to discourage those that strayed too far from his original thoughts. The playwright proved flexible in this connection; he was always willing to listen to Blin's views, which mostly concerned the theatricalisation of his work, and even adopted some of the agreed changes to the text for his English translation of the play. Perhaps the most notable of these is the omission of the letter from Monsieur Godot brought on by the boy in the original text, which was deemed to convey too concrete a notion of that character who never arrives. Another casualty was the reference to Bim and Bom 'the Stalinian comedians' which was thought to disturb the timelessness of the piece.[18] Also, for Beckett's curt instruction 'échange d'injures.' ('exchange of insults'), Blin and his cast put their heads together and came up with a list including 'filth', 'cretin', 'curate' and pinnacling with 'architect!'[19] The origin of this last, obscure but suitably surreal insult was a cab journey taken by Jean Martin in Brussels, where the driver used the insult to hurl at other drivers, explaining to his passenger that the profession of archi-

17   Blin, 'Trente-trois ans après', in *Le Nouvel Observateur*, 26.9.81, p.60.
18   Beckett, *En attendant Godot* (Paris, Éditions de minuit, 1952), pp.47–8 and p.56 of the prompt copy. A photocopy of the prompt copy (the October 1952 edition of the play) is kept at the Beckett Archive, Reading University Library.
19   Beckett, *En attendant Godot*, p.106. 'Andouille, Tordu, Crétin, Curé, Dégueulasse, Micheton, Ordure, Architecte' is written by Blin in the margin of p.127 of the prompt copy.

tect was not held in high esteem after the post-war restructuring of the Belgian capital.[20] The word, famously, was subsequently replaced by the retort 'crritic!' in Beckett's English translation, for straightforwardly similar reasons.

The surviving prompt copy of the play attests to further, more substantial, cuts. The most significant of these are a striking out of two whole pages of the original script in the first act and two thirds of a page and then a further page and a half in the second. None of these omitted sections made the transfer to the English or later French editions of the play. The first cut in act one (immediately preceding Estragon's 'Nothing happens, nobody comes, nobody goes, it's awful!')[21] was of a passage in which Pozzo attempts to explain, amid interruptions and appeals to continue from Estragon, that it is uncertain whether or not Lucky will carry out the requests he makes of him. Its loss permits Lucky's speech to arrive sooner after his dance than originally conceived. The page cut in act two was to material following Pozzo's failed attempt to get up and concerned a short discussion between Vladimir and Estragon as to whether Pozzo has died or not and whether they ought to have been so brutal.[22] The final notable cut follows Pozzo's request that Estragon go and check on Lucky was a short passage in which Estragon articulates his fear of approaching Lucky due to his having been kicked on their previous encounter, and was presumably removed for being a redundant repetition of this fact.[23] Also here, Pozzo's line 'Ah, mais il ne faut jamais être gentil avec ces gens-là. Ils ne le supportent pas' ('Ah, but you must never be kind to such people. They can't stand it')[24] must have seemed an over-statement of a theme which had already been presented more vividly visually and therefore risked being something of a burdensome and clumsy clarification.

20   Jean Martin to Mark Batty, 11.1.95.
21   Beckett, *En attendant Godot*, pp.57–8, *The Complete Dramatic Works* (London, Faber and Faber, 1986), p.41 and pp.67–70 of prompt copy.
22   Beckett, *En attendant Godot*, p.116, *The Complete Dramatic Works*, p.77 and pp.139–40 of prompt copy.
23   Beckett, *En attendant Godot*, p.123, *The Complete Dramatic Works*, p.81 and pp.148–50 of prompt copy.
24   p.149 of prompt copy.

Blin's approach to directing may at first have disconcerted Beckett, who quite possibly had conventional preconceptions about a director's functions. Normally, Blin would turn up to rehearsals without having prepared a section to work on beyond having read it through. To Blin the place to prepare a play for the stage was in rehearsal, bouncing ideas off actors and trying out movements and nuances of delivery and reaction within a process of improvisation. For him, note-taking was unnecessary as directing was not so much a cognitive process as an instinctive one, feeling the text and the way it should come across to its audience. For Beckett this approach may well have appeared approximate and disorganised. Deirdre Bair notes how he would watch on nervously as Blin spent a whole day's rehearsal concentrating on just one small segment of the dialogue:

> Blin never had a definite schedule in mind, but would come into the theatre ready to rehearse whatever lines interested him most at that particular moment. Then he would spend several hours making the actors move their bodies and voices until he brought them to the point where they naturally conveyed the expression and movement he wanted. He seemed to be distracted and vague, to drift off into mental reaches known only to himself, but this was the only method that worked for him.[25]

Blin seems to have been well aware of the perplexing, not to say anxious, quality of the experience for Beckett but was unable to address the task in any other way. 'He was disturbed by my working methods. I should really say my lack of working methods,' he later confessed. 'I never prepare a day in advance; I soak myself in the play and things fall into place through successive approximations, trials, alterations. [...] I try to integrate the verb, thought, sentiment into a choreography that I discover in rehearsal with the actors.'[26] Undeniably, Beckett's own approach, when he later came to direct his own plays, showed nothing of the spontaneity of this 'take it as it comes' method, and this difference in their attitudes must have been the cause of some uncertainty, and perhaps some friction, in those early rehearsals. The author nevertheless had implicit trust in Blin's

25 Bair, *Samuel Beckett*, p.423.
26 Blin, *Souvenirs et propos*, pp.97–8.

ability and must eventually have been satisfied with the progress he saw unfold as he watched more and more rehearsals.

The Babylone, previously the refectory of a political youth movement, had been converted into a theatre by a group including Jean-Marie Serreau, Maurice Jarre and Éléonore Hirt. Situated at 38 Boulevard Raspail, it could boast seating for 250 but a stage measuring only six metres by four. Within this restrictive space, only slightly more generous than the dimensions of the Poche where rehearsals had begun, Blin had the unenviable task of creating the open wilderness of Beckett's play. Faced with this challenge, his craftsmanship came to the fore:

> The work of a director involves fitting complete circuits and all the movements implied in a text upon a stage measuring six or eight metres. The stage is always without limits in the author's mind. For example, when Beckett says: 'Vladimir, who is beside Estragon, speaks to him then goes to the centre of the stage and keeps walking towards the other wing' – to effect such an indication you need the stage of the Paris Opera. That's what directing is also about; finding ways of walking about that replace what a thirty metre stage would allow in one small detail, and which does the text justice and respects the author's ideas in spite of the constrains of the theatre's stage.[27]

As with the idea of the circus ring and the dressing gowns, Blin was not above suggesting slants to the play in performance that were not apparent from the written text but constituted, rather, modes of interpretation or developments of perceived shapes within it. These might be arrived at in the enthusiasm of a reading or inspired by images in the world around him, and could subsequently be applied if they proved apt in rehearsal or just as easily abandoned if they seemed to jar or get in the way. Beckett, having virtually no practical experience of the theatre, allowed Blin the flexibility to develop his own impulses and discoveries in rehearsal; indeed he came to trust them and would not interfere unless he felt that a certain imposition was contrary to what he had intended:

> [Beckett] had indicated the movements and the timings perfectly well in his text, but these indications were for the reader first and foremost; once on the

27   Ibid., p.99.

stage things are different; you have to take into account the unfathomable personality of the actor, material requirements, the expressive value of certain words [...] he graciously accepted my ideas, looking *a priori* for a stylisation, and approved the adjustment they demanded in the execution. He proved not to be against discoveries, but he insisted that they were totally, organically, justifiable.[28]

Notable insertions of Blin's into Beckett's action included, for example, having Pozzo and Lucky do a complete circle around the perimeter of the stage, a deliberate allusion to clowning practice, before they left the two vagrants alone to face the night at the end of Act One. In the second act, Blin directed Vladimir and Estragon to walk over the fallen bodies of Pozzo and Lucky, as if oblivious to the pain they might inflict, and in fact stamping the words 'all mankind is us' into Pozzo's back (the original French text is more rhythmic, uninterrupted by the descending cadence of English delivery, permitting both comedy and horror to the moment: 'l'humanité c'est nous'). Far from being intrusive, such moments served to accentuate not only the non-naturalistic nature of the performance but also the tensions within its portrayal of the human condition.

Being an amateur painter, Blin thought very much in terms of images, which for dramatic purposes meant an emphasis on the creation of moods and atmospheres directly through the devising of visual pictures, the manipulation of distances and groupings and the application of non-realistic physical business (such as the stamping of Pozzo's back) capable of speaking poetically or with a palpable emotion, evoking human experience. This approach perhaps matched Beckett's attraction to the 'shape of ideas' and 'fundamental sounds',[29] replicating his own way of capturing the essence of a statement as much pictorially as in words, affording us some of the most potent stage images of this century. As a starting point for the 'physicalisation' of Vladimir and Estragon, Blin looked first at their ailments,

28   Blin in Mélèse, *Samuel Beckett*, p.140.

29   'I am interested in the shape of ideas [...] It is the shape that matters.' Beckett to Harold Hobson, in Hobson, 'Samuel Beckett – Dramatist of the Year,' *International Theatre Annual*, 1 (1956), p.153. 'My work is a matter of fundamental sounds [...] made as fully as possible, and I accept the responsibility for nothing else.' Beckett to Alan Schneider, in Harmon, *No Author Better Served*, p.24.

real or imagined. He saw Vladimir, with his prostate trouble, as being in constant movement and correlated this uneasy, uncomfortable stalking with his constant vigil for Godot, sending him frequently to the wings. Estragon, always hungry and sleepy, and with hurting feet, would therefore move as little as possible; he would be 'a block of refusal, with a leaden arse',[30] always seeking to sit down, rest and stay put. The key to their relationship was their interdependence, and the ambiguous and often painful nature of that mutual necessity:

> There is a certain cruelty in the Vladimir/Estragon relationship, but also a certain tenderness. Their friendship is not based on much. Like a couple, they are bound together by habit; they can't bear each other, but they cannot separate. Beckett told me that in this filth that surrounds us [in spite of his pessimism about the human condition], there are nevertheless moments when one can take someone's hand, when something authentic happens.[31]

The now iconic Vladimir/Estragon relationship was only then being sculpted, tried out and understood for the first time, and Blin was the first to find the physical means of presenting this ambiguous and strained friendship out of the words of Beckett's text. Working from images that he found inspiring he sought first to formulate the notion of interdependence: for instance, the way they were trapped together and mutually comforting reminded him of two embracing monkeys, 'interlaced with a kind of infinite distress',[32] which he had seen at the zoo, and this image was incorporated in his production at moments where the two tramps hugged for comfort. He was also reminded of John Steinbeck's couple in *Of Mice and Men*, where the poetic asymmetry of the smaller protecting the taller and stronger appealed to him. The physical contrast between Raimbourg as Vladimir and Latour as Estragon allowed Blin to play with this highly pertinent image and to weave it into the fabric of the two characters' interaction on stage:

> Those two tramps seemed to me to have to blended physically each to the other, because their relationship is like that of an old couple which operates with a

---

30   Blin, *Souvenirs et propos*, p.88.
31   Blin in Aslan, *Roger Blin*, p.35.
32   Blin, *Souvenirs et propos*, p.88.

simultaneous physical attraction and repulsion. They need each other, they can't be apart for long, but they can't stand each other either. When they're happy, let them come together, their hugging becomes analogous with the systole and diastole of the beating heart. The physical connection which takes place at moments like that is so strong that, in their embrace, the image of the two of them coming together as one being is created.[33]

For the character of Pozzo, Blin wanted a physically domineering actor, not only in order to establish a clear visual contrast between him and Lucky but also, more explicitly, to inspire fear in Vladimir and Estragon. To play Beckett's 'lump of flesh'[34] Blin expressed his fantasy casting of Charles Laughton alongside Charlie Chaplin's Vladimir and Buster Keaton's Estragon. Less unrealistically, he would have liked to employ Michel Simon – who had become famous under Jouvet and who enjoyed a high profile in French cinema in the early 1950s – but he dared not approach him without the means to pay an actor of his stature. Dissatisfied with most of those who tried out the role in rehearsals, and deserted by the actor he did finally take on to play the role (who left less than a month before the play opened) Blin reluctantly took the part himself. He entrusted the role of Lucky, which he had been rehearsing until then, to his friend Jean Martin, telling him mischievously but not inaccurately that he would only had the one line to learn.

To become Pozzo, the slim-framed Blin had to transform himself completely. He had a false stomach constructed and wore a false bald forehead over his hair. Rather than his size (with Raimbourg towering over him) he employed his voice to dominate the others on stage. He saw the character not as a powerful and intelligent landowner, as the role might be interpreted, but as the stupidest of the whole group, the most naïve, the one who is least aware of his situation and who therefore falls foulest of it in the second act. Blin had little trouble in envisaging how such an impression might be conveyed:

[I]n spite his desire to come across as authoritarian in front of the others, in spite of his frequent shouting, he botches the effect all the time. He's a bit of a ham. He smokes his pipe and runs out of breath because he's overweight, with

33   Ibid., p.89.
34   Ibid., p.90.

a heart condition. He's got flat feet too. He walks with difficulty, with his feet open. He is led by his stomach. He's always performing in front of the others. He's sly but is so in love with himself that he suffers when he doesn't get the admiration he feels he earns from his spectators.[35]

The way Blin chose to physicalise Pozzo's personality is a good illustration of his preferred method of working from images first externalising those elements that he saw as true to the character, as with the way he showed Vladimir and Estragon how to walk from their physical ailments, and thus creating a picture or stage-shape of the character, like a sculptor moulding the most apt shape to embody his thoughts. From the physical relationships that grew between the characters in rehearsal the emotional connections between them became more apparent to the actors. These Blin developed simply, couching his explanations in plain terms, avoiding any manner of intellectualising the text:

> I know that from a semiological point of view there are various levels in *Godot*. When I was working on the play, I had to see all these levels, think them. In practice, I only ever wanted to make use of the primary level, that of immediate understanding. But in working with my actors we were able to reach at times another level, an anti-realist one. We achieved, sought a stylisation, not a rigid one, but starting from the humblest of points.[36]

Supporting him in this, his actors did not demand clarification on the hidden meanings and perhaps part of the success of this first production lay in the sustained innocence that the performers brought to their characterisations. Martin recalled how 'Raimbourg, to the end of his days, never understood what he was performing in *Godot*, and he was superb. And that's why Blin liked him a lot because he never needed to explain to Raimbourg why he was performing *Godot*.'[37]

The character of Lucky, in Blin's view, was first and foremost a servant, and although he did not want to politicise Beckett's text in any way, he felt that it was necessary to make this relationship between oppressor and oppressed apparent. Beckett himself did not

35 Blin, *Souvenirs et propos*, p.90.
36 Blin to Fady Stéphane, in *Le Safa*, 15.8.73.
37 Jean Martin to Mark Batty, 11.1.95.

see the necessity in this – his characters were not reflections of society and the play was not intended to comment on social issues – but Blin was insistent that his interpretation could not be avoided. 'Beckett didn't want the Pozzo-Lucky couple to have any social resonances,' he remembered, 'yet that's how Vladimir and Estragon see it, the yolk of exploitation, social oppression; that's what they have coming to them.'[38] Blin explored thoroughly all the possibilities available in their relationship, notably their interdependence and their cruel game-playing. In particular, the servant was made fully conscious of the power he had over his master and Blin had him glancing bitterly at Pozzo, exacting revenge for his maltreatment through disobedience, gleefully aware of his ability to dominate his persecutor. The director also approved of an effect introduced in rehearsal by Jean Martin himself, to whom Beckett had described the kind of posture he saw Lucky adopting and the muscular quivering he envisaged for the character. After consulting a friend who was a doctor Martin realised that in effect Beckett was asking him to reproduce the physical symptoms of Parkinson's disease:

> I remember that Blin told me: 'look, I can't say I don't like it, I can't say I like it either, I just don't know,' and said, 'keep doing it.' So I kept on doing it. Beckett didn't say anything. One day we were rehearsing in front of the theatre's wardrobe mistress who was married to the man who collected the bins and who had got some props for Lucky for us. To thank them, we'd invited them to see a rehearsal. They were simple folk, by which I mean they'd probably never been to the theatre. And I remember that when I started Lucky's monologue, the lady was overcome by a fit of nervous laughter and all of a sudden she began to retch, saying 'It's intolerable!' That's when Blin said to me: 'Right, that's how it has to be done!'[39]

Costuming did not pose too many problems for Blin. Beckett had not specified in the text how Vladimir, Estragon, Pozzo and Lucky should look, and since he could offer little advice on the subject beyond being sure that they wore bowler hats, Blin was simply left with the task of choosing the most effective costumes for the types of character to whom his actors were giving stage flesh. Once the clown

38   Blin in Mélèse, *Samuel Beckett*, p.147.
39   Jean Martin to Mark Batty, 10.1.95.

notion had been rejected, the inclination to see the two key figures as tramps became all the stronger: the clues provided by the text, that they were two unemployed wanderers sleeping in ditches and dressed in tatters, certainly seemed to justify that interpretation:

> Vladimir – You should have been a poet.
> Estragon – I was. [Gesture towards his rags.] Isn't that obvious.[40]

Playing Vladimir and Estragon as tramps also accentuated the ambiguity of their history and their background. From his manner of speaking Blin imagined that Vladimir had once been a professor and this was suggested vaguely in the morning coat that hung to his knees and the stiff collar and tie around his neck. This interpretation was virtually ratified by Beckett in a response provoked by the critic Vivian Mercier's charge that he had made Vladimir and Estragon both speak as though they had PhDs: 'How do you know they hadn't?' was his curt riposte.[41]

Pozzo was dressed as a John Bull figure, in boots and leggings, an elegant cravat and collar, a waistcoat with a watch and chain, and a hooded cape. For Lucky, Beckett had suggested the uniform of a railway porter, but Blin found this image far too obvious and he proposed instead the picture of Lucky which had come to him in a dream, wearing the apparel of a French lackey. Jean Martin was accordingly clothed for his role in a shabby large red jacket with gold braiding, a striped sailor's vest underneath, trousers that were a foot too short and shoes that were a size too big (a nod, perhaps, to the original circus clown inspiration). Under his bowler hat was hidden a wig of white hair that would fall to his shoulders at the given moment.

The design of the sparse set was handed over to Blin's friend Sergio Gernstein, who was given an unenviable budget of 'pas un sou de merde',[42] restricting him to scraping together the set from what he could borrow or scavenge. The backcloth which was to hang at the rear to screen off the back wall of the building had to be sewn together from remnant pieces of material. The tree, twisted and scrawny as

---

40   Beckett, *The Complete Dramatic Works*, p.14.
41   Enoch Brater, *Why Beckett* (London, Thames and Hudson Ltd, 1989), p.75.
42   Bair, *Samuel Beckett*, p.422. 'Bugger all' might be a close translation.

Blin had designed it, was constructed from wire wrapped in crêpe paper and held upright in one of two elongated blocks of foam rubber which were placed upstage as mounds to break the evenness of the stage floor. In accord with this impoverished design most of the props and costumes had been picked up for nothing or borrowed; Lucky's suitcase had been found discarded in a dustbin and Pozzo's jacket had been covertly appropriated from Blin's father's wardrobe.

As for lighting this set, Blin decided on a prevailing and fairly realistic quality of dusk, to achieve which he placed lamps at floor level, concealed by the foam blocks, to illuminate the backcloth. This effect he coupled with starker front lighting which cast a less naturalistic glow over the scenic action itself. Side-lighting was also used on the tree to give the effect of the setting sun. For the moon's appearances at the end of both acts Blin had a stagehand manipulate a blue light behind the backcloth, physically raising it into position to conjure a stylised moon that rose as rapidly as the text demanded.

As the winter of 1952–3 grew colder, all the elements of the *Godot* project were coming together and the small group of actors began the final leg of their rehearsals. Before the first night, on 5 January 1953, Beckett took off to his small rented house in Ussy-sur Marne, neither willing nor able to face the public performance of his work. He wrote to Blin asking him to forgive his absence and sent Suzanne along to note what success the performance might achieve and to assess the public's reaction. From her report he learnt how Latour had not fully dropped his trousers at the end of the second act, as he had been directed to do, and this was the subject of the letter he wrote to Blin the following day. Even in rehearsal Latour had been reluctant to drop his trousers to the floor, but the forcefulness with which Beckett's letter insisted on the action as being of paramount importance persuaded him to give way and perform accordingly.

Despite the little publicity that could be afforded on the budget at Blin's disposal a sizable group of thirty critics turned up at the press night, intrigued perhaps about the first dramatic work by the author of *Molloy* and *Malone meurt* (*Malone Dies*), both of which had been published in 1951 and had received considerable critical attention. Despite the notable absence of the Parisian press's most influential critic, Jean-Jacques Gautier of *Le Figaro*, who would anyway have been unlikely to give the play a favourable notice, the journalistic turn-out at the première of this experimental play in a small non-mainstream theatre was far more impressive than might have been expected and, in the event, the vast majority of reviews were favourable both towards the play and its author. Most agreed on the fine performance of the actors too, with Raimbourg in particular being singled out for his interpretation of Vladimir.

The so-called 'succès de scandale' often attached to the first performance of *En attendant Godot* was perhaps more the creation of a bemused and shocked public than of the reviewers. One concerted attempt to disrupt the performance was even reported in the press. *Le Monde* carried an article headed 'Demonstrations at the Théâtre de Babylone', which described how certain of the spectators, outraged by the play, had virtually sabotaged the performance one evening:

> A group of feather-wearing spectators, looking obviously as though they'd come in from distant suburbs, protested noisily last night against Samuel Beckett's play *En attendant Godot*. Whistles, insults, nothing was left out. Roger Blin, the play's director, had the curtain dropped before the end of the first act. In the interval, discussions between those for and against the piece grew in pitch, and it wasn't until the departure *en masse* of the discontented members of the audience, as the second act began, that we were able to listen to the rest of Samuel Beckett's remarkable play in peace.[43]

Publicity of this kind, bringing notice of Beckett's play out of the arts section of a newspaper and into current affairs, helped to promote greater interest in the work and opened up a public debate that could not have been incited by the mere opinions of critics. That *En attendant Godot* was able to disturb people to the point of offending them became common knowledge and consequently attracted larger audiences. *Arts*, recognising the 'Controversy surrounding *Godot*', published in late February letters received on the subject: 'I go to the theatre to experience a couple of hours of art and spirituality', protested one audience member, '[and] if I whistled at M. Beckett's play it is because it offered me no such thing, but disgust.' 'The lady sitting next to me did not stop murmuring 'horrible! horrible!' wrote

43   *Le Monde*, 2.2.53.

another, 'and I agree with her completely. What is the use of this piece? What is the point of this play?'[44]

This first incarnation of *En attendant Godot* was a powerful mixture of the comic and the tragic in Beckett's vision, leaving the audience both disturbed and enthralled. Blin had successfully carved out the play's grim and demanding picture of the human condition and with it managed to provoke a full spectrum of reactions, the approval far outweighing the outrage. The critic of *Le Monde*, for example, applauded the play: 'I left the theatre with my heart swollen, full of sighs,' he stated, 'I had hardly noticed that the room was poorly heated; I had frozen without noticing.'[45] Though the greatest critical attention was reserved for the author, Blin's achievement also received recognition, most notably from Jacques Lemarchand who, though not always generous to the avant-garde, had always been supportive of Blin's work:

> For a long time Roger Blin has been to thank for excellent and all too rare evenings. I don't believe his success has ever been as complete as with his *mise en scène* of Beckett's play. To achieve this simplicity, this clarity and powerful expression, a certain emotional intelligence and generosity is required, without which talent and experience are useless.[46]

The long gestation period of three years' rehearsal, for different venues and with different actors, exploring and applying ideas to the play, had finally paid off in the performance. It is to Blin's credit that within that time he had been able to focus his energies so devotedly:

> A profound and intimate unity of text, *mise en scène* and performance is a rare thing. Such a miraculous coming-together has nevertheless occurred with *En attendant Godot.*[47]

---

44   Gustav Sachs and 'D.M.-C' in *Arts*, 27.2.53.
45   Robert Kemp, *Le Monde*, 14.1.53.
46   Jacques Lemarchand, *Le Figaro littéraire*, 17.1.53.
47   René Saurel, *Les Lettres françaises*, 15.1.53.

An even worse affair: *Fin de partie*[48]

In letters to Blin during 1955 and 1956, Beckett alluded to a new script earmarked for his direction, finally announcing in a letter dated 30 May 1956 that Suzanne would leave the play for him to read within the week. Blin was immediately taken by *Fin de partie*, a tighter, bleaker, more claustrophobic vision of the human condition than *En attendant Godot* had been. Later he would maintain that the play was his favourite amongst Beckett's dramatic writings. He was more than happy to take on the role of Hamm, which had been written specifically for him, and called again upon Jean Martin to play the other half of this new Beckett couple, the tormented servant Clov. He saw a keen similarity between the Hamm/Clov relationship and that of Pozzo and Lucky, which he and Martin had interpreted three years before, and felt that the two of them could build upon their endeavours with the earlier play. Rather more difficulty was experienced in finding actors to play the two remaining roles of Hamm's spurned parents, as many of the elderly actors he approached were understandably reluctant to be confined to dustbins in a stage appearance that may well prove to be their last. Finally, Georges Adet accepted the part of Nagg, while Christine Tsingos, Blin's old colleague from the Gaîté-Montparnasse, agreed to play Nell.

Despite the huge international and commercial success of *En attendant Godot*, Blin was exasperated to find that none of the numerous theatre managers to whom he offered the script proved willing to risk underwriting production of a Beckett play. Eventually, Lucien Beer did agree to make the Théâtre de l'Œuvre available and rehearsals were able to begin in the winter of 1956–7, but no formal contract was signed and on receiving a more lucrative proposition, Beer announced that Blin and his cast would have to vacate the rehearsal space and look for a stage elsewhere. Maurice Jacquemont's Studio des Champs-Elysées was able to accommodate the play, but

---

48   Referring to *Fin de partie*, Beckett explained in a letter (dated 11.1.56) to Alan Schneider that he was 'writing an even worse affair', in Harmon, *No Author Better Served*, p.9.

was enjoying a successful run of Lorca's *La Maison de Banarda Alba* (*The House of Banarda Alba*) and Blin was told that he would have to wait until audiences began to dwindle, reminiscent of his trouble with the Théâtre de Poche four years previously.

That Beckett could not get a theatre in Paris for his second play, despite his now established international reputation, seemed beyond belief. Amongst others, Ionesco and Adamov lent their voices to a public protest at this state of affairs. 'It is clearly scandalous,' wrote Adamov, 'that a representation of a Beckett play should pose such problems. If not even the success of *En attendant Godot* is enough, one wonders what it will take for Parisian theatre managers to risk – finally! – a bit of money.' '*Fin de partie* is perhaps better than *En attendant Godot*,' added Ionesco, 'It is a masterpiece and I believe that all the theatres should be fighting over it.'[49] Learning of Blin's difficulty in finding a venue, George Devine, director of the English Stage Company at the Royal Court Theatre in London, offered him an eight-day run from 3 April 1957, within the framework of a scheduled fortnight of French culture. *Fin de Partie* was arranged to be presented alongside Beckett's short *Act Without Words*, performed and directed by Deryk Mendel, with music by Samuel's cousin John Beckett. Cast and author crossed the channel to continue the rehearsals that had begun at l'Œuvre.

Blin saw in *Fin de partie* the theme of the death of kings, relating the blind Hamm to a tormented Lear or an arrogant Oedipus figure. In accordance with this view, he elaborated slightly upon the costumes suggested by Beckett in the text and wore a long velvet dressing gown, bordered with strips of fur. To intensify the decadent image he glued copious aristocratic whiskers to his cheeks and sat in a large wooden chair resembling a throne, with a tall back and armrests at the level of his chest. Of designer Jacques Noël he requested a curved set, with a concave back wall, which would place Hamm more visibly at the centre of the world over which he ruled, also creating the impression of the interior of a human skull, with two windows like eye-sockets gazing out at the desolated land and coast, as does the madman whom Hamm remembers visiting in his asylum. All these

49   *Arts*, 6.3.57.

details helped to lend a regal air to Hamm and Blin took the dominant, hierarchical attitudes of this character as a basis for all the relationships within the piece: Hamm as the remorseless tyrant who relishes his position of power over Nagg, Nell and Clov. Beckett had little objection to Blin developing the imperial side of Hamm though he had never really imagined the character as much more than a vain, overbearing bourgeois and claimed never to have considered a possible connection between what he had written and the themes that Blin had detected.

Blin chose not to accentuate too heavily the comedy with which the text was impregnated. He felt that the humour was fundamentally different in purpose from that of *En attendant Godot*, in which he had seen the protagonists' situation as essentially comic. *Fin de partie*, he felt, offered a more sardonic presentation of the human predicament, the characters' humour acting as a form of restraint, a means of retaining a modicum of dignity in the face of their terminal plight. 'For both Beckett and me, laughter is a form of propriety,' he claimed, 'it's the constant terror of being alive.'[50] He endeavoured to create a caustically funny tragedy, using the humour to torment rather than relieve the audience: '*Fin de partie* is a drama with a circus watermark beneath', he believed. 'It's a natural comedy played to the second degree – the sincerity has to be ambiguous: if the spectator sees the circus in advance, then he's not on board.'[51]

Beckett discovered through rehearsals how well his structure held up in performance and, perceiving weaknesses in his text, suggested some minor cuts. The arrival of the child for example, as seen by Clov outside the 'shelter' which houses Hamm and his servant, was much reduced for this première and did not survive at all into Beckett's English translation. The two men did not always agree fully on a formalistic interpretation of the text, however. Blin had difficulty in relating to the purely schematic fashion in which Beckett wanted lines to be delivered, such as Hamm's lamentable cry for Clov and

50   Blin to Stéphane Fady, *Le Safa*, 18.8.73.
51   Blin to Myriam Louzoun, '*Fin de Partie* de Samuel Beckett. Effacement du monde et dynamisme formel', *Les Voies de la création théâtrale*, 5 (Paris: Editions du C.N.R.S, 1977), p.443.

Clov's repeated assertion that things had run out, which he wanted to be pronounced in precisely the same manner each time. Speaking of Beckett's work on the Berlin production a decade later, Ruby Cohn reveals that Beckett persisted in his demand that repeated lines be spoken identically: 'Beckett didn't care whether the word was spoken dispiritedly or euphorically, but it must be repeated in the same tone' she points out.[52] Blin's early resistance to this instruction was due to the impact it had on him as an actor and director, denying him any opportunity fully to chart a progression in the situation or a development between characters. 'I have the feeling that Beckett saw *Fin de partie* like a Mondrian painting, with very clear partitions, geometric separations, geometric music,' he complained. 'And I rebelled against that a bit in rehearsals, which provoked some passionate discussions between Beckett and me.' 'I thought it was a *vue de l'esprit*, it made it all very harsh. Originally, he didn't think there was any drama or suspense.'[53]

Beckett's suggested method certainly accentuated the game-like quality of the play, embedding the suggestion that the 'farce', as both Nell and Clov declaim, truly is repeated day after day. Blin, though he recognised the legitimacy and ambition of the interpretation, nevertheless felt that he and his fellow actors could demonstrate just as effectively that their characters were aware of the falsity of what they were saying without totally detaching themselves from the dramatic flow of the play as he perceived it. Reluctantly following Beckett's instructions, Blin and Martin struggled to come to terms with the performance that the author wanted:

> It took us a while to master the rhythm, even though this was indicated by the author's numerous indications, with which this sort of musical score is stuffed. Not one measure is missing, not one crotchet, not even a key: 'The end is in the beginning and yet you go on'. That was what was so difficult – to construct a

52   Ruby Cohn, *Just Play* (Princeton: Princeton University Press, 1980), p.242.
53   Blin, *Souvenirs et propos*, p.113 and in Tom Bishop and Raymond Federman (eds.), *Samuel Beckett* (Paris: *L'Herne*, 1976), p.145. For a discussion of Blin's expression *vue de l'esprit*, see pp.248–50.

dramatic crescendo, a semblance of progression in the action, in spite of that initial pessimism.[54]

Such development was precisely that which Beckett seemed to want to stifle, continuing all the time to insist that the play contained 'no drama'.[55] Blin was concerned that if he were to follow Beckett's wishes to the letter the power of the play would be so sterilised as effectively to disengage the audience from the drama which should, he thought, be working upon them. In order to serve the text to the optimum degree, he felt obliged to disagree with Beckett and convince the author to trust his actor's intuition. He knew that a play in performance demanded a different quality of engagement from its audience than does a novel from its reader, yet Beckett's proposals seemed to him to require of an audience the reader's cool detachment; the clipped, monotonous delivery Beckett solicited from his actors would induce in the spectator a measured contemplation of the drama as it unfolded and not, as Beckett claimed was his aim, allow it to 'work on the nerves of the audience.'[56] Blin believed that the play could not function in the manner in which its author was advocating and reasoned that, even though the audience are informed during the play's opening monologue that all is finished, the painful wait for something to happen was in itself a dramatic progression that should be seen to have a toll on the characters just as much as upon the audience. Hamm's increasingly tormented desire to have evidence of change outside the shelter, the subtly escalating power struggle between him and Clov, the decline of the parents' will and energy, the arrival of a small boy outside the shelter – all of these together represented progression of sorts, and they therefore demanded a development of the relationship between the characters. Blin argued that within their slow wearing down of each other Hamm and Clov must be able to express increasing degrees of irritability and impatience, not only with each other but also with the situation in which

54   Blin to Claude Sarraute, in *Le Monde*, 27.4.57.
55   Quoted by Blin to Fady Stéphane, in *Le Safa*, 18.8.73.
56   Beckett to Jessica Tandy, in Linda Ben-Zvi, *Samuel Beckett* (New York: Twayne Publishers, 1986), p.30. This quotation is extracted from a conversation about the intended effect of *Not I*.

they are both trapped. This required a range of different intonations for each of their repeated phrases and an intensification of the tension between them (demonstrating their distorted mutual affection and interdependence). Beckett, however, simply wanted his text to be recited, intoned in the manner of a monotonic ecclesiastical reading of the psalms, and expressed little concern that the audience might decide to leave during the performance. For his part, Blin felt that the likely effect on the audience of this sort of delivery would be worse than making them leave: 'They wouldn't have left', he argued, 'they would have stayed... but frozen!'[57] Later, he and Martin came to the conclusion that Beckett had imagined his play in the rhythms of English, and that this was the cause of difficulty for them. Jean Martin recalls the problem:

> Beckett's French was impeccable, sublime, wonderful, but he thought in Anglo-Saxon. At the beginning of rehearsals he was there every day and he wasn't at all happy with things, especially me, with Clov's monologue. He gave me examples and I thought to myself that it really made an extremely artificial way of talking; artificial, not my thing at all. Sam said 'but it isn't complicated... [demonstrating] "Fiiiniiir"' and all of a sudden Blin and I, we were quite embarrassed in fact, we said 'Sam, what you can do with the English language you can't do in the French language, there is after all a phrasing that is only possible either in one or in the other'.[58]

Blin, then, wished to induce the sense of progression and the tension that he felt were integral to the dramatic success of *Fin de partie*. From his own point of view as an actor, this required him to identify with and engage with his character, and not detach himself from it or simply intone the text as though a musical instrument. In attempting to please Beckett, Blin felt that he and Martin had played their roles too austerely and blamed this for the poor response the play received from the English audiences who saw the première. Typical of their reaction was the description of the performance as 'a rather

57   Quoted by Guy Verdot, *Figaro littéraire*, 12.3.60.
58   Jean Martin to Mark Batty, 11.1.95. Beckett wanted the vowels of the French 'finir' to be extended as one might with the vowels and the 'sh' in 'finished'. See Beckett, *Fin de partie* (Paris: Éditions de Minuit, 1957), p.15 and *The Complete Dramatic Works*, p.93.

horrible evening.'[59] The following year, when London critics compared the première to George Devine's own production, they reflected back on the stilted acting of Blin and Martin, recalling how '[w]hen Mr. Samuel Beckett's *End-game* [sic] was presented at the Royal Court Theatre in its French version the production was heavily stylised [and] as such it was hard to accept.'[60] Beckett himself was less than satisfied with the reception and wittily described the experience as 'rather grim, like playing to mahogany, or rather teak'.[61] Disappointed at the harsh criticism he received in London, Blin concluded that perhaps the English preferred subtler, understated acting. Undoubtedly, Beckett's insistence upon a particular style of delivery had been partly responsible for the heavily stylised production. Back in France, at the Studio des Champs-Elysées, 'the hooks went in' and Beckett felt that 'Blin, after a shaky start in London, is now superb as Hamm.'[62] The more intimate theatre suited the atmosphere of Beckett's play better and the company were able to give a much better account of it than they had in London.

The improvement was not simply due to the more congenial performance environment. Once in Paris, Blin saw to it that the faults that he had perceived in the London performance were ironed out and eased the whole dramatic structure more towards his own inclinations. By following Beckett's directives the actors had found themselves making contrived alternations between anger and laughter which jarred with audiences. After two or three performances, Blin noticed that as Hamm he had begun instinctively to accommodate his performance to the presence of an audience, to soften some of the stilted switches from one mood to another that Beckett had required. To act as if he were a musical instrument had served to cut him off from the internal flow his performance required to justify the developing build or fall of emotion the character must display. '[T]o pass from laughter to anger, for example,' he argued, 'one goes through intermediary organic states,

59   *The Times*, 4.4.57.
60   *The Times*, 29.10.58.
61   Letter (12.8.57) from Beckett to Schneider in Harmon, *No Author Better Served*, p.15.
62   Letter (30.4.57) from Beckett to Schneider. Ibid., p.14

which is human.'[63] Such actorly phenomena Blin referred to as 'harmoniques', the inner resonances which must be given adequate space to resound within the performer in order to create a true performance where, for example, anger could either be dissolved by the effect of humour or else maintained as a residue that might then inform the laughter. As an actor, he could not help but seek meaningful progressions of mood between segments of the play and by the time *Fin de partie* had settled into a run in Paris the performance had matured and become more flexible. He came to feel more at ease with his work and Beckett had to concede that the play had evolved well. Looking back, in 1973, Blin recalled:

> Effectively, Beckett does not have the same vision of *Endgame* today that he had in '57, about the geometric construction, that verbal architecture that he thought was of the utmost importance. He concedes that there is a drama where back then he refused to see one, insisted on as much with us [...] It was a *vue de l'esprit*.[64]

The play enjoyed a long, successful run of three months over the summer of 1957 and managed a short revival in October of the same year, with a minor cast change by which Germaine de France replaced Christine Tsingos as Nell. The French critics, on the whole, responded positively to the play. Pierre Marcabru's response, typical of the more enthusiastic reviews, described the play as 'performed with a disquieting, destabilising, cruel rage, with shapeless bodies, with ravaged nerves, with a convulsive sincerity.'[65]

In 1968, Blin had the opportunity to revive *Fin de partie* at the Théâtre 347. The arrangements for this production were made so quickly that Jean Martin could not be released in time from the television contract to which he was bound and his part was offered instead to André Julien. Georges Adet and Germaine de France returned to recreate the Nagg and Nell couple. For this revival Blin received a

---

63   Blin to Christine Vymétal-Jacquemont, in Odette Aslan, *Roger Blin – Qui êtes-vous?* (Paris: La Manufacture, 1990), p.163. The French edition of Aslan's text is a more substantial volume. This shall be cited where material is not in the English text.
64   Blin to Fady Stéphane, in *Le Safa*, 18.8.73.
65   *Arts*, 8.5.57.

letter from Beckett (dated 3 April 1968) specifying a number of significant alterations to his original text and to his original cuts of 1957. Firstly, there was to be no blood on Hamm's handkerchief. Clov's opening business was to be reduced to climbing the stepladder at each window, and he should no longer forget it nor take it with him towards the dustbins. The *lazzi* of dropping the eyeglass and the gag of seeing 'une foule en délire' ('a multitude... in transports... of joy') were to be cut.[66] Similarly, the sighting of the child was to be severely abridged, omitting all dialogue from its being spotted to Clov's decision to go out supposedly to exterminate it (thus effectively cutting back the French text back by a page to match the English published version). Beckett assented to this cut in rehearsals 'because Blin couldn't bring it into line with his interpretation of the role,' he admitted, revealing his willingness now to consider the actor's needs, adding that 'I think the play is better without it.'[67] Finally, he wanted Clov's song to be taken out, along with Hamm's interruptions ('Articule' and 'Assez'), leaving a single long diatribe from Clov following Hamm's desire to hear a few words from his heart.[68] Blin complied with these suggestions which, on the whole, seemed designed to reduce the comedy in the play and allow certain sections to run more smoothly. They arguably seemed to have been inspired by a recognition of the dramatic progression that Blin had originally perceived in the play. Blin welcomed these changes on the whole, especially the final one which allowed the resolution of the play – Clov's threatened departure – to arrive more swiftly, and also permitted him to follow the interpretation of Hamm's character which he had originally sought to pursue. Hamm's lack of interest or concern at the arrival of the child and his slackening insistence on control over Clov (as originally manifested by his interruptions) facilitated the more subdued, defeated Hamm that Blin wanted to build towards, or rather wane into, by the end of the play:

66 Beckett, *Fin de partie*, p.45 and *The Complete Dramatic Works*, p.106.
67 Beckett, letter to Alan Schneider (dated 17.3.58), in Harmon, *No Author Better Served*, p.41
68 Beckett, *Fin de partie*, p.107–8 and *The Complete Dramatic Works*, p.131–2.

The cuts were necessary because there was a wearing down of attention; it was necessary to arrive at a provisional solution: Clov's departure. Also, the character of Hamm loses his vitality throughout the play; he receives a series of tough blows: nothing changes outside; his father doesn't reply; his mother dies. Hamm is too tired to go back to his questions and his jibes once the child arrives. The actor can't either go on playing and starting the role over again.[69]

Matias provided the décor for the revival and, with him, Blin toned down his original conception of Hamm; gone were the side whiskers and the throne-like chair, replaced by what appeared to be more of a luxury office chair on castors. His characterisation now approached Beckett's definition of Hamm as 'a worn-out bourgeois, disoriented, trapped in a kind of pillbox.'[70] Everything on stage was tinted grey: Hamm's costume, the gaff, the chair and so on, according to Beckett's wishes. Such details, along with the cuts, created a tighter and perhaps grimmer performance, more demanding for the audience than the original production of eleven years earlier. Blin felt more at ease with the play and that his own performance had improved.

On tour in Austria, Blin received a well-wishing letter from Beckett which demonstrated the trust and satisfaction the author had in his work:

I'm very happy that you're over there – as long as you are a little too – and to know with certainty that there will be at least one German language *mise en scène* that is both intelligent and intelligible. This adds to all that I owe you and for which I hope one day finally to be able to repay you with a real play.[71]

Beckett's modest implication that none of the plays he had so far offered Blin were good enough seems to suggest that he hoped one day to offer his friend a strong role worthy of his talent. If this was the case, such a role was never to materialise; at this time (1968) Blin had not yet taken on the part of Krapp, which Beckett had originally hoped to see him play, and had already directed his last Beckett production, *Oh les beaux jours*.

---

69   Blin to Myriam Louzan, in *Les Voies de la création théâtrale*, 5 (1977), p.443.
70   Ibid., p.433.
71   Letter dated 26.1.58, sent from Ussy to Roger Blin at the Theater am Fleisch-markt, Vienna, Fonds Blin, IMEC, Paris.

The 'mise en terre' of *Oh les beaux jours*[72]

When Samuel Beckett completed his own translation of *Happy Days* in December 1962, there was no doubt in his mind who should direct the French language première of the play. The choice of an actress to play Winnie was more open to question. Having seen Brenda Bruce in the English première in London, Blin at first sought a comic actress, or one who would project a comic image – a round-faced, large-chested, 'larger than life' woman, crammed painfully into the earth mound which is both her home and prison. His thinking adhered to Beckett's own vision of the character as 'perhaps a little podgy, a comic figure, ludicrous, more fleshy than wasted away.'[73] He reasoned, however, that a comic appearance would only have any vitality in the first moments of the play and would wear thin and undermine other more potent aspects of the dramatic texture. He felt that Winnie's tragedy, as displayed in her moments of insight, demanded an actress of sterner qualities, one 'who might have the futility she shows in the first act, a kind of bird-brain, bourgeoise, who natters away in her hole as though still in a *salon de thé*, who might still project all the tragedy and depression of the second act when only the head is above ground.'[74] His thoughts settled quickly on Madeleine Renaud and he lost no time in having a copy of the play sent to her at the Odéon – where he was already busy preparing a production of Ramón del Valle-Inclán's *Divines Paroles* (*Divine Words*) – and informed Beckett of his choice of actress for the role. Hesitant at first, the author acquiesced to Blin's suggestion. Jean-Louis Barrault was keen to incorporate the play into the forthcoming season, as it fitted perfectly into the cross-cultural repertoire he had striven to achieve since assuming the directorship of the theatre in 1959. He programmed the play into the Odéon's 1963–4

---

72 The expression 'mise en terre' ('putting in earth', as opposed to the 'putting on stage' of *mise en scène*) was coined by the critic Paul Morelle in his review of *Oh les beaux jours* in *Libération*, 2.3.63. Blin himself was reluctant to use the term *mise en scène* for his work on the play, his credit in the programme for the production reading instead 'présentation de Roger Blin'.

73 Blin in Waintrop, *Les mises en scène de Beckett*, p.39.

74 Ibid.

schedule, and also offered to play the part of Willie. Lending a good measure of fresh credibility to Beckett's reputation, not as yet acknowledged in the Parisian 'mainstream', Madeleine Renaud accepted the role of Winnie happily, if with a certain initial apprehension. Later, she declared that the opportunity to play Winnie had been a high point in her long career:

> Listen well, I mean what I say. I've said to myself quite often: 'Will no author give me a real woman's role?' That role has been written by Beckett. No other dramatist, I maintain, has yet demonstrated such a great, profound and moving understanding of women... Roger Blin has given me a memorable gift in bringing the manuscript of Oh les beaux jours to me.[75]

Renaud tackled the role with the excitement of having at last found a vehicle that lent a vital means of expression to her identity as a woman, an actress and a human being, and later claimed: 'There is total identification between Winnie and me; I'm not playing a character, I'm playing myself. That has perhaps never happened to me before, not to this point.'[76]

The first problem the Renaud/Barrault Company faced in mounting the play was the unsuitability of the Odéon's stage, which all concerned agreed was far too large for Beckett's static monologue. The play was written with the pocket theatres of the Parisian Left Bank still in mind, as the author continued to do throughout the 1960s and 1970s, providing dramatic material that was best suited to small theatres where the audience enjoyed an intimate relationship with the stage action. The smaller stage of the petit Odéon had not yet been constructed and the huge volume of the Théâtre de France had to undergo rather drastic adaptation before it could offer a suitable performance space for Oh les beaux jours. To reduce the size of the auditorium, the second and third balconies were obscured by sheets of canvas, whilst the stage was extended out over the orchestra pit to meet the front rows of the stalls. Madeleine Renaud was to sit in her mound of earth at roughly the position of the downstage edge of the theatre's fixed stage. This arrangement not only facilitated a greater

75   Madeleine Renaud to Maurice Tillier, in Le Figaro littéraire, 14.11.63.
76   Renaud in Paris-Presse l'intransigeant, 17–18.11.63.

intimacy between actress and audience, crucial to the performance, but also gave the designer, Matias, considerable depth to suggest the expanse of the wilderness in which Winnie is trapped.

From *En attendant Godot* to this latest work there was already a clear development in Beckett's dramatic writing towards reducing the voice and restricting the mobility of his characters. The reduction in mobility, coupled with a more precise and meticulous detailing of pauses and inflection, were to become characteristic of Beckett's dramatic style, and reached an early extreme with *Oh les beaux jours,* in which one third of the written text is made up of stage directions. In this way, arguably, Beckett progressively achieved a greater degree of control over the interpretation of his work, reducing the role of the director. Many critics and analysts have not only construed this combination of proliferating stage directions and close overseeing of rehearsals as evidence of Beckett's tightening of authority over the live incarnations of his writings, but have concluded from this that he effectively directed these French premières himself, Blin's role being perhaps one of simply providing experience and theatrical know-how in dealing with the technical aspects of production. If Jean-Marie Serreau is to be believed, there could have been little more than this for Blin to do with Beckett's tightly-knit drama: 'At his side, the director can scarcely make the work his own, he is merely the author's representative, serving as a pivot between author and actors, and has nothing other than the technical realisation of the play at hand.'[77] Such an assessment was offered in the context of some of Beckett's later plays, such as *Comédie* (*Play*, which Serreau directed in collaboration with Beckett in March 1963), in which the actor is reduced to a near static collection of facial muscles and dialogue has been pared down to a bare minimum of fragmented soliloquy. Nevertheless, even when Beckett went so far as precisely to dictate the use of lighting, as the fourth 'character' of the interrogator in *Comédie*, or the details of stage blocking, as for example he did later in the published version of *Footfalls*, there was still painstaking and trying work left for director and actors in making sure, in the words of Alan Schneider 'that the

77   Serreau in Mélèse, *Samuel Beckett*, p.150.

nonessentials don't creep back in.'[78] In this sense the director's work consists of 'editing' the actors, by guiding them into the text from which the role emerges. This is perhaps an appropriate description of Blin's work alongside Beckett on *Oh les beaux jours*, developing a characterisation for Winnie with Madeleine Renaud. He frequently described his work as that of a craftsman attending to small and intricate details, an entirely appropriate approach on this occasion: 'My work has above all consisted of trying to find, with Madeline Renaud, the form of stylised diction that is imposed by the text, constructed on needle points. A real milliner's task!'[79]

As a point of departure, and to give Madeleine Renaud firm footholds for developing Winnie's reaction to her situation, Blin first worked on the fine textual detail provided by Beckett as a guide to delivering the lines, particularly his marking of pauses and indications of inflection and stress:

> Throughout rehearsals, I laid stress on the punctuation of the text. Beckett's texts are stuffed with full-stops and these full-stops have to be played. 'This will have been another happy day! (Pause.) After all. (Pause.) So far.' In their very precise order, those phrases go from joy, to a diminished joy, to nothing.[80]

With complete deference to the text, then, and ensuring that she respected the construction of Beckett's lengthy monologues, Blin eased Renaud into her role. The process was a long and exacting one, the actress gently cultivating a performance from her understanding of the character and the director acting as her mirror, adding and subtracting details in the evolving characterisation. Next, having made sure that Beckett's words and stage directions were strictly adhered to, Blin was on the lookout for any 'nonessentials' that might creep into the performance of an actress schooled in the Conservatoire style. Above all, he had to discourage the naturally cheerful and optimistic Renaud from applying too light a touch to her characterisation. For

78 Schneider, 'Symposium on Rockaby', quoted in Enoch Brater, *Beyond Minimalism – Beckett's Later Style in the Theater* (New York: Oxford University Press, 1987), p.174.
79 Blin to Maurice Tillier, in *Figaro littéraire*, 14.11.63.
80 Blin, *Souvenirs et propos*, p.167.

example, at the moment when Winnie notices an ant crawling on her hill, Renaud instinctively played the revelation as joyous, whereas Blin counselled her that a response of disgust or horror at the persistence of life might be more appropriate to Beckett's vision. The discipline required of Renaud, an actress at this time more accustomed to a dramatic diet of Molière and Feydeau, was rigorous:

> Roger Blin – [...] I was able to torture you at will.
> Madeleine Renaud – You met with no resistance from me. The authority was that of the text alone. Arguments were impossible between us.
> Roger Blin – All the same, I had to force you to forget certain things. For example, hadn't you always been told not to have your mouth open in moments of silence.[81]

This close attention to detail ensured that every physical movement or shift in tone of voice was dictated by the text or was wholly appropriate to it. Yet, despite the apparent specificity and restrictiveness of the script, Blin asserted that there was still a great deal left for him to do, and, while occasionally grumbling at Beckett's expanding use of directions in the printed versions of his plays, he maintained that his job was to infuse the text with a life that no author could supply. Blin acknowledged that *Oh les beaux jours* resembled a musical score even more than had *Fin de partie*, a score for one voice with repeated leitmotifs, refrains and different tones of utterance, and yet he maintained that an orchestral score can nevertheless be interpreted in a variety of ways, and that no two performances of it could ever be truly identical. Its execution is wholly dependent on the interpretation the conductor of the orchestra brings to it, the competence of the individual musicians and their collaborative work as a performing group. This can clearly be directly paralleled to the work of actors and directors in the realisation of a dramatic work. However explicit the playwright's text, Blin argued, there will still be a great deal of scope for interpretive talent. Indeed there is an absolute need for it, as much for the effective performance of an orchestral concerto as for the ensured success of a presentation of a play such as *Oh les beaux jours*. Rehearsing with Madeleine Renaud for the first time in

---

81   Renaud and Blin to Maurice Tillier, in *Le Figaro littéraire*,14.11.63.

1963, Blin recognised how much work was still required of him to bring the optimum performance out of this most accomplished of French actresses and that the text itself, however fastidiously constructed, did not hold all the answers:

> [W]hen Beckett indicates a pause, that might be for a fraction of a second or for a minute. There are moments when there is a question of rendering something with a double meaning, of mixing sadness with a joyous word. You have to 'oil' things, adapt it for the actress [...] We had to find a truthful way of speaking, a manner of articulating, a way of expressing Beckett's style which employs very short phrases and assonance, raised to a kind of music.[82]

Elaborating upon this precisely shaped diction, Blin provides further insight into the process of grafting visual actions on top of Beckett's densely layered text:

> It seemed to me that certain phrases could be spoken slowly, others very quickly, and that above all it was important to accentuate each come-down. She has to, each time, before saying 'And now', always followed by a come-down, of despair, of weariness, falling asleep a little, sometimes even closing the eyes, and being brought back to attention by the alarm, then off again: 'And now!' Madeleine really didn't like those moments. I'd asked her to go into each come-down with her breathing, with a movement of the face towards the ground and to hold herself totally still for just a few seconds.[83]

The esteemed actress proved a willing student, both to Beckett's fastidious directions and to Blin's dedicated coaching, and spent two months being coached by the director and listening to the author. She remembered 'going over each word, each reply by heart, in absolute trust' and recalled: 'I already have a long career behind me, and yet Blin and Beckett have opened a new window onto my craft for me.'[84]

Blin left behind some rare examples of rehearsal note-taking on his work with Renaud for act one of the play. These notes are scribbled out over eight pages of foolscap and much of what is written is in a barely legible hand (a trait Blin shared with Beckett). Scribbled and terse as these notes are, they not only confirm Blin's attention to

82   Blin to Catherine Valogne, in *La Tribune de Lausanne*, 27.10.63.
83   Blin, *Souvenirs et propos*, p.164.
84   Renaud in *Les Nouvelles Littéraires*, 2008, 24.2.65, pp.6–7.

detail, but also provide some insight into his own reading of the play.[85] On one page, for example, seemingly associated with Winnie's long story/reminiscence, there is a brief comment on the similarity between Winnie and Hamm, and one can imagine that Blin and Renaud discussed the comparative tasks of playing the two roles, notably the need that both characters' manifest to construct narratives as modes of coping with or clarifying their experience. The notes also reveal much of the work done on the tone of Renaud's performance. Aware that the actress did not present the visually comic image that Beckett would initially have wished, Blin advised her to 'in a general manner, reconsider the character as grotesque, as there is nothing physically ridiculous', while often encouraging her to intensify the severity of her approach or to achieve a balance between the despair and the moments of hope that Winnie experiences: 'keep an eye on the unsteadiness – hold it back for moments of depression or distraction.' Usually the suggestions he made were not so much express instructions as hints at directions in which she herself could take her interpretation of the role. He seems to have been intent on making her aware of any excesses in her performances or of any moments that needed accentuating: 'Find a way of feeling the fear or the sensation of a danger of being drawn upwards.'[86] On the other hand, Winnie's lighter side, her futile optimism, was clearly significant to Blin, as there are a number of notes urging Madeleine Renaud to take the character's jauntiness still further: '"Fully guaranteed..." – a certain triumph in having found one more word with the help of the magnifying glass.'[87] He clearly considered it important that any hope the character experienced should be visibly inspired by objects and incidents, emphasising Winnie's dependence on external stimulation to feel perceived and recognised. For example, her early expression of joy at Willie's withdrawal from his hole and installation behind her is

85   The notes are held in the Blin Archive of the Bibliothèque Nationale, département des arts du spectacles (Arsenal), Paris. In my transcriptions of the notes, where an estimation of the original wording is made (or a word is assumed from the context of the sentence) this is given in square parentheses.

86   See Beckett, *Oh les beaux jours* (Paris: Éditions de Minuit 1963), p.40 and Beckett, *The Complete Dramatic Works*, pp.151–2.

87   See *Oh les beaux jours*, p.23 and *The Complete Dramatic Works*, p.143.

glossed thus: 'Cold cream – "this is going to be a happy day" more connected with what's just been heard.'[88] The strained relationship between husband and wife is also emphasised in Blin's notes. Winnie's manner of speaking to Willie was to be cool and without affection: 'Always maintain a little vocal distance to Willie, even when he is at his closest to you.' Conversely, Blin notes twice that Willie's lines too should be spoken with more hostility ('Willie: "Sleep!" – louder and more aggressive' and 'Louder attack Willie')[89] and he also hints at the vacuity of Winnie's relationship with Willie, firstly by undermining the manner in which she talks to him: '"I hope you caught something of that" as a rupture... comic, pretentious voice for the ruptures.'[90] Later, it is conveyed more darkly when Blin explicitly relates the revolver in her possession to an annoyance with her husband: 'Perhaps a glance towards Willie when, instead of putting the pistol away she puts it back in front of her.'[91]

These few notes provide a tantalisingly brief insight into Blin's approach to Beckett's text. They seem to belong to a late phase in rehearsal where most of the interpretative work has been completed, lines are learnt and set and props are more or less in place. But they do offer us a glimpse of Blin's work as 'editor' to his actors, and are therefore significant for our appraisal of his methodology, which will be dealt with in the concluding chapter of this study.

88   See *Oh les beaux jours*, p.29 and *The Complete Dramatic Works*, p.146.
89   Ibid. In his French translation, Beckett has Willie instruct Winnie to sleep ('Dors!'), dismissing her question about the grammar of 'à Dieu et à soi' and I have translated this French instruction here in Blin's notes. In the original English text, though, Beckett has Winnie respond at this point to Willie's query over whether hair should be referred to as 'it' or 'them' with a blunt 'It!'
90   See *Oh les beaux jours*, p.46 and *The Complete Dramatic Works*, p.154.
91   See *Oh les beaux jours*, p.53 and *The Complete Dramatic Works*, p.158.

'A solidarity between meagre men' [92]

Roger Blin and Samuel Beckett's friendship was to bind them until the director's death in 1984. Their casual correspondence over the three and a half decades of their association is imbued with warmth and affection and dotted with numerous invitations to dinner or arrangements to meet and pass the time together at the Dôme, 'chez Lipp' or in the other cafés of the Left Bank that the pair would frequent. Hospitalised for the final time in December 1983, Blin received visits from Samuel and Suzanne Beckett and the couple attended his cremation at Père Lachaise some weeks later. Though the two men were not constant companions, their fondness for one another was genuine and had grown from a reciprocal respect and a recognition of shared attitudes.

Those who knew Blin well would expect him to indulge in periods of silence and knew that the greatest mark of comfort he could show in another person's company was an ability not to need to communicate. Matias reminisced about times Blin would go for a stroll, leaving his second arrondissement home to cross the river and come and sit in his apartment on the rue Mazarine to sip wine or coffee in silence.[93] Hermine Karagheuz, Blin's long-term partner, spoke of their being able to pass each other in the corridor of the flat in the rue St Honoré without even exchanging an acknowledging word.[94] Beckett's passion for silence and privacy was well known and one can imagine the nature of the affinity between these two modest, shy and intelligent men. Beckett was certainly confident in their alliance, stating once simply that 'Roger and I have no need of seeing each other' as a seemingly paradoxical manner of expressing the bond they shared.[95]

---

92 The title here is borrowed from that of Blin's article on his relationship with Beckett: 'Une solidarité entre maigres', *Arts-Spectacles*, 418, 3–9.7.53, p.5. He held to the expression, repeating it thirty years later in the collated *Souvenirs et propos* (p.83). Bradby translates this as 'a solidarity in leanness' (*Waiting for Godot*, p.57).

93 Matias to Mark Batty, 10.1.95.

94 Hermine Karagheuz to Mark Batty, 5.1.95.

95 Reported by A.Simon in *Esprit*, April 1984, p.142.

As with any protracted relationship, the two men were capable of demonstrating temporary annoyance with one another. As an example, Beckett had taken offence, unbeknown to Blin, at his refusal in 1960 to play the part of Krapp. Blin's initial disinterest in the part was complicated: on a personal level, he was uncomfortable with the idea of growing old and the consequences of senility and, though publicly he joked as he explained that he was tired of playing Beckett's old men ('I've stopped playing Beckett's old fools because it was getting too close to reality for me'),[96] more privately, he felt it inappropriate to play the role of Krapp in 1960 in the light of a recent romantic entanglement. Conversely, in 1975, Blin was mildly indignant when he saw Beckett's Berlin *mise en scène* of *Warten auf Godot*, claiming that, despite the notable differences between this and his own productions of the play, Beckett had consciously or not directly lifted many of his own discoveries.[97] The trust and respect between the two men remained nevertheless constant. Blin was accorded the right, usually vested exclusively in the author, of his permission being required by companies seeking to stage *En attendant Godot* and *Fin de partie* in the Parisian region. A further example of the esteem in which Blin was held is provided by a letter he received in 1969 in which Beckett politely explained that he had given Jean-Marie Serreau permission to mount *Act sans paroles II* (*Act without Words II*) on the assumption that his friend would not have wanted to direct the work. Such respectful deference on the part of an author to a director is indicative of the depth of regard Beckett held for Blin, both as a friend and an artist.

The two were prone to disagree over the necessary tone to be realised in productions of the plays which followed *En attendant Godot*. Such disputes offer us some insight not only into Beckett's response to his own work, but also into the nature of Blin's approach and his attitude to the staging of the works of living authors. In spite of the differences in interpretation that might arise during rehearsals, Beckett continued to confide his plays to the instinctive and un-

96   Quoted by François Weyergans, in *Les Nouvelles*, 2.2.84.
97   '"Sam's copied me, he's copied my *mise en scène*!" He felt that Sam had done the same things he had.' Matias to Mark Batty, 10.1.95.

conventional director who had first demonstrated a dedication to his work and done it such justice. Following the successes of *En attendant Godot* and *Fin de partie*, Blin was given the newly translated (by the author) monologue *La Dernière Bande* (*Krapp's Last Tape*) which he presented in March of that year at the Théâtre Récamier with Jean-Réné Chauffard in the role of Krapp, and, in 1963, he presented his last *mise en scène* of a Beckett play, *Oh les beaux jours* (*Happy Days*). His involvement with the works of Beckett did not end there however; he went on to direct and perform in numerous revivals of *En attendant Godot* and *Fin de partie*, as well as being recalled to advise Madeleine Renaud whenever she returned to the part of Winnie, to which her name had become indissolubly linked. In 1977 he finally played Krapp in a Swiss television production of *La Dernière Bande* and harboured a secret desire after all to play the role in Paris one day.

Though he could be enthusiastic in his praise of their poetry, Blin declined to direct Beckett's later plays, a decision attributable in part to a desire to support new and unknown authors, but also in part to a diminished interest in working on these later plays to which his input could only be minimal. He did contemplate directing Madeleine Renaud as the mouth in *Pas moi* (*Not I*) in 1973 but, after having travelled to London with the actress to see the European première there, realised that rehearsals for such a play could offer him little satisfaction.[98] The playwright still clung to the hope that he could interest him in mounting his new work. In 1974, for example, after sending a copy of *Cette Fois* (*That Time*) to Madeleine Renaud, Beckett contacted Blin expressing a desire for him to direct the piece. Similarly, in 1977, Blin received a copy of a freshly translated *Pas* (*Footfalls*) with a note attached in which Beckett explained that he saw their mutual friend Delphine Seyrig in the role of May, clearly expecting to extract a response.

Blin did undertake a number of roles in some of Beckett's radio pieces, including *Cascando*, *Tous ceux qui tombent* (*All that Fall*) and

---

98   Blin saw the British première of *Not I*, with Billie Whitelaw as mouth, directed by Anthony Page at the Royal Court Theatre, London in January 1973. Renaud finally took the role in the French première in 1976 at the Théâtre d'Orsay directed by Jean-Marie Serreau.

Cendres (Embers).[99] The latter, in which he had played Henry opposite Delphine Seyrig as Ada, he declared to be one of his favourite of
Beckett's writings and he maintained that the piece could work
visually. Pondering how he might adapt the work for the stage, he
believed he could surmount the problem of the necessary ambiguity
surrounding the existence of the female role, an ambiguity which constituted the chief reason for Beckett's objection to a stage production.
Blin hoped to be able to convince him, but the project, regrettably,
was never to be realised. This proposed production might originally
have been conceived for the 'Beckett cycle' project that Blin had
began to plan in 1969.[100] Later, in what were to turn out to be the last
years of his life, Blin had hoped to mount a one-man Beckett show,
incorporating numerous elements from a selection of the author's
dramatic works, but such a homage was to be constructed instead by
Barry McGovern with *I'll go on*, a dramatisation of sections from the
trilogy of novels *Molloy, Malone Dies* and *The Unnamable*.[101] Had
Blin's planned montage of Beckett's prose and drama ever seen the
light of stage, in certain (if reluctant) collaboration with the author, it
would surely have been a definitive tribute to the work of Samuel
Beckett.

Blin's name will always be associated with that of Samuel Beckett, the ephemeral achievements of the former obscured by the impressive reputation of the latter. Indeed, their association participated very
much in cementing Blin's reputation as a director of the 'nouveau
théâtre'. This was a hindrance as much as it was an accolade; so much
so, for example, that when Blin and Martin played Davies and Aston
in the French première of Harold Pinter's *The Caretaker* in January
1961, their Pozzo/Lucky and Hamm/Clov personas were still fresh in
critics' minds and they were accused of having 'perhaps exaggerated
the pitiable and morbid tone of the play, obsessed as they are by

---

99   *Cendres* was broadcast by O.R.T.F. in January 1961, *Tous ceux qui tombent* in
      January 1963 and *Cascando* in October 1963.
100   The cycle opened on 16.3.70 at the Theatre Récamier, running for three
      months, and included *En attendant Godot*, a Beckett-directed *La Dernière
      Bande* with Jean Martin as Krapp, *Acte sans paroles* and *Oh le beaux jours*.
101   This was first presented at the Gate Theatre, Dublin, in 1985.

Beckett's vision of a decaying humanity'.[102] Conversely, Beckett recognised how much of his early exposure was due to Blin, and, as the earliest token of his gratitude, the published text of *Fin de partie* (éditions de Minuit, 1957) was dedicated to Roger Blin. The production of that play was crucial to Beckett's continued pursuits as a playwright and its difficult period of gestation was to prove an invaluable experience for both him and the director he trusted. Indeed, one might even conjecture the degree to which the nature of Beckett's subsequent dramatic writing was shaped by his early experiences in rehearsal rooms. In this regard, the precise extent of Blin's influence on Beckett's development both as a dramatist and as a director of his own plays is perhaps incalculable. Nevertheless, it is curious that this influence has hardly even been considered within the mass of biographical, analytical and critical material that has accumulated around Beckett's work over the past few decades. Without Blin's enthusiasm for both *Eleuthéria* and *En attendant Godot* in 1949, and his persistence in seeing to it that the latter reach the stage, Beckett himself declared that his encounter with Blin had been one of the most significant turning points in his career:

> Meeting Roger Blin was one of the great opportunities of my life. By accepting *in extremis* and with open arms a play that nobody else wanted, he unlocked the door for me. Towards adventure. More than assistance, deliverance. I owe an incalculable debt to that man of the theatre and dear friend.[103]

Given such sentiments, Beckett would have no doubt been the first to admit that, had it not been for Blin, he may not have achieved the world-wide recognition and acclaim that was generated by the success of his first play. Indeed, it was the triumph of *En attendant Godot* in itself which led directly to his nomination for, and reluctant

102 Bertrand Poirot-Delpech, *Le Monde*, 28.1.61. Though the programme named Martin as *metteur en scène*, and Blin recalls the same (*Souvenirs et propos*, p.297), Harold Pinter, who saw the production, remembers that it was Roger Blin who directed the play (Harold Pinter to Mark Batty, 16.9.2004). It is not inconceivable that Blin assisted Martin who, playing Aston, would rarely have been off-stage in rehearsals to direct.

103 Beckett in *Blin Beckett*, Atelier de Création Radiophonique (France Culture), 622, 3.2.85, p.4.

acceptance of, the Nobel Prize for literature in 1969. At the time some journalists went so far as to attribute some of the credit for the award to the director, one stating that 'Blin should today be quite excited; he's just been given a well-deserved share of a Nobel prize, for to crown Vladimir is also to crown Estragon.'[104] Though one can imagine how horrified Blin would have been at this suggestion, there can be no doubt that Beckett was truly aware of the debt he owed his friend. André Bernold, in *L'Amitié de Beckett*, pointed out that

> Beckett's predominant attitude as regards those (such as Roger Blin and Alan Schneider) who had made his work known was a gratitude that was as emotional as it was touching; without them, he would repeatedly say, nothing would have happened, he would never have been heard, his work was refused everywhere, he owed them everything.[105]

The precise nature of any debt that Beckett felt he owed Blin, and others who carried his torch afterwards, was however not simply that of having helped stamp his name firmly on the theatrical map. The accumulated knowledge that Beckett gained about the nature of the stage through witnessing the rehearsal and gradual taking shape of his work clearly informed the development of his writing and the nature of his personal approach to the possibilities of the stage. When writing his first plays Beckett mischievously claimed a lack of knowledge in all things theatrical. In 1952, for example, he publicly stated: 'I have no views on the theatre, I know nothing about it, I never go, it's appalling.'[106] It is of course untrue that Beckett never went to the theatre, though he certainly had no significant practical experience of stage practice at that time. Furthermore, he would insist when quizzed that there was little or nothing he could do to assist with the rehearsal of his plays, for example stating to Schneider: 'You know by experience what little help I am with my own work.'[107] His maturation from such confessed ignorance of the practice of the

104 Claude Roy, *Le Nouvel Observateur*, 3.11.69.
105 André Bernold, *L'Amitié de Beckett* (Paris: Hermann, 1992), pp.98–9.
106 Beckett, preamble to extracts from *En attendant Godot*, recited by Roger Blin, broadcast by the O.R.T.F., 17 February 1952.
107 Letter from Beckett to Alan Schneider, dated 12.8.57, in Harmon, *No Author Better Served*, p.15.

theatre to his markedly increased interest in overseeing productions during the 1960s and 1970s, culminating in his decision to direct his plays personally, is clearly of significance to the Beckett scholar. His ventures into directing can only have been the result of a growing concern for the precise execution of the vision he wished to convey: this lies at the core of any understanding of his dramatic achievements and calls for a study of all the practical circumstances that informed his education in the machinery of performance. Knowlson asks whether 'Beckett's dramatic methods [were] developed pragmatically? Were they guided perhaps by working with a director who was also an expert on lighting techniques, like George Devine, or by somebody with all-round theatrical expertise, like Roger Blin?'[108] In the light of such uncertainty one might have expected greater interest in the possible influence of those such as Roger Blin who served to furnish Beckett with a basic empirical schooling in the resources of the stage and the building of a performance from the written text. His inability at first to appreciate Blin's approach was demonstrative of his inexperience in the theatre and, though contact with Blin's methods initially troubled him, and though they were a far cry from the approach he himself was to adopt later, he must slowly have been reassured by their effectiveness as he saw the performances Blin constructed develop and assume their final form.

As has been shown above, their collaboration on *Fin de partie* was to prove less than peaceful, as Beckett started to leave his back seat and take a more active role in the rehearsal process. This conflict was crucial to his development. In drafting this play, with the confidence of an international success behind him, Beckett conceived the text more in terms of the life it would adopt on stage and even cultivated definite views as to the delivery of the dialogue. Some of these *vues de l'esprit*, as Blin called them, formulated in the cool atmosphere of solitary composition, were to prove inappropriate to the reality of performance from the director's standpoint. The resultant friction, and Blin's stubborn insistence on giving the work full credit, as he saw it, and in spite of its author, must have played a major part

108 Knowlson, 'States of play: performance changes and Beckett scholarship', *Journal of Beckett Studies*, 10 (1985), p.116.

in instructing Beckett about the nature of the interaction between text and audience, the needs of actors and such requisites as rhythm, pace and pitch. The lessons learnt were invaluable. One may speculate that it was as a result of this experience that he came more fully to terms with drama as an experiential art, and with the consequential acceptance of the taxing effect of time upon the spectator. From this Beckett undertook further formalistic investigation to achieve a mode of expression that would not overstretch an audience's attention, nor be overly dependent on an actor's interpretative faculties, and we can see in his work subsequent to *Fin de partie* a pronounced reduction in overall length and in the amount of dialogue together with a greater concentration on movement and visual information. Textual repetition is employed far more mechanically and to greater effect, for example, in *Play* and *Come and Go*, and the potency of visual imagery in relation to spoken words is clearly demonstrated in *Happy Days*, *Not I*, *Footfalls* and *Rockaby*.

Perhaps most significantly, Beckett learnt from the stubborn Blin the need to accept the collaborative nature of dramatic art. 'Like all practising playwrights,' Schneider recalled, 'he was gradually discovering that all actors have personalities and get ideas which may seriously affect the intentions of the author.'[109] The attempt to discover the means of control of his artistic mode of expression is characteristic of Beckett's career. Ironically, it was perhaps through his collaboration with Roger Blin, the director who felt the need to struggle with Beckett in order to forge his vision to the most compelling degree, that Beckett decided further to limit the possibility of alien interpretations of his work through the scrupulous noting of stage directions in the text. He certainly discovered that resolute actors and directors had the sole power of relaying his vision to the public, and though he was more than satisfied with Blin's contribution and trusted the latter's intuition, he may have realised that specific measures were needed to ensure that his work was safe from the tampering imaginations of more egoistic practitioners. The next logical step, that of directing his own productions, caused its own problems. Blin was not

109   Schneider, 'Waiting for Beckett', *The Chelsea Review*, 2 (Autumn 1958), p.12.

sure quite how Beckett would fare in his pursuit of tighter regulation over his scripts:

> We've never argued, Beckett and I, but we did have to discuss long and hard all problems of interpretation. Since then, he's done many *mises en scène*, and has undoubtedly come up against actors more attached to their craft than I ever was.[110]

Beckett himself was not unaware of the inadequacy, or at least the potential negative effect, of his own intervention in the work of a director. Responding to an invitation to participate in the 1978 revival of *En attendant Godot*, he wrote to Blin to decline the proposition: 'As I've told you, I want to stay away from this revival. I'd only get in the way and cause confusion.'[111]

It is possible to argue, then, that Beckett's presence at the rehearsals of Blin's productions of *En attendant Godot*, *Fin de partie* and *Oh les beaux jours* contributed in some form to Beckett's apprenticeship in the practice of stage craft beyond that of dramatic writing. From these first encounters with professional actors he developed the knowledge and confidence that enabled him ultimately to assume the full responsibility of directing as a way of guaranteeing fidelity to his work. The nature of the author/director interface in Blin's case, where he tended to take on the role of surrogate author in re-imagining plays from text to stage, allowed for some seeping of inspiration to cross both ways, and the fruits of this method can only have been of benefit to those, like Samuel Beckett, whom he first brought before the public and who had alongside him their first experience of the practical considerations of rehearsal and working with actors.

---

110 Blin, *Souvenirs et propos*, pp.117–18.
111 Letter from Beckett to Blin, dated 7.12.77, Fonds Blin, IMEC, Paris.

Jean Genet

Les Nègres

Roger Blin proceeded from the successful tour of *Fin de partie* to the creation of the first production of Jean Genet's *Les Nègres* (*The Blacks*) and was to consolidate his standing as a key exponent of the avant-garde by emulating the close rapport with Beckett, first by directing *Les Nègres* to Genet's extreme satisfaction and later by collaborating with the playwright on a production of *Les Paravents*. With Genet's plays, Blin was to embroil himself in further controversy, and of a more political nature than the critical scandal provoked by some of Beckett's work.

By the time Blin produced *Les Nègres* in 1959, Jean Genet was already an established artist, the bulk of his literary output having by then been completed. His first novel *Notre Dame des fleurs* (*Our Lady of the Flowers*), his first plays *Haute Surveillance* (*Deathwatch*) and *Les Bonnes* (*The Maids*) and his autobiographical *Journal d'un voleur* (*A Thief's Journal*) were all published in the 1940s. *Le Balcon* (*The Balcony*) and *Les Nègres* appeared in print in 1956 and 1958 respectively and Genet was at work on his last play, *Les Paravents* (*The Screens*) as Blin and his company were in rehearsal. *Les Bonnes*, the first of his plays to be performed, had been mounted in 1947 by Louis Jouvet at the Théâtre de l'Athénée while *Haute Surveillance* had been produced two years later at the Théâtre des Mathurins. By the 1950s, then, Genet had achieved a measure of financial security and had attracted a good deal of critical attention. He had seen his plays performed in leading Parisian theatres and, with the patronage of such as Cocteau and the friendship of Sartre, had become quickly accepted in literary and intellectual circles.

Blin had first encountered the writer at Genet's bookstall by the Seine and they were often to meet one another through mutual friends of the Saint-Germain-des-Prés group. He was one of a number of people who publicly supported Genet (alongside a campaign by the *Combat* newspaper) when he received a life sentence in 1948 for accumulated petty thefts, and the weight of that support helped lead to the pardon granted by President Auriol. Though he had not been able to see Jouvet's production of *Les Bonnes* owing to his other engagements that year,[1] Blin admired Genet's work and, as a friend of Olga Barbezat, the wife of Genet's publisher, had often was able to read his plays before they were printed.[2] Their overt theatricality, however, had not altogether appealed to him and he had never been motivated to stage any of them. Before plans for a production of *Les Nègres* came to light, Blin had been cast in Peter Brook's production of *Le Balcon*, which was originally scheduled for performance in 1958 at the Théâtre Antoine but postponed when the manageress, Simone Berriau, grew concerned about the controversial nature of Genet's work, and withdrew her backing.[3]

A play written specifically for black actors, *Les Nègres* would never have become a viable project for Blin had he not made the acquaintance of a group of black amateur theatre enthusiasts. During the run of Beckett's *Fin de partie* in 1957, Blin was approached by Toto Bissainthe, Aba Bakar Samba and Thimeté Bassouri. These young black actors, along with Sarah Maldoror, then comprised the entire membership of a company named La Troupe des Griots.[4] They asked Blin to be their patron, to give them actor training and to take

1   In *Souvenirs et propos* (p.125), Blin claims to have been unable to see *Les Bonnes* due to his engagements at the Gaîté-Montparnasse. In 1947, however, he was engaged at the Noctambules and later at the Vieux-Colombier. He may certainly have missed *Haute Surveillance* due to his mounting of Johnston's *La Lune dans le fleuve jaune* at the Gaîté-Montparnasse in 1949.

2   Blin had made the acquaintance of the actress Olga Barbezat at the time when they both studied under Dullin.

3   Brook's production of *Le Balcon* finally reached the stage at the Théâtre du Gymnase opening on 18 May 1960 with Blin in the role of the Envoy, after having been considered for the part of the Bishop. It was partly due to the overwhelming public and critical reception of *Les Nègres* under Blin's direction that Brook finally had the opportunity to mount *Le Balcon*.

4   A griot is a traditional West African poet, singer, and wandering musician, engaged in an oral tradition of story-telling.

them into production, hoping they might interest him in directing a play by Aimé Césaire. A letter to Blin from Maldorer testifies to the group's hope that he might help them to organise themselves:

> Next week we will be able to begin rehearsals for *Et les chiens se taisaient* [*And the Dogs Fell Silent*]. There are three of us at present. I am to meet a fourth one day soon. I am counting very much on you to train us, but we will call on you when there are eight of us and when we have found a kindred spirit who would be the heart of the T.P.A. I would very much like for you to be the director.[5]

Having previously mounted only two plays, Sartre's *Huis clos* (*No Exit* or *In Camera*), as there were only three of them at the time of producing it, and Pushkin's *Don Juan ou l'invité de pierre* (*The Stone Guest*), on account of Pushkin's Ethiopian roots,[6] the young apprentices wanted to broaden their experience and aimed, with Blin's help, securely to establish their small group as the first professional French black theatre company. Their chosen policy of promoting the work of black authors and poets began with a few texts by black writers including poems by Césaire and Léopold Sédar Senghor, for which they concentrated on training voice and delivery. That they should have approached Blin is indicative of the reputation he enjoyed for the engaged and non-mainstream attitude he adopted to his work. Once he had agreed to take the group on his initial concern was to help them develop an awareness of their own cultural identity, as opposed to any specifically French or Eurocentric form of training:

> We're lucky. He's a man with great intelligence and understanding. He is giving us his time. And what work! He has to both maintain out natural manner and teach us how to speak. Do you know what he wants to do? Instead of making us recite from *The Misanthrope*, in order to be sure we aren't corrupted

5   Letter from Sarah Maldorer to Roger Blin, undated (though clearly from 1957), Archives Roger Blin, Bibliothèque Nationale, département des arts du spectacle (Arsenal), Paris.

6   The company won second prize of the concours régional when they entered *Huis clos* into the Septième Concours National du Théâtre Universitaire in 1956 and presented *Don Juan ou l'invité de pierre* in May 1957 at the Théâtre de la Maison de l'Etudiant.

in any way, so as not to just copy you whites yet again, to keep us as 'black' as possible, he makes us read extracts from newspapers out loud.[7]

Under Blin's tutelage the group were invited to participate in a theatre festival devoted to African culture in Douvaine in the Haute-Savoie. They were offered as a stage the interior of a barn in which a collection of African art was being exhibited. There they presented a montage of poetry with a strong anti-colonial flavour, compiled by Jean-Jacques Morvan, and a play by Senegalese play-wright Abdou Anta Kâ entitled *La Fille des dieux* (*The Daughter of the Gods*) in which Blin himself took a role. They later took the whole programme to the Festival de Parme. By this time the troupe had begun to establish a sense of identity and had managed to procure the patronage of a number of significant literary figures.[8]

It is unclear when the notion of mounting Genet's *Les Nègres* with this unique group of actors first struck Blin as feasible. Sarah Maldorer had certainly nursed the ambition of performing Genet's play from her very first contact with Blin; it was she who had ap-proached Genet and had been given permission by him to take it into production. Sarah Maldorer was not to appear in this première pro-duction of *Les Nègres*, though she was very much involved in the initial stages of its creation, originally playing the part of one of the queens in early rehearsals. Internal conflicts caused her to leave the group. Of her departure Blin simply states 'it didn't work out'.[9]

The play was beautifully written, carefully crafted and contained such anti-establishment venom that it immediately attracted Blin. A blatant assault upon an audience's expectations and their middle-class attitudes, it appealed to his spirit of revolt, while the originality of its construction, the vigour with which it approached its subject matter and 'the insolence of its (very crude) words and situation' could not

7   Sarah Maldorer to Marguerite Duras, in *France Observateur*, 20.2.58.
8   In February 1958 the company, with Maldorer as its president, had a five mem-ber 'Comité Directeur', on which Blin sat, and a 'Comité de Patronage' which included Marcel Aymé, Aimé Césaire, Jean Dasté, Marguerite Duras, Jean Genet, Langton Hughes, Gérard Philipe, Jacques Rabemananjara, Jean-Paul Sartre, Léopold Sedar Senghor and Pierre Aimé Touchard.
9   Blin, *Souvenirs et propos*, p.130.

fail to excite him.[10] One of the supreme ironies of this first production is that, as the most challenging of mid-century works directed at European colonial misconceptions of Black peoples, it was written by a white man, at the request of another, and directed by a third.[11] That the Griots should have approached Blin to help them establish their company suggests that they trusted him to provide the impetus with which to achieve their objectives. That they should have so fully embraced Genet's work suggests that they considered it a potent representation of their own anger and experience. The fact that the two men could be identified as suitable 'allies' for Black artistic consciousness might perhaps be explained by their particular reactions to the culture of which they were part. Genet's cryptic introduction to his play ('But what exactly is a black? First of all, what's his color?')[12] embraces all those who find themselves rejected by society and suffering prejudices. Genet the outsider, was adequately acquainted with the social alienation inherent in being of another race in mainstream European culture, and even stubbornly refused to accept his 'whiteness', declaring himself, as Paule Thévenin recalled 'to be a black man at all costs, despite coming across as the whitest, the pinkest of carnations'.[13] Blin as a radical militant voice, choosing, through the medium of the theatre, to express his marginalisation from a society whose values he refused to endorse, adequately demonstrated his suitability for the task through his uncompromising rejection of convention and middle-class attitudes. Speaking of Genet at the time of *Les Nègres* Blin explained the appeal of the play to him and how, to his mind, the author had been accepted by his cast:

> He has the sadistic (to use the word in its most acceptable manner) euphoria of a punished schoolchild who exacts his revenge from the inside. Genet, white-black man, feels himself to be more intelligent than those who punish him or might punish him, and he has the elegance to exact revenge elegantly. The

10 Blin to Noëlle Greffe, in *Combat*, 7.8.59.
11 In *Le Figaro*, 12.10.55, Raymond Rouleau announced that he had asked Genet to write a play solely for black actors.
12 Genet, *The Blacks: A Clown Show*, trans. Bernard Frechtman (New York: Grove Press, 1960), p.3.
13 Paule Thévenin, *Magazine littéraire*, 313 (September 1993), p.36.

actors have sensed that extremely euphoria well: they have understood that Genet is a white-black man and they have felt, as have I, the euphoria that I hope to communicate to the audience.[14]

Whether *Les Nègres* was or is any longer a legitimate vehicle for Black anger is much in question; its approach of the subject matter within today's cultural climate and its affirmation of the concerns of racism and Black cultural identity are arguably defective. Genet himself announced at the time that his play was predominantly anti-white rather than pro-black, being no more than a medium for his own anger and not an expression of political revolt.[15] Only later in his life did he mobilise his anger in political activity, adding his voice and support to the causes and activities of numerous subversive groups in Europe and America. The nature of the text, and the way in which blacks are presented so harshly by Genet, upset and disturbed some of the troupe, especially, Blin noted, those who had lived the longest in France or in Western culture. 'One actor gave up her role rather than utter the words: "My mother shat me standing up",' he recalled.[16] Lydia Edwandé, playing Vertu, initially had difficulty with the barrage of insults against the white race that her character gives vent to, and Toto Bissainthe (Bobo) felt too reserved to perform the kind of obscene dance Blin requested of her. Despite such qualms about the text and the presentation of blacks as a crude magnification of white misconceptions, Blin noted how deeply the company felt about their own experiences of casual or institutional racism and how profoundly the play affected them in rehearsal. He commented how they 'did not have to scratch too deeply to discover that they had suffered the tortures of racism and persecution, the immense pain of being considered inferior. Fundamentally, they agreed with every word in the play, with

14   Blin to Jean Duvignaud, in *Les Lettres Nouvelles*, 18.10.59, p.24.
15   Jean Genet in Jean-Bernard Moraly (ed.), *Les Nègres au Port de la Lune* (Paris: Éditions de la Différence, 1988), p.100.
16   Blin to Jean Duvignaud, in *Les Lettres Nouvelles*, 18.10.59, p.26. The offending words ('C'est debout que ma mère m'a chiée!') were rendered less crudely in Bernard Frechtman's translation as 'My mother spawned me standing up!' (*The Blacks*, p.73.)

the spirit of the work.'[17] For the Griots, *Les Nègres*, for all its flaws, offered a unique opportunity to examine the narratives of identity they manufactured, or which were imposed upon them, and fully to comprehend the consequences of white culture upon them. For some the performance they were working toward took on a significance that would affect them beyond the experience of rehearsal and performance:

> All I know is that I have a need to feel black, and to play on my own imperfections as I will play on the imperfections of whites. *The Blacks*, for me, can only be a farce – for once we're going to be blacks, be proud of it, we're not going to worry about whether or not we have any hang-ups.[18]

Their commitment to Blin developed, too; in him they found an outrage that equalled theirs in strength, if not in origin, and were motivated by his enthusiasm. 'There was Genet's great desire to provoke that they obviously felt,' Blin remembered. 'But they felt that I, a white man, I felt it too and that I wanted to pursue it as much as they did, if not more.'[19] His personal attachment to the project stemmed from an intellectual curiosity about other cultures and an anger rooted in his humanistic repugnance for racist attitudes:

> My taste for Africa and exoticism goes back a long way. It was in 1931, at the time of the so-called 'colonial' exhibition. 'Savages' had been brought from Africa and Melanesia on the promise that they'd get to see Paris. Once they arrived in Marseilles, they were stripped of their clothes to be exhibited in cages in the zoological gardens. Together with some friends, I arranged to get them some clothes and show them around Paris. I wrote of their plight in a vaguely humanitarian African journal. My article even provoked a question in parliament.[20]

The respect which he commanded from the Griots grew, then, not just from his talents as an instructor and director but also from this uncompromising rejection of the corrupt values embedded in the history and practices of his own culture. That he was white was im-

17 Blin to Bettina Knapp, in *Tulane Drama Review*, 1962, 7.3, p.115.
18 Sarah Maldorer to Marguerite Duras, in *France Observateur*, 20.2.58.
19 Blin, *Souvenirs et propos*, p.133.
20 Blin, in *Nouvel Observateur*, 30.3.66.

material. Asked by a journalist whether it was any concern 'to be directed by a white man, showing you how to be 'Blacks'?', Robert Liensol replied; 'No, Blin is a friend. And what's more, he leaves us enough leeway to express what we ourselves feel.'[21]

If the play contained enough revolutionary spirit and artistic merit to arouse Blin's interest, there was, however, also enough about it to mark it out as distinctly different from the kind of play he had so far opted to mount. The structure of *Les Nègres* relied heavily on artifice: its cast have to portray characters each of whom in turn takes on a role in a fictitious scene of their own making; the re-enactment of the supposed murder of a young white girl, witnessed by a white court who in turn are massacred. This brutal ritual is revealed to be a staged event created by a group of black performers impersonating both black and white characters in order to live out their hatred of their oppressors. These, in turn, are being played by real actors who are also black. This highly self-reflexive theatricality called for decisive input from a director: various techniques were required to demonstrate the artifice; a pronounced style of acting would be necessary; the audience would need to be made to invest in the action and distanced from it in successive motions. In short, what was required of Blin was a highly visible *mise en scène*, and the script called for a certain degree of interference and indulgence on the part of a director.

> This is the first of Genet's plays that I have wanted to direct. Usually, I despise the 'play within a play', the winks at the audience. But in this case the actors' theatricality, the possession they are performing, needs to be repeatedly broken: if the audience become attached to the play, you have to construct fractures in that attachment and disrupt any credibility to constantly remind them that it's about thirteen actors enjoying themselves! [...] Now, by their very nature, these continuous disruptions call for a real *mise en scène*.[22]

For Blin, this represented a reappraisal of his directorial relationship with a text in rehearsal. In the event it occasioned an unleashing of his imagination, permitting him legitimately to work his own creativity into the play. He used the initial stages of what turned out to

21   Robert Liensol to Maria Craipeau, in *France Observateur*, 22.10.59.
22   Blin to Jean Duvignaud, in *Les Lettres Nouvelles*, 18.10.59, p.24.

be a one-and-a-half year rehearsal period to give the Griots simple actor training, concentrating for the most part on voice. Other young black professionals had been recruited and the original group expanded in number to the thirteen needed to populate Genet's play. The company was a mixture of people from France, the Americas, the Caribbean and Africa and the diversity of their accents presented an initial problem to overcome:

> Now things start to get difficult. We need months and months to mount a play such as this. It's a difficult one. We have to find a lyrical tone which is not that of the Comédie-Française but which comes truthfully from the black persona. Now, the Griots all come from different countries: Africa, Guadeloupe, The Antilles, Haïti, Madagascar. They all have different accents. It will be necessary to make these accents work in harmony with one another and with the accent that the text requires.[23]

In an effort to instil some measure of uniformity and render the complexities of the text fully comprehensible in performance, Blin gave the actors vocal training exercises to improve the command of diction and breathing necessary for tackling Genet's long poetic constructions. He did not attempt to iron out their individual accents or promote an Île-de-France French – such an endeavour would have contradicted the point of the exercise – but instead he wanted to overcome certain differences in the manner of speaking of the separate contingents. For example the Caribbean actors had the habit of eliding the 'r' whereas the Africans would roll the consonant quite heavily. Working around a table with newspapers and poems the group studied under Blin to achieve a composite accent that would then graft easily into Genet's language.

Blin's initial concentration on the necessary unification of the varying French accents, followed by encouraging the actors to adopt a 'lyrical tone which is not that of the Comédie-Française', was his intuitive reaction to Genet's poetry, full of rich imagery, with which the characters of the play express themselves. In 'Pour jouer *Les Nègres*' Genet echoes Blin's words, if with a hint of sarcasm: 'In what tone of voice should they speak: imitate well tragic actors, and above

23   Blin, in *Arts,* 8.1.58.

all French tragic actors. Adding talent to that, of course.'[24] He has his oppressed black characters speak in a rich, poetic and well-mastered French, the language of their oppressors, the bourgeois white, to create a more venomous and disrespectful effect:

> Before saying such remarkable, such exceptional things, I could not express them in anything other than a language recognisable to the dominant class. It was necessary to have those whom I refer to as 'my torturers' listen to me. So I had to attack them in their own language. If I'd used slang they wouldn't have listened.[25]

The atmosphere at the rehearsals was a relaxed and jovial one, Blin often commenting upon how much he had enjoyed working with the young troupe on such a long project. With no theatre yet in prospect, they rehearsed at a Caribbean dance club when it was not in use, at the Foyer des Étudiants A.E.F in the rue Platon and at the Théâtre de la Maison de la Médecine in the rue du Faubourg St. Jacques. Enjoying the indulgence the play offered them, they rehearsed without concern over funding. For their physical warm-ups they would bring along musical instruments to create atmosphere, and prepare for rehearsals with jazz music and African rhythms.

Luckily, Blin made the acquaintance of the new proprietor of the Théâtre de Lutèce, which was undergoing refurbishment. Lucie Germain offered to assume responsibility for the production and committed herself to providing salaries for Blin and his actors, arranging for the play to open in October 1959. Now with a clear target at which to aim, Blin finished the casting and set about tuning the work for performance.

An examination of where his *mise en scène* strayed from Genet's own written indications reveals Blin's capacity to build upon the playwright's raw material to create an effective shape for the stage action. Prior to the start of the play proper, the flower-covered coffin, which was to serve for the dark rite of the performance was visible, placed in full view in front of the closed curtains. In this way, even

---

24   Genet, 'Pour jouer Les Nègres' in *Les Nègres* (Paris: L'Arbalète, 1960), p.10.
25   Genet to Bertrand Poirot-Delpech, in *Jean Genet – Dialogues* (Paris: Cent pages, 1990), p.60.

before the actors were on stage, the barrier between performance space and auditorium had already been eroded, the coffin announcing the presence of the drama in the real world. As the curtains opened Blin had his actors enter dancing a minuet to Mozart's *Divertimento,*[26] but incorporating short leaps into the otherwise orthodox European dance steps. This immediately served to underline a non-conformist and derisory attitude of the characters as they appeared in coat tails dancing to European classical music. They scattered the flowers they were carrying around the stage before placing what remained of them on the coffin, as the text indicated. For this balletic introduction, Blin enlisted the choreographic help of Edé Fortin, whom he had met when they both studied dance under Jean Weidt and who was cast in the role of the valet. The White court then entered, not 'above' as Genet suggests in the text but instead walking through the white territory of the auditorium and installing themselves downstage left, confronting the blacks who were already in position for their presentation, before finally climbing the steps to their position on the upper level of the scaffolding structure which constituted the set. Such an entrance forced an identification between audience and the 'white' characters and, employing the established opposition, emphasised physical and spatial confrontation in the first stage meeting of the two groups.

All the props that were to be used at any point in the following performance were on stage from the start, effectively transforming the stage into a pocket of theatrical activity, a den where the actors might come and act out their fantasies. The handkerchiefs used to wave goodbye to Diouf on his departure were tied to a rail of scaffolding, as were the wig, mask, jumper and other accessories that he was to adopt shortly afterwards in order to play the role of the raped and murdered white girl. A tom-tom which would accompany the actors in a final outburst of manic laughter at the play's close was also visible on stage from the start. The puppets of the court, which Bobo retrieves, were concealed under the costume of the white queen and plucked out from beneath her skirts one by one, culminating with the final doll, a

26 Genet states in *The Blacks* (p.7) that the actors should enter to 'an air of Mozart'. Blin tried various pieces, using Kay Dergueloi's *Lamento* for a while until a friend brought him Mozart's *Divertimento*.

likeness of the queen herself. Rather than have the puppets produced from under the skirts of the Mask as Genet does in his script, Blin created a more powerful image of the queen 'giving birth' to these voodoo-inspired figurines. After the love sequence between Vertu and Village and the scenes of judgment near the end of the play, Blin orchestrated a liberating peal of laughter which matched similar outbursts throughout the performance. These menacing, self-indulgent bursts of inane laughter intensified the haunting and uncomfortable atmosphere with which Blin wished to assail his audience.

André Acquart provided the setting for *Les Nègres* and this venture was the first demonstration of the mutual suitability of the director and the designer who were subsequently to work together on other projects.[27] Blin had first met Acquart through Jean-Marie Serreau, for whom the designer had constructed a set for Kateb Yacine's *Le Cadavre encerclé* (*The Encircled Corpse*) at the Lutèce some years previously. He was employed at the Lutèce by Germain and had originally converted the place into a theatre for her in 1956. In this space he knew so well, Acquart created a scenic environment within which the actors could move and with which they could interact. As solid wood would have been too expensive, he built his three-tier construction from iron scaffolding that he acquired from an ironmonger he knew. The framework was accessible from the stage by a series of stage-left steps that were part of the structure and which led up the levels to the space for the court backstage right. The white queen's throne was set upstage centre on an intermediary level, overlooking the triangular stage space defined by the framework of the structure. This scaffold décor, innovative for the time, provided the perfect setting for Genet's metadramatic scenes. To begin with, it eschewed any notion of precise location, divorcing the action from the real world and thereby aiding the ritual element. More importantly, it offered Blin and the actors a non-naturalistic environment that suited

27   Acquart was to work with Blin on a further five productions: *Le Lion*, at the Théâtre de Lutèce (1960), *Divines Paroles*, at the Odéon-Théâtre de France (1963), *Les Paravents*, at the Odéon-Théâtre de France (1966), *Minimata and Co.*, at the Théâtre de la commune d'Aubervilliers (1978) and *Triptyque*, at the Odéon-Théâtre de France (1983).

the artificiality of the play's action and plot. To underline this further Blin considered having the actors finish off the construction of the scaffolding as the audience were entering the theatre and taking their seats, but this would have proved impractical, not least from the point of view of safety, and would also have undermined the more important ritual entrance of the blacks. To this metal framework Blin attached strips of white cloth to break the rigidity and linearity of the tubing, thereby humanising the abstract décor, and making it more tangible for the performers.

Acquart also designed the production's costumes and masks. Constructed by his wife, Barbara, the costumes fitted the 'homemade', seemingly improvised quality that Blin sought for the production. Those playing black characters wore frilled and laced white shirts under tailor-made tailcoats and shoes of different colours, whilst those playing the white court had costumes appropriate to their respective roles: the governor wore a pith helmet and a white embroidered knee-length jacket; the judge had an exaggerated ermine collar and a strangely oversized hat; the missionary was given a long white sleeved chasuble, quartered at the chest by a large white cross, and the valet wore traditional livery and a white powdered wig. The ladies' dresses, made from furnishing fabrics, were highly decorated, tasselled garments more reminiscent of nineteenth-century clothing than modern French style. The white queen wore an elegant long white dress and cloak and was given the largest and most elaborate of the masks provided for the white court. It was Claude Acquart, the designer's son, who made the masks after his father's sketches. These met Genet's written demands, covering half the black actors' faces but allowing their own skin to remain much in evidence. The masks all sported caricature expressions intended to undermine the authority that the assumed roles are allowed to exercise: the queen's had a large nose and long, ridiculous eyelashes, the governor's had exaggerated eyebrows and moustache and a drooping nose whereas the valet's had a long, comically upturned nose and large innocent eyes.

When, subsequent to Blin's production, Genet wrote the directive 'Pour jouer *Les Nègres*', first published in the 1960 French re-edition of the play, he began by paying tribute to the work of the director who, he felt, had shown such understanding of his play:

Imitate Blin? His success was close to perfection, to imitate him would be to defile him. His *mise en scène* is nothing less than an example of daring and rigour.[28]

He goes on to describe how he would have the actors made-up, how they would gesticulate and articulate; he explains also how he wants lighting to be used at certain points in the play and how he envisages an outdoor production. It is tempting to speculate how much of this may have been influenced by the satisfaction he experienced at what he stated was the first entirely acceptable interpretation or performance of any of his plays to date. In the version of the play published after this first production, Genet explicitly refers to Blin's work three times, once in that adjoining preface 'Pour jouer *Les Nègres*', and twice in footnotes to the body of the text. Having seen photographs of Blin's Paris production which corroborated reports of the effectiveness of the *mise en scène* before he saw the work himself,[29] Genet insisted that these photographs be printed with any subsequent publication of the play, indicating that Acquart's set satisfied him as much as the *mise en scène* that it served.[30] Such direct acknowledgement of the contribution made by a director of his work, captured in the printed edition of a play by a playwright, is rare and all the more remarkable in view of the fact that Blin guided the play through the rehearsal period free of advice or comment from Genet, corresponding with him on an irregular basis. In fact, Genet never even saw the first production, only the revival of the same *mise en scène*, with British actors, in London in June 1961. During the première of *Les Nègres* Genet was in Athens, revising yet again the script that was already shocking audiences in Paris. In 'Pour jouer *Les Nègres*' he recounts how Blin ended the play by having Ville de

28   Genet, 'Pour jouer *Les Nègres*', p.9.
29   'It's Blin – I felt it from the critical responses to *Les Nègres* and from the photos – who has best understood what I had felt: that stifled delirium that rears up.' Genet in a letter to Bernard Frechtman, quoted in Jean-Bernard Moraly, *Jean Genet – La Vie écrite* (Paris: Éditions de la différence, 1988), p.253.
30   In 'Pour jouer *Les Nègres*' (p.11) Genet says of the set: 'I am leaving the descriptions of the set that I had imagined in this book, but by setting these against those that André Acquart made, it is clear that it is with these latter that one should set out.'

Saint-Nazare (named Newport News in the Frechtman translation) leave the stage while the rest of the cast were dancing to a strong African rhythm which slowly segued into the Mozart minuet with which the play had opened. The character then returned bearing the white coffin covered with flowers, which he carried downstage between two rows formed by his fellow actors to the front of the stage where it had originally stood before unopened curtains. The actors then danced the minuet until the curtains closed. This is in contrast to Genet's original ending where Village and Vertu simply walk upstage, having finished their piece of dialogue, to join the others dancing around the coffin. Of Blin's version he wrote: 'I prefer this way of accomplishing the play.'[31]

In the later published version of *Les Nègres*, two inserted footnotes relating to Blin's *mise en scène* represent observations by Genet on how Blin had enhanced the presentation with small details that clearly must have impressed him. The first concerns the positioning of Vertu underneath the white queen on the latter's intermediate rostrum, thereby associating the two figures. Later, when the two queens confront each other, Blin had them begin as far apart as possible, again associating the two characters this time through visual symmetry, then asked them to advance slowly towards each other and downstage towards the auditorium, thus gradually building the tension between the two while increasing the sense of danger to the audience as their verbal battle escalates. The second footnote is nearer the end of the play, where the valet is killed, at which point Blin had him do a parodic version of the dance of the death of the swan from Tchaikovsky's *Swan Lake*.

Genet's play relied heavily on structures of ritual, an element that had become distinctive in his work. In *Les Bonnes* and *Le Balcon* characters take on other identities and act out roles that are not properly theirs but which are nevertheless exaggerated facets of their own personalities. It is through enactment and role-play that Genet's characters can fully realise themselves and it is the extra dimension that Genet brought to characterisation that is one of his main achievements. Role-play also serves as a medium of liberation for the op-

31   Ibid.

pressed, providing them with a cruel, satirical voice with which to express the sufferings of servitude. This layering of personality through role-play naturally lent itself to dramatic expression and reached its most successful manifestation in *Les Nègres*. The ritual aspects of Genet's text which enhance this play-acting were taken by Blin as being of the utmost importance to the whatever meaning the play might project to its audience. It was necessary to create such a sense of ambiguity within the layers of role-play present in *Les Nègres* that the conventional idea of theatrical character was completely destroyed, and the audience should have difficulty in discerning the thresholds between the black actor and the black character he is portraying, between the role within the ritual that character is playing and the character itself, even between the role and the performing black actor: at one point Genet has the confused Archibald, after Ville de Saint Nazare's announcement of the execution of a traitor, declare: 'is he still acting or is he speaking for himself?'[32]

Blin saw this ambiguity as crucial to the play in performance and elaborated on it, using uncertainty to disorientate the audience, to shock them or at least prevent them from finding any comfort within the action. At first the actors would permit the audience to experience a complacent sense of ease, as witnesses to a seemingly innocent clown-show, only to tug the mat of reassurance rudely from beneath them. Into his *mise en scène* he wove details aimed at creating and sustaining the impression of a protracted liturgy, at once seductive and disturbing. This required a stylised mode of acting, a specifically elevated form of delivery and various alienation effects to protect the audience from any illusionistic tendency in the performance. An example of this strategy is the manner in which Blin dealt with the crossing of the jungle by the masked white characters to reach the blacks. He had Mamadou Condé (Archibald) operate a lantern from the side of the stage, manually turning a disc which contained a number of different coloured gels; in this way the actor was not simply stepping outside his role to display the workings of stage lighting, but using his position external to the situation to assume a threatening control over the position of his on-stage opponents. On the

32   Genet, *The Blacks*, p.114.

152

stage itself, meanwhile, the other actors, still visible to the audience, mimicked the cries of jungle creatures to add to the disconcerting atmosphere. Earlier, when Village is being prepared for the re-enactment of the rape of the white maiden, Blin had Toto Bissainthe (Bobo) mime applying make-up to his face, indulging in the theatricality of the stage circumstances. Blin's success in creating a sombre liturgy punctuated by overt theatrical references can be measured by one of the critical reviews the play received:

> The (black) mass becomes theatre and the theatre, in memory of Antonin Artaud, becomes black mass. You are not watching the show, you are taking part in it. And, upon an excellent scenic scaffolding, though somewhat cramped on the Lutèce stage, the black actors of the compagnie des Griots seem also to be playing outside of the performance – it's a kind of alienation, but an alienation towards the interior of the actor.[33]

The journalist employs the French word 'distanciation' (clumsily but conveniently translated here as 'alienation'), a term intended to evoke the objectives of Bertolt Brecht's *verfremdungseffekt*.[34] Brecht had been championed in Paris in the few years prior to the *Les Nègres* production chiefly by Jean-Marie Serreau and Arthur Adamov. Blin, however, refused to make any connection between Brecht's 'de-familiarising' *verfremdungseffekt* and Genet's theatrical articulation. He had not been enthused by Brecht in the same way as his friends and, although he sought in his *mise en scène* of *Les Nègres* to pur-posefully expose some of the workings of the theatre, as Brecht advised, the effect was not intended to be the same as Brecht's undermining or subverting audiences' identification with the char-acters as a mode of encouraging reflection on the necessity of narrative elements. On the contrary, Blin recognised that a perform-ance of *Les Nègres* could become more challenging and unnerving through the detachment of the performer from the action, precisely because the play evokes as it unravels the presence of a threat, which

---

33   Robert Kanters, *L'Epress*, 5.11.59.
34   Translation of *Verfremdungseffekt* has a history of controversy. The word is sometimes rendered as 'estrangement' or 'distancing' and most commonly, but least satisfactorily 'alienation'. Owing its roots to Russian Formalist Viktor Shklovsky's *ostranenie*, 'defamiliarisation' is a preferred compromise.

may be real or unreal, to the captive white audience before which the play should ideally be performed.[35] The more loosely the actors are attached to their roles, and the greater the multiplicity of levels in their onslaught, the more powerful is the suggestion that they may descend from the stage and attack the white audience, which they are clearly meant to insult and menace. In this way, for example, it is significant that the white court discover no corpse when searching for evidence with which to convict the blacks. As on-stage spectators of the action they have believed in the death of the young girl, whereas the real audience would not have done so; thus, by having the actor/spectators renege on their willingly suspended disbelief, the threat is brought palpably closer to the real world and the true audience are pulled closer to the panic of the white court. In such a case, the growing awareness of an audience that they are witnessing actors, investing in the anger of the play, can only increase the fear they may feel for their own safety and the tension that surrounds the generation of that fear throughout a performance.

That Blin chose to have the white court process through the audience at the play's opening served, therefore, two principal theatrical purposes: firstly, it established the dramatic identification between the court and the audience of which they were cruel exaggerations; secondly, it served to detach the spectators from the illusion of theatre while having the doubly disturbing effect of introducing them to the black actors at close range, yet behind their ritual masks of white faces. That Blin strove to achieve this theatrical assault on an audience's security is attested by the anecdote he offered Bettina Knapp concerning one performance that Eugène Ionesco attended:

> Many people are shocked by Genet's plays. They are frightened when confronted with a world they know really exists – a complete world. Ionesco, for instance, never stayed to see the end of *The Blacks*. As a white man he felt uncomfortable; he felt he was being attacked; he sensed the great pleasure the

35 Genet states in a preface to the play that the play is specifically written for a white audience and that, if this were not possible then at least one white person should be invited or that the audience should accept to wear white masks or that a white mannequin be placed in the auditorium. (*The Blacks*, p.4.)

actors took each time they insulted the whites. [...] Even those who feel they are being mocked and ridiculed are struck by the 'truth' and burning sincerity of his poetry and are held by a sense of 'fair-play'.[36]

For Blin, the need to use any identifiable *verfremdungseffekt* in the *mise en scène* evolved directly from the text, from the way in which Genet had written his play in order to assault an audience. This, he felt, was quite different from the more calculated compilation method of Brecht:

> Genet found a solution without having recourse to realism. In his writing, the poetical element remains essential and understanding is always complete. He seems to have been able to arrive at this even better than Brecht... Today, there is no need any more for what used to be called 'social realism' to be able to reach the audience. Everyone has been shaped by how the cinema and cartoons have made us used to those temporal contradictions, those quick-moving passages that you find in *Les Nègres*. Bergman's films have people from different eras in the same picture, and we all understand. The theatre shouldn't be able to do less than the cinema. [37]

Writing to his editor Pauvert on publication of *Les Bonnes*, Genet spoke of the attempt he had made in that play to ensure the closest possible degree of communication of what he had to say to a prospective spectator. His manner of writing was, for him, a means of cementing that link: by eliminating psychology of character he could be sure of the power of the signs he had created, and they might then be immune from the interference of any director on whom they were ultimately dependent. The defamiliarisation built into the structure of the play would strengthen its impact on an audience:

> I attempted to achieve a displacement which, facilitating a declamatory tone, would bring theatre into the theatre. I hoped in this way to achieve the abolition of character – which psychological conventions usually sustain – in favour of signs that are as far as possible removed from what they should principally signify, but nonetheless linked to them in order for the author to connect to the spectator in the only way possible. By which I mean to achieve characters on stage which are more than just the metaphor for that which they are supposed to

36   Blin to Bettina Knapp, in *Tulane Drama Review*, 1962, 7.3, pp.112–13.
37   Blin to Jean Duvignaud, in *Les Lettres Nouvelles*, 18.10.59, p.24.

represent. To get the project to work as best I might, I of course had to invent a tone of voice, a manner of walking, a way of gesturing.[38]

This tone of voice, gait and stylised gesture were successfully developed by Blin for *Les Nègres*, to Genet's entire satisfaction. The play achieved critical acclaim and sustained a long and profitable run at the Lutèce, playing there to full houses for five months before transferring to the Théâtre de la Renaissance for a further month, totalling 169 performances in all. A tour in France and abroad was organised, and the entire *mise en scène* was subsequently recreated by Blin for a company of black actors in Britain. His London production of *The Blacks*, for which Blin used Bernard Frechtman's English translation, tempered to suit the Lord Chamberlain's censorship, opened at the Royal Court Theatre on 30 May 1961. It was here that Genet finally saw Blin's work and was adequately impressed by it, stating that 'Blin is the only director who satisfies me. He has understood everything. His work is very beautiful.'[39] Originally Genet been unwilling to see Blin's work:

My dear friend, You've succeeded, I'm sure [...] if I haven't come to Paris, don't see that as ingratitude. I've told you, I refuse to know the physical face of my plays.[40]

The critical success of the production, which transferred to the Théâtre de la Renaissance, helped to secure the Grand Prix de la Critique for 1959. Blin's handling of the ritual and his manipulation of the audience within a highly 'visible' *mise en scène* were recognised as a triumphant account of Genet's difficult play:

The director is constantly there, so much so that he often speaks through the actor's mouth; the director is the organiser, faithful and precise, of a ceremony the mysterious developments of which follow the sequence of a mass which flows right up to the final burial.

38   Genet, 'à Pauvert', in *Obliques*, 2 (1972), pp.2–4 (p.3.)
39   Letter from Genet to Marc Barbezat, dated 13.1.61, in *Lettres à Olga et Marc Barbezat* (Paris: L'Arbalète, 1988), p.207.
40   Letter from Genet to Blin, dated November 1959, in Lynda Bellity Peskine and Albert Dichy (eds.), *La Bataille des Paravents* (Paris: IMEC, 1991), p.12.

The least one can say about this performance is that it tears us from our usual expectations as an audience with a singular originality [...] Roger Blin has given to this lyrical poem a stage expression which seems to me to translate it entirely. He has naturally placed the greatest emphasis upon the ceremonial element implied in the text, and has done so with no holds barred; he blends and unites his 14 black actors whilst all the time respecting the nuances of an attitude which he has entered into wholly, if not even more solidly than the author.[41]

Blin's theatrical realisation of Genet's *Les Nègres* earned him the trust, respect and lifelong friendship of the most enigmatic of twentieth-century playwrights. Once the first draft of *Les Paravents* was available Genet thought immediately of Blin for the *mise en scène*:

Dear Roger Blin,

The production you have put together, I tell you, has given my play an extraordinary power, which in places made me a little afraid. You must mount *The Screens*. I'm trying to construct it, squeeze it, cram it in – and prune it, unpick it, fix it [...] For the new edition [of *The Blacks*] that Barbezat wants to do, I'm correcting the *mise en scène* instructions and am making use of yours. Dear Roger Blin, let me express once again my gratitude and admiration. You are dear to me, you know it. I shake you by the hand.

Jean Genet.[42]

41   Pierre Marcabru, *Arts*, 11.11.59 and Jacques Lemarchand, *Le Figaro littéraire*, 7.11.59.
42   Letter from Genet to Blin, dated June 1961, in Peskine and Dichy (eds.), *La Bataille des Paravents*, p.15.

Les Paravents and scandal

Roger Blin's production of *Les Paravents* at Barrault's Odéon-Théâtre de France in April 1966 might be considered the artistic zenith of his career. Alongside his liaison with Beckett, it assured his place in theatre's history books, though in this case as much for the controversy surrounding the production as for his directing achievements. The play, one of epic proportions, gave him the opportunity to experiment with certain conventions of Oriental theatre and called for a disciplined and painstaking *mise en scène*, coordinating the work of more than sixty actors and actresses. As a powerful expression of anti-colonial sentiment it must also have greatly satisfied Blin's thirst for radical provocation. *Les Nègres* had been written for black actors to be performed before any white audience, but *Les Paravents* specifically targeted the French. Its subject matter and the location of its action in colonised North Africa had a particular sensitivity for French audiences at the time of its creation. Indeed, even before it had been published The Minister of the Interior had made it clear that the play should not be produced, a remarkable act of stage censorship.[43]

Set more or less overtly against the backdrop of the Algerian War of independence (1954–62), *Les Paravents* in part calls into question the precepts of patriotism and the mechanisms of colonialism. Although it has a much broader theme (and a more profound human interest) than the simple examination of a period of recent French history, the issue was still raw enough in France for any treatment of it to stir controversy with relative ease. The Algerian war of independence had resulted in over 100,000 casualties and caused the reluctant repatriation of over a million ethnic French Algerians. Added to these tangible consequences was a pervading sense of national humiliation. This background, allied to Genet's lack of delicacy in his choice of vocabulary, was the recipe for the most violent of critical responses to any production in twentieth-century Europe. From the outset the author was prepared for the reaction his play

---

43   In 1959, Blin was forbidden by the minister of proceding with a proposed future production of *Les Paravents* at the Théâtre du Vieux-Colombier.

would provoke. 'If my most recent play, *The Screens*, isn't being performed in France,' he told Madeleine Gobeil, 'it's because the French apparently find something in it that isn't there but that they will think they see: the problem of the Algerian War.'[44] The main bone of contention in the controversy occasioned by the production was that such a 'subversive' piece should be mounted by a state owned and subsidised theatre. Barrault had cleared his decision to include the play into the Odéon repertoire with the minister of culture, André Malraux, and the results of this ministerial decision became a factor in the ensuing discussions on freedom of expression and censorship in the press on French television and even at the Assemblée Nationale.[45]

Though Genet's theatrical writings are at core intentionally provocative pieces, they are never specifically political: Genet's concern was never to censure any existing political systems – which he considered merely symptomatic of faulty social structures – but rather to satirise the very fabric of the societies and the cultures which gives birth to these systems. To interpret his plays simply as modes of political commentary would involve a mis-reading of their focus and target and might result, in production, in a dilution of their potency. In his preface to *Le Balcon* Genet emphasises this himself in a comment applicable to any of his dramatic works: '[...] don't present this play as though it were a satire of this or that. It is, and should therefore be presented as, the glorification of the Image and the Reflection. What it has to say – by way of satire or otherwise – will only then become evident.'[46] *Les Paravents* is an artist's contemplation on death, on the nature of evil and on the human activity of constructing and indulging in sign-systems and not at all a dramatised political treatise on the Algerian war or even colonialism in general. When asked directly if *Les Paravents* was a political play, Blin addressed this head-on. 'Of course, in a way,' was his immediate response, then quickly qualified;

44   Genet to Madeleine Gobeil, quoted in Albert Dichy (ed.), *The Declared Enemy*, trans. Jeff Fort (Stanford: Stanford University Press, 2004), p.7.

45   The parliamentary debate took place on 26 October 1966. A transcript of the proceedings is printed in Lynda Peskine and Albert Dichy (eds.), *La Bataille des Paravents*, pp.85–91.

46   Genet, 'Comment jouer Le Balcon', *Le Balcon* (Paris: L'Arbalète, 1962), p.12.

'But Genet is not really concerned with social order – he is against any established government. Genet told me, "This play is not an apology for betrayal; it is an aesthetic theatrical experience."'[47] The joy of working on *Les Paravents* must have been twofold for Blin: firstly he could contrive a theatrical life for this most theatrical of plays and, secondly, he could breathe life into any controversy that was held dormant within it. This delight of Blin's in being given license to annoy a conservative faction in the audience did not, however, impede his collaboration with Genet:

> He was aware of my political leanings, he knew that I was attached to the Left far more than he was and he was fully aware of certain decisions I had taken. He also guessed that one of the reasons for my being involved was to piss off those on the Right. We spoke about all that several times and he wrote me numerous letters, in one of which he said 'whatever you do don't make my play an agent of the Left' [...] As opposed to some of the texts I've directed, which seemed to me to express important matters from a political angle, I never wanted to make a militant piece of either *Les Nègres* or *Les Paravents*. But I was, of course, very happy to do those plays, at those times precisely, because they had extraordinary repercussions and because that, to me, is what theatre is all about.[48]

There was more than an element of agreeable irony for Blin in his being able to mount this play with funding from the very same government that had deprived him of work as a punitive measure for his signing of the notorious 'Declaration of the right to insubordination during the Algerian War'.[49] As a result of his having added his signature to that petition, Blin found that he was unable to obtain work on radio or television for a period of a year, and films in which he had appeared were not transmitted on TV. He took particular exception to the underhand manner in which he understood the 'ban'

47   Blin to Bettina Knapp, in *Tulane Drama Review*, 11.4 (1967), p.109.
48   Blin, *Souvenirs et propos*, p.202.
49   The 'petition of the 121' (Roger Blin was the 121st signatory) was a statement of support for deserters from and conscientious objectors to the war with Algeria. Among others to sign the declaration were Simone de Beauvoir, André Breton, Alain Cuny, Bernard Dort, Marguerite Duras, Jérôme Lindon, Jean Martin, Alain Robbe-Grillet, Nathalie Sarraute, and Jean-Paul Sartre.

had been executed, producers and directors having been contacted by telephone and advised against employing the signatories.

Genet's longest play requires specifically theatrical means to be staged; in conception it demands the construction on a large-scale of meaning-bearing systems in space, in the choreography of actors and in the execution of an integrated design. It is written in a mixed style of everyday speech, crude gutter language and a highly poetic idiom, which lends its characters a grand, mythic quality. The plot progresses in an episodic manner, but one that splays out in three inter-related narrative routes, developing from the petty concerns of one Arab family to the portrayal of a society in revolution against the forces of colonialism. The poetry of the Genet's writing and the provocative nature of the material made *Les Paravents*, like *Les Nègres*, a play that was tailored to Blin's artistic and political temperament:

> What appeals to me theatrically about this play is that it represents a veritable anti-realistic declaration for a reality of another order, proving that everything can be dared and meaningful beyond realism. What is special about *The Screens*, is that the words are comic and the whole is tragic: it's a tragedy in the language of burlesque.[50]

> Will the play shock the public? I don't want to know. I haven't worried about that kind of thing for a long time. It's an insolent work, moving, but one that does not demand emotionality of its actors. It's a celebration, a ceremony. Pure theatrical ritual. The whole thing should suggest that which Genet wants: a lucid, consensual abjectness, pushed to the limits.[51]

Genet had begun writing *Les Paravents* in the mid-1950s, first alluding to it in a letter to Olga Barbezat in February 1956.[52] He was to spend four years writing and revising his manuscript until he was satisfied with it enough to permit its publication in February 1961. During this period of gestation it changed titles regularly, becoming first *Saïd*, then *Les Mères*, *La Mère*, and *Ça bouge encore...*,[53] only to

---

50   Blin to Nicole Zand, in *Le Monde*, 16.4.66.
51   Blin in *Nouvel Observateur*, 30.3.66.
52   'I've nearly finished my play about the Arab. It's very beautiful.' Genet in a letter to Olga Barbezat, dated 6.2.56, in *Lettres à Olga et Marc Barbezat*, p.149.
53   *The Mothers*, *The Mother* and *It's Still Moving*.

end up with a title that, instead of reflecting its characters or themes, referred essentially to the manner in which it was to be staged, to its formalism (though this, in itself, invokes issues of representation and authenticity). There were several points of departure for Genet's conception of the play and its different narrative strands. The relationship between Saïd and Leïla, for instance, was based on the true misfortune of an Algerian mason working on an extension to a house where Genet had stayed as a guest. This workman had been robbed of his savings and bemoaned having to return to Algeria without sufficient funds, he claimed, to be able to attract a beautiful wife. This story was adopted as the basis for a relationship that would underpin all elements of a broader story, which itself was intended to be a part of a larger work that was never completed, a cycle of plays that was to be entitled *La Mort* (*Death*) and of which *Les Paravents* was to be the first section.

Before Blin's production of *Les Paravents* reached the stage in 1966 the play had already been mounted four times, but never in the original French, and not to Genet's satisfaction. The première had taken place in Germany at the Berlin Schlosspark-Theater in 1961 and the same German translation was used again two years later at the Vienna Volkstheater. Peter Brook took the first twelve (of seventeen) tableaux and gave a performance of them at the LAMDA Theatre in London in 1964, whilst a Swedish translation was mounted uncut over two nights at the Stockholm Stadsteater later the same year.

Though the play had been in Blin's hands since its publication there had been no clear opportunity for him to stage it. In France, few companies dared to suggest mounting *Les Paravents*, not least because of the financial outlay that would be involved. Genet had been able to find an Italian producer willing to fund a production of the play in New York and a contract was signed on 16 August 1961. His immediate impulse was to ask Blin to direct the piece and their collaboration on the project can thus be traced to the beginning of the decade.[54] During 1961 Genet spent time in Italy revising his play and

54 'He [Roger Blin] is going to mount *The Screens*, but he doesn't yet know where.' Letter from Genet to Marc Barbezat, dated 13.1.61, *Lettres à Olga et Marc Barbezat*, p.208.

corresponding with Bernard Frechtman who was to provide the English translation for the prospective production in New York. Through Frechtman, Genet had copies of his amended text sent to Blin for his approval. The producer Aldo Bruzzichelli, a friend and admirer of Genet's, paid Blin a small retainer to enable him to concentrate solely on the project and in the summer of that year invited him to his villa in Tuscany to discuss the play and their forthcoming production more fully. Unfortunately, Bruzzichelli was finally unable to come up with sufficient funds and the production had to be cancelled. The seed of the collaboration between Blin and Genet had already been sown and they had already spent much time revising the body of the play together. Though it cannot be suggested that Blin had any claim to authorship, he was able to exert, in an advisory capacity, a degree of editorial influence upon details in the text in the course of discussions with Genet in both Italy and France between 1961 and 1963. That he had the closest knowledge of the play besides Genet, and that the latter trusted his judgement, is demonstrated by the fact that in 1966, when Marc Barbezat began to prepare a re-edition of *Les Paravents*, Genet asked Blin to correct the proofs.

According to Paule Thévenin's account of the genesis of the Paris production, it was a chance meeting in an elevator between herself and Simone Benmussa, the cultural advisor to the Compagnie Renaud-Barrault, that first got *Les Paravents* onto the agenda of possible future programming at the Odéon-Théâtre de France.[55] Her suggestion was met with enthusiasm by Jean-Louis Barrault and the possibility of mounting the play was immediately followed up. Genet was contacted for the rights and permission was given for work to go ahead, on the condition that the *mise en scène* be the responsibility of Roger Blin. Barrault remembered the decision over who was to direct to have been a suggestion of his own,[56] but Blin recalled the terms of Genet's double-edged assent:

55   Paule Thévenin, 'L'Aventures des *Paravents*', in Peskine and Dichy (eds.), *La Bataille des Paravents*, pp.5–11.
56   'The director I had suggested to Genet was Roger Blin.' Barrault, *Memories for Tomorrow*, p.293.

Genet told Barrault: 'I am very happy that you accepted to put my play on in your theatre, but I really don't like what you do and I absolutely insist that Roger Blin should be director. I hope it goes well.' That's how it went. It was quite cold.[57]

There was, of course, no problem with Blin working at the Odéon as this was by no means his first encounter with the company, and his friendship with Barrault was well established. His previous three productions there had in fact been under Barrault's patronage. The first of these was in 1963 when Barrault chose to produce Valle-Inclán's *Divines Paroles* and engaged Blin to direct the piece; later in the same year came the première of *Oh les beaux jours*, and then in 1965 Blin returned once again, this time to mount Jean-Pierre Faye's *Hommes et pierres*. Consequently, when he came to concentrate on *Les Paravents*, Blin was directing a number of people whom he knew well and, in casting the piece, he used all the suitable members of the troupe who were available and willing to participate in the venture (as some actors preferred to have nothing to do with the play and others felt they could not afford to get involved because of their acquaintance with certain politicians).[58] With Barrault's consent, Blin also introduced actors from outside the company. The engagement of outside actors for lead roles caused a ripple of discontent within the established company, as did some of Blin's other decisions: he felt obliged, for example, following Genet's extreme disapproval of her work in rehearsal, to ask the much respected actress Tania Balachova to stand down from the role of Ommou and re-cast the part, giving it instead to Marcelle Ranson. Barrault stood firmly behind Blin's judgements, and took the role of the rebel Si Slimane himself as a way of demonstrating full confidence in the director's work. As an act of solidarity with her husband and with Blin, Madeleine Renaud proposed that she should play the prostitute Warda.[59] Blin was grateful for their support. 'They could have told me: we'll lend you the theatre, we'll give you

---

57   Blin, *Souvenirs et propos*, p.176.
58   'Jean Desailly and Simone Valère had refused to speak such a filthy text.' Michèle Oppenot to Anne Laurent, in *Libération*, 10.6.83.
59   Previously Blin had contemplated taking the part himself, after also having dreamed of Marlene Dietrich in the role.

some cash, sort it out,' he remembered, 'but they insisted on acting in the play. They were fully aware of the risks they were courting and they were both extremely courageous.'[60]

The success of Blin and Genet's creative partnership through rehearsals stemmed perhaps from the degree to which they complemented each other functionally, not only in the actual realisation of the staged play itself but also in the way the work was approached by both on a very personal level, as distinct from a purely intellectual or professional level. The nature of the collaboration between the two men was a mixture of unquestioning trust and precise instruction from the author to director. Genet was notorious for his unpredictable and temperamental character and the concern he showed for the mounting of his epic would fluctuate from the pettiest anger over the smallest of details to apparent apathy, leaving Blin to his own devices in finding solutions to problems. The production was nevertheless extremely important to Genet and he was fully involved in all aspects of the preparation of this first staging of his the play in France. This participation begun with the casting process and he insisted on approving Blin's choices before they were finalised. For the key role of La Mère, Blin approached the celebrated Spanish actress Maria Casarès, with whom he had worked in 1947–8 in Pichette's *Les Épiphanies* and Artaud's *Pour en finir avec le jugement de dieu*. Genet knew Maria Casarès well and was pleased that she should be involved.[61] For the part of Saïd, Blin's thoughts settled on a young Moroccan actor, Amidou, whom he had recently seen and admired in Claude Lelouch's 1964 new wave gangster film *Une fille et des fusils* (*To be a Crook*). Genet had made it clear that he wanted no truck with realism, and had specifically instructed Blin not to cast any North Africans in the roles of the Arabs. Hesitant therefore about his director's choice of lead actor, he invited Amidou to spend a week in his company before then declaring that he felt he would be suitable for

---

60   Blin, *Souvenirs et propos*, p.183.

61   Maria Casarès was originally under the impression that Genet himself had chosen her for the part, which is not improbable. He later persuaded her to reprise the role of the Mother in Patrice Chéreau's production of *Les Paravents* at the Théâtre Amandiers in 1984.

the part.[62] Blin sent for Paule Annen to play Leïla alongside Amidou. For the legionnaires Genet instructed Blin simply to find twelve similar looking actors, all over six feet in height, but Blin had to make do with those who were available, distributing the roles of the Arabs amongst the darker haired members of Barrault's company and those of the legionnaires amongst the remainder to avoid having to use wigs. Those playing Arabs were also required to double, playing some of the colonialist figures. For the part of the Sergeant, Genet would have preferred a blonde actor, but later suggested that Blin himself should play this character. The role is an important one as the European mirror of Saïd and Genet wanted a strong actor for it. In the event Bernard Rousselet of the Renaud/Barrault company was given the part, Blin clearly having enough on his plate as matters stood.

The most revealing testimony to the collaboration of Blin with Genet is the published correspondence *Letters to Roger Blin*, a collection of letters and notes sent to Blin throughout the rehearsal process. They not only document the author's concern for detail and for the precise communication of the play's themes but also the trust and friendship he felt for Blin during this whole period. These letters offer a backstage glimpse into the nature this significant collaboration between playwright and director. The tone of the majority of the letters is one of amicable discussion. The two men had worked together on the body of the text off and on for over half a decade and Genet knew that the thoughts and ideas he was jotting down on paper would be fully understood and thoughtfully analysed by his colleague. The contents of this correspondence can be read as appendices to his written work; a recognition that the process of playwrighting need not end with edited proofs but might continue through full participation in the visualisation and embodiment of his characters and themes. As such, the letters did not constitute a series of demands upon Blin – rarely does Genet lapse into impatience or write with any urgency in them –

---

62   'I went away with Genet for eight days. He did not – absolutely did not – want to talk about the theatre. Nor did he want me to work on the play. He didn't even want to hear me read the role. We just had our breakfasts and our dinners. And we talked. After eight days he said, "Yes, I think you can play Saïd."' Amidou to Bettina Knapp, in the *Tulane Drama Review*, 11.4 (1967), p.105.

instead they represented an enthusiastic expression of support for Blin's work, whilst acting as a reassuring umbilical chord between Genet and his creation, ensuring his continuing nurturing of its evolving form. In the first letter, Genet stresses the importance of creating a theatrical occasion, a celebration of death powerful enough to invoke the whole of humanity, including the dead and future generations:

> In order for this event – the performance or performances – without disturbing the order of the world, to impose thereon a poetic combustion, acting upon a few thousand Parisians, I should like it to be so strong and so dense that it will, by its implications and ramifications, illuminate the world of the dead [...] If you stage *The Screens*, you must always work with the notion of a unique spectacle in mind, and carry it as far as you can. Everything should work together to break down whatever separates us from the dead. We must do everything possible towards creating the feeling that we have worked for them, and that we have succeeded.[63]

He goes on from there to suggest how these elements of festivity and celebration should be brought to the fore, addressing the style of acting necessary, the painting of the screens, the costumes and the make-up. To make his point he stretches to the untenable suggestion of working towards a one-off, single performance of the work,[64] underlining with this impracticable notion the emphasis he wanted laid upon the magical aura any performance must have – each being a unique occasion that must achieve perfection. Blin knew better than to take the suggestion literally, interpreting it instead as Genet's statement of absolute commitment to his work, and a call for solidarity with that commitment; the work should be spectacular and leave a profound mark on those who see it:

> At the end of the day he was saying: 'I don't care, get hold of the money however you can, you want to put this on, good, but there will only be one performance and it should be beautiful.' Genet knew perfectly well that if Barrault had thrown so much cash into the project, if we'd taken on so many

63   Jean Genet, *Letters to Roger Blin*, in Genet, *Reflections on the Theatre*, trans. Richard Seaver (London: Faber and Faber, 1972, p.57.), pp.11–12.

64   'A single performance properly staged ought to suffice' 'I think that a single performance is enough, rather than five. But one polished and perfected over a period of six months' Ibid., pp.17 and 19.

actors from inside and outside the troupe for an extremely long and arduous rehearsal period, if Acquart had constructed beautiful, costly decors, all that could not have been done for just one performance. But it's a little like when Artaud said 'the actor should perform just once and then explode'. You understand perfectly well what he means. And you understand perfectly well what Genet means, that the performance should be successful, that it should be beautiful: 'love that which you shall never see a second time.' As it was, the Parisian audiences were able to see *The Screens* fifty or sixty times.[65]

Genet's immoderate demands and extreme propositions, Blin knew, were expressions of the utmost zeal and a determined need to maintain a tight grip on artistic presentation of his work. The first letter reveals a wealth of enthusiasm for the project, an enthusiasm that Genet sensed also in his director. In it Genet gave voice to the vigour he knew he shared with Blin and used a poetic language to describe the methodology he expected of him and the actors. He was secure in the knowledge that Blin understood his play better than anyone else:

> Of course, everything I'm telling you, you already know. All I'm doing is trying to encourage you in your detachment from a theatre which, when it turns its back on middle-class conventions, goes in search of its models: gestures, tone, in the visible life and not in the poetic life, that is, the one we sometimes find near the confines of death. There, faces are no longer ruddy, one no longer has the ability to open doors – or else it is a strange door indeed, opening upon what! In short, you really know what it is I should like to say, without finding the appropriate words.[66]

The *Letters to Roger Blin*, for the most part, represent a body of notes on details of the production and Genet's reflections and reactions after having witnessed rehearsals and work in progress. Many of the notes are intended as concrete suggestions, either to be adopted by Blin for the *mise en scène* or rejected.[67] Others demonstrate

65 Blin, *Souvenirs et propos*, p.196.
66 Genet, *Letters to Roger Blin*, p.15.
67 'These, my dear Roger, are the only notes that I have which I leave to you to accept or reject' 'The two preceding pages are some suggestions offered with a view towards rectifying, but the play taken as a whole is for astonishing.' Ibid., pp.21 and 36.

168

frustration with certain actors or with the screen paintings and give precise, curt statements of his will and, occasionally, impatient reminders as to the authorship of the work that is in preparation: 'Of course I am completely ignorant when it comes to theatre in general, but I do know enough about my own.'[68] There is an evident faith in Blin running through the letters and notes, even a slight conspiratorial tone in some cases where he discusses his response to the work of individual actors. On the whole there is no question of Blin simply acting as Genet's puppet-director, a powerless surrogate held up by the strings of the notes and letters he received. Historically, Blin's reputed self-effacement in the shadow of someone like Genet creates a distorted and enfeebled impression of his input. The letters were not an arrogation by Genet of ultimate artistic control; rather they served him as a moderating factor, ensuring his ability to fine-tune Blin's work, work with which he was more than satisfied and which he commends, and even praises, at intervals throughout the correspondence.

The artistic vision of the two men was unified and Blin rarely faced any real discontent on the part of Genet, his adaptations of the original material being wholly appropriate to the overall structure. A writer such as Genet, however, is so personally attached to his work, as a manifestation of his own spirit and personality, that he could not resist feeling concern about the extent to which he was reliant on the work of other artists for his plays to achieve optimum effect in performance and this ultimate lack of control could only have been cause for anxiety. This is inevitable, and if Genet voices such anxiety in the *Letters to Roger Blin*, it is a result of his need to have his voice heard in all aspects of the production process. There is, for example, an obvious sense of frustration to be found in 'Another Letter', an assortment of notes and reflections that in parts seem discouraged, defeated even, after having seen a run-through of the play that failed, in his eyes, fully to attack its anticipated audience. He wonders whether he and Blin are guilty of complacency and questions some of the direction:

68   Ibid., p.51.

I surrendered on several occasions to Barrault's objections, and to your own. Your knowledge of the theatre threatens to make you avoid any errors of taste; my ignorance of this same profession should have led me towards them.[69]

If Genet was ever seriously dissatisfied with any element of Blin's production it was with the screens themselves and the work of André Acquart. To be precise, it was the work of Acquart's son Claude, who painted the screens according to his father's designs, that sometimes provoked Genet's annoyance. Twice in the first of the letters he comments on the design of the screen paintings,[70] and, insensitively telling Blin to go to Rodez (where Artaud, of course, had been interned) insists that the images should resemble the work of madmen,[71] and in later letters he criticises the paintings as executed. Wherever feasible Blin made changes to the production when asked by Genet, but in the case of the screen designs, which were approved before work began on them, once the final paintings had been completed even modifying the smallest screen would have been too costly. When, however, the designs were transferred to Berlin, where Claude Acquart's screen paintings were faithfully reproduced, Genet was delighted with the work, apparently unaware that there had been no change.[72]

A feature of the overall conception of the play was that the actors themselves should paint pictures on the screens, most notably in the arson attack on the orange trees in the tenth tableau and in the scene of violent revolution during the twelfth tableau. For the fire Acquart had arranged a system of cloth flames attached to the screens that could be manipulated from behind by stage hands: Blin had the Arabs creep on with sparklers to 'light' the fires and the strips of cloth were then released and jolted in the manner of flames as the sound effect of fire

69   Ibid., pp.52–3.
70   Ibid., pp.13 and 16.
71   In an unpublished interview with André Acquart, Jacques Bioules explained how he himself experimented by visiting an asylum and, in a room set aside for the inmates' artistic therapy, read them segments of *Les Paravents* and asked them to draw pictures but the results were disappointing, being for the most part realistic and lacking imagination. (André Acquart to Jacques Bioules, Fonds Blin, IMEC, Paris.)
72   André Acquart to Mark Batty, 23.5.93.

came out over loudspeakers. An interesting detail of Blin's *mise en scène* at this point was to have the stage hands wearing red socks that would briefly catch the audience's eyes as the screens were folded and carried offstage at the end of the scene. For the violent and graphic depiction of revolution on the screens in the twelfth tableau, Blin gave the actors aerosol paints and had them cover the entire surface of five or six screens with their drawings, climbing rostra or sitting on one another's shoulders to reach unpainted sections. Earlier, in the ninth tableau, where Genet indicates that Leïla should draw a clock she has stolen onto a screen, Blin had the actress delineate the clock with her finger and had the clock appear through the canvas of the screen, painted from behind by another actor with a spray paint can. The mother then held a candle up to light Leïla's handiwork in a beautiful scene of complicity between the two women before the arrival of the Gendarme.

Make-up was employed in such a way as to elevate the actors' appearance beyond the realm of realism. Blin asked those playing Arabs to apply a thick black line under their eyes to set them apart and to use patches of small crosses on their cheeks to give an unshaven impression. For the women, especially the prostitutes, he wanted mask-like patterns suggestive of Oriental theatre, featuring lines and colours that twisted across their faces. The soldiers adopted plain untextured colours. For the dead, Blin spent a long time trying to devise a simple characteristic that would evoke the transition from life. After toying with crosses and a thick line across the forehead he hit upon the Omega sign by simply following the contours of the actor's face with a stick of make-up: he felt this would be effective for the upstage appearance of the dead in the play's final tableaux.

The costumes were designed by Acquart and constructed by his wife, Barbara. Genet discusses them at length in *Letters to Roger Blin*, explaining the kind of expressive beauty he wanted them to possess:

> Not a beauty of the streets but an essential beauty, the same as with the make-up and the altered voice, so that the actors can throw themselves into the adventure and emerge victorious from it.[73]

---

73   Genet, *Letters to Roger Blin*, p.12.

Blin was anxious that the costumes should not too clearly locate the action in North Africa and discouraged Acquart from employing a documentary approach. A balance had to be struck between deliberate and provocative reference to the Algerian war of independence by means of the costumes and their abstraction from any specific historical or cultural context. Genet himself seemed undecided on this point, at times warning Blin against politicising his play and at others declaring that there should be clear reference to the war.[74] Blin concluded that above all the style of the costumes should be as theatrical, and as functional to the action, as were the décor and the comportment and delivery of the actors:

> Genet wanted the characters to be pushed in a theatrical manner, made-up beyond all realism and with costumes that only very vaguely suggest Algeria. Acquart, who lived in Algeria for a long time, could very easily have made a documentary reproduction, but that's not what we wanted. The French soldiers' costumes are pale green and their Bugeaud caps integrated all the history of the period of conquest.[75]

It was the work of the actors that preoccupied Blin and Genet most of all and the greater part of the *Letters to Roger Blin* deals with various individual interpretations or an ensemble approach for the company. Genet had a very precise notion of what he wanted from a performance and was at considerable pains to make this clear, conveying his thoughts eloquently in the letters:

> Therefore the actors and actresses must be induced to put aside cleverness and to involve the most secret depths of their being; they must be made to accept difficult endeavours, admirable gestures which however have no relation to those they employ in their daily lives. If we maintain that life and the stage are opposites, it is because we strongly suspect that the stage is a site closely akin to death, a place where all liberties are possible. The actors' voices, moreover,

74   Genet insisted on several occasions that a visual link needed to be made with the Algerian war: 'A few details here and there should remind one of Algeria.' Ibid., p.12.

75   Blin, in 'Les Paravents de Jean Genet presenté par Roger Blin', transcript of a public debate, in *Entretiens sur le théâtre*, 18 (September/October 1966), p.7. Thomas Robert Bugeaud de la Piconnerie was the French marshal who led the invasion and annexing of Algeria in 1836.

will come only from the larynx: this is a difficult music to find. Their make-up will, by transforming them into 'others', enable them to try any and every audacity: as they will be unencumbered by any social responsibility, they will assume another, with respect to another Order.[76]

Such passages are reminiscent of Artaud's writings, evoking the potential power of a performance through a colourful, abstract prose. Genet's proposal of 'difficult endeavours' and 'admirable gestures', like Artaud's 'moving hieroglyphs',[77] call for the creation of a theatre of charged signs capable of impressing their meaning upon an audience. In the structure of his play Genet had set the tone of performance by his emphasis on the screens as designators of location, while his language created a world of unnaturalistic exclamation and sordid poetry. Blin's task was to craft an overall performance style, seeking out particular signs and movements that made dramatic sense of the text, and to acclimatise the actors to this very individual yet highly effective form of theatrical expression, in order to push them towards the polished performance that both he and Genet envisaged. It was a major challenge:

> I have to say that Genet's language and style afford a more exciting work than the straightforward visual imagination of directing. The work on 'long' and 'short' for example. You can't play it cinematically, nor make do with immediate emotionality. Actors used to a certain type of realism, to human emotion, have to ingest something different.[78]

The difficulty of working with some permanent members of the Odéon company who demonstrated an inflexible approach to the job in hand compounded Blin's problems, whereas the actors from outside the company, with whom he rehearsed longer, had less difficulty in finally achieving the kind of performance required of them. The reasons for this shortcoming in performance seem to lie in their reluctance to invest the large amount of emotional energy that they play demanded. Some, also, were disenchanted with Blin's unconventional methods and, with a cast of fifty-seven, most of whom were in smaller

76   Genet, *Letters to Roger Blin*, p.12.
77   Artaud, 'On the Balinese Theatre', *The Theatre and its Double*, p.37
78   Blin in *Arts*, 6–12.4.66.

roles, there were the inevitable differences of opinion and a periodic waning of enthusiasm on the part of certain groups of actors.

> As the rehearsals progressed, a sort of rift came about between the two families. The Renault-Barrault team were a little hostile towards the text and what he [Genet] wanted in the last 15 days, they revolted against Roger Blin's working methods and pressure was put on to have Jean-Louis Barrault take over the *mise en scène.*[79]

Barrault, however, totally supported his friend's work and many of the personal and personnel problems were ironed out during the rehearsal period. Nevertheless, Blin felt that in the final product there was a disparity of achievement among the cast. Genet himself criticised the contribution of some actors, demanding in one letter that they learn to indulge in the ugliness of their roles and temporarily suppress their egos. In another he complained to Blin of the state of their offstage etiquette and apparent lack of commitment.[80]

The poetry of Genet's language required a form of diction that was not that of the standard French classical actor, despite the richness of the text. Instead it called for a whole range of changing tonal attacks, rhythms and paces of delivery, more akin to the way in which a musical score may be organised into movements and governed by changes of tempo and intensity in performance. In fact, Blin likened the delivery required to that of a song, layered in a way quite different from the customary 'hum' of poetry, stating that 'Genet's lyricism is the opposite of what you hear in so-called poetic language'.[81] In a part of a section of *Letters to Roger Blin* that was written earlier and not originally addressed to Blin, Genet outlines the demands he would make of a director to provide his actors with a way into this musicality. Effectively, he is describing the method Blin was to adopt some years later:

> The director, taking into account the various tonal qualities of the different actors' voices, will have to invent a manner of speaking which ranges from murmurs to shouts. Sentences, a tempest of sentence, must be delivered like so

79   Michèle Oppenot to Anne Laurent in *Libération*, 10.6.83.
80   Ibid., pp.49 and 54
81   Blin in *Arts*, 6–12.4.66.

174

many howls, others will be warbles, still others will be delivered in a normal conversational tone.[82]

When rehearsals first began, Genet left Blin alone to find his way in to approaching to the play. The initial stages of rehearsal involved only Amidou, Paule Annen and Maria Casarès and extended over a period of four months, other actors being called to join the three principals when appropriate. The actors experienced acute growing pains when first faced with the script. Maria Casarès had great difficulty with the role of Saïd's mother, stating that she had 'never been confronted with a theatrical text which has demanded such an engagement nor such courage to be able to get into it',[83] and '[f]or a whole month, I really thought that I had to give up the part of the mother' until she was persuaded to stay on by Genet himself.[84] Amidou had trouble at first in shedding his natural gestures and Blin spent some time selecting from the actor's instinctive body language the movements suitable for the role of Saïd: Blin worked on promoting gesture only where this was wholly fitting, as a kind of punctuation for the scripted words, giving the actors freedom to try out ideas but then paring back their work to meet the requirements of his *mise en scène*. Amidou told Bettina Knapp: 'When you do what Genet and Blin tell you to do you realise how weighted with meaning each word and movement becomes. The personality of the character does not budge.'[85]

At first Genet rarely attended rehearsals, fearful perhaps of disturbing the actors or of getting in Blin's way. Amidou's account of the early rehearsals tells us as much ('At first he didn't want to spoil things so he stayed away. He has great confidence in Blin. Genet said that aside from himself, Blin understands his play best')[86] though on the occasions when he did come to the theatre he would not hesitate to

82   Genet, *Letters to Roger Blin*, p.24. 'Daily notes' had originally been entitled 'Notes on how to play *Les Paravents*' and had been written shortly after the play was first published in 1961.
83   Maria Casarès, *Résidente privilégiée* (Paris: Fayard, 1980), p.396.
84   Casarès in *Masques, revue des homosexualités*, 12 (Winter 1981–82), p.30.
85   Amidou to Bettina Knapp, in *Tulane Drama Review*, 11.4 (1967), p.105.
86   Ibid.

make his opinions known. Maurice Tillier in an article for *Le Figaro littéraire* recounted what happened on one such occasion:

> It begins with words quickly whispered in the ears of some of the actors, called over one after the other. A little later, there is the author standing beside to his director. More confessional mutterings. Then, all of a sudden, Genet speaks out loud, astonishingly clearly, high-pitched, urgent. Those going through an ensemble movement on a piece of rostrum in the middle of the stage are captured where they stood by this.
> Jean Genet – I would very much like not to hear the floor creak.
> An actor – What if we took our shoes off ?
> Jean Genet – No! Try to make no noise with them on. It's quite possible to walk without making the floor creak. Have none of you ever burgled a room ? [...]
> To get the troupe back on track, Roger Blin makes use of one of those artistic-cum-poetic-cum-literary references of which he is fond.
> – As you move, create a sort of atmosphere of indulgence. Have you read Guillaume Apollinaire's *The House of the Dead*? That's the atmosphere we need.[87]

Here, the journalist neatly captures the atmosphere of the later rehearsals of *Les Paravents*, showing how Blin managed to complement Genet, communicating to the actors the atmosphere required of the scene, acting as a middle man and at times a buffer to Genet's less than delicate suggestions or impatient interjections. The incident also catches Genet voicing one of his main concerns – the amount of unwanted noise inevitably made on stage by large groups of actors or by the shifting of the screens. At times such as these his ideas were clearly impractical; it being impossible entirely to suppress so much extraneous noise, especially when, as in the case in question, the actors were shod in hobnail boots. As has been shown, the relationship between the two men was at once professional and one born of friendship. Nevertheless a person of Genet's character can never be totally easy to please and Blin was kept constantly on his toes:

> He had a good shout at me plenty of times. He's also very temperamental. One day he even said: 'All these decors are useless. If there's money to be spent on

---

87   Maurice Tillier, *Figaro Littéraire*, 7.4.66.

this, it'd be better for Madeleine Renaud to have enormous golden shoes.' But when it came down to it these were his usual gags. We all got on very well.[88]

The impression sometimes given of an intolerant and impatient Genet, impossible to please and giving brusque instructions to all he came into contact with, is perhaps a distortion of this kind of sense of humour. Ultimately he was capable of demonstrating great flexibility:

> He was very precise, but is capable of changing. He changed some things, he accepts modification, even in the text to facilitate Roger Blin's directing which was much more interesting than what he had proposed. That's where Genet is marvellous, he's very open, he doesn't hold on to every full-stop or comma like many authors do, and that's really very rare.[89]

Blin's task in bringing *Les Paravents* to the stage and making its themes both vital and compelling was perhaps one of the most demanding experiences of his career. It has already been argued that the kernel of the collaborative relationship he shared with Genet is to be found in the fact that fundamentally the two men were engaged in pursuing the same end: both knew they would not have to operate at odds with one another and that the final creative product of their work together would answer each other's expectations. The letters he received and the suggestions that Genet would make during rehearsals helped to sharpen Blin's awareness of the function of individual scenes within the drama and of the through-lines around which the play had been constructed, but his work as director was essentially to do for *Les Paravents* what Genet himself could not: to convert it from a written text into a performance event. This, of course, had its habitual difficulties:

> An author like Genet, when writing, does so both thinking of the tiny pocket theatre and of a stage five times bigger than that at the Opéra. He doesn't always realise, for example, that an intimate scene taking place at the back of the stage with the actors' backs turned cannot be heard by the audience. It was therefore necessary to find solutions, which allowed us, whilst always remaining faithful to the text, to make it work.[90]

88   Blin in *Masques*, 12 (Winter 1981–82), p.36.
89   Acquart to Jacques Bioules, Fonds Blin, IMEC, Paris, p.23.
90   Blin to Catherine Valogne, in *La Tribune de Lausanne*, 17.5.66.

Though Genet's indications, such as can be found in *Letters to Roger Blin*, read very much like the notes that a director may give his cast, they are concerned on the whole with the secondary details of precise tuning. *Les Paravents*, however, posed a number of primary problems in terms of its staging: for instance, that the dead should exist on stage and that they should comment on the action, including action that has not yet occurred in real time, were then concepts not familiar to the average Western playgoer. Blin had to devise a stage vocabulary that would deal with this problem in performance and which an audience could both accept and rapidly digest:

> Using oriental conventions, everything would have been straightforward, but such conventions do not exist in Europe. I created a number of them which the audience could pick up as the play unravelled [...] I'm interested in what an actor can do on his own with the most modest of means (I don't imply that what we had at the Odéon was a problem for *The Screens*) because mechanistic procedures which derive from film don't seem truly to serve the theatre, to my mind.[91]

An approach of this order was most appropriate for the non-naturalistic characters and situations created by Genet. *Les Paravents* demanded a stylised interpretation but one which did not regress too far into theatricality or demonstrative 'show' for its own sake. Devices discovered in rehearsal and subsequently used in performance had to be effective and immediately understandable, avoiding both the fussily cerebral and the unnecessarily obtrusive. Genet's means of scene-setting, the numerous screens themselves, acted as straightforward indicators of locale and became thereby the principal ingredient of the type of theatrical vocabulary that a performance of the play must have:

> Screens are an important element of oriental theatre and Genet is strongly influenced by the ceremony of that theatre. For this play in particular, I tried out a few discoveries in the same spirit and, for example, to demonstrate that it is night time, an actor playing one of the Arabs at one point tears up a paper sun. For *The Screens*, I tried to find effects of an extreme theatrical type, which were all perfectly understood by the audience.[92]

91   Ibid.
92   Blin, *Souvenirs et propos*, p.200. For the tearing of the sun, Blin is referring to Habib in the fourth tableau.

178

The simple beauty of this theatrical demonstration of sunset (one that also lends incidental subversive agency to an Arab character) is exemplary of Blin's contribution. In a similar vein, in the eighth tableau, he had Jean-Louis Barrault bring on a rolled up rug which he laid out in front of him to create the space of Si-Slimane's tomb. In a display of dislocating real space and effectively frustrating audience expectations, the legionnaires in the final tableau shouted out into the auditorium when addressing the dead, who were in fact situated behind them on an upstage raised level. An extraordinarily beautiful effect was created in the fourteenth tableau when Blin had Leïla slowly disappear into her costume at the end of her speech, instead of receding upstage as originally indicated by Genet.

Such simple techniques and devices locate the action within an environment that visually confesses its theatrical conceit whilst maintaining the integrity of its illusion of representation, heightening the attention of the spectator through the imaginative collaboration produced by the recognition and acceptance of the meaning-making systems being constructed before them. Blin developed a network of similar devices involving actors, screens, costumes and properties either to heighten the action or the impact of Genet's poetry. Actors might be required to address one another without facing one another, or with an unnatural distance between them, or they might anticipate the arrival of others from the wings only to have to accept as normal these same characters entering from the opposite side of the stage. In response to Genet's request that Saïd and Leïla should express themselves physically with beautiful gestures, Blin choreographed their confrontation in tableau eleven as a succession of swaying movements of closeness and rejection, Leïla being repeatedly picked up and held close but then dropped and allowed to fall to the ground by Saïd. Details of this kind demonstrate Blin's concern for a distinctive form of stage reality, conjuring up the world of *Les Paravents* by overtly theatrical means. On the other hand a total absorption of stage convention was to be avoided:

> Genet wanted there always to be one or more real objects on stage to stand against the objects or landscapes painted on the screens. No doubt because in the theatre the most extreme convention in itself equally permits a certain con-

vincing quality. Now, we wanted to constantly break with what is convincing, such as realism of course, but also convention itself. He wrote me some very beautiful letters on the subject. In one of these he said to me: 'true and untrue but not false, the play has its truth.' That's what we were looking to find, the truth of the piece. We took every precaution to disrupt the emotional character of the play whilst constantly keeping in mind that it was theatre. But despite everything, emotion found its way out, and above all laughter. The show because it worked, the text because it is beautiful and powerful, all that let us pull it off. It worked, even amongst those annoyed by the production, because they laughed a great deal. The audience had a great time because there were plenty of gags, and because as the show progressed, it constantly brought with it surprise after surprise.[93]

By disrupting the audience's capacity to become fully engaged in the action at an emotional level, a balance was maintained between the poetry of the text and the harshness of the socio-political situations with which it engaged. The effect Blin strove to achieve served to heighten an audience's emotional response rather than to activate their critical faculties and did so in a way that was consistent with Genet's own method.

As for other, apparently minor details of *mise en scène*, it was Blin's sensitivity to the theatrical requirements of the text and the need for an overall unity of style that overruled Genet's wish to have all the scene changes done within short periods of blackout. Genet felt the true meaning of the play would become more apparent if the scenes were punctuated by darknesses but Blin convinced him that the same effect would be achieved by the gliding on and off of the screens at the end of each scene in preparation for the next. He therefore had all the scene changes carried out in full view of the audience, thus maintaining a continuously overt theatrical framework around the dramatic action. A similar policy was adopted in blocking entrances and exits: where Genet had indicated that actors should simply come on or leave the stage via the wings, Blin arranged, wherever it was feasible, for them to exit or enter behind the screens.

On very few occasions did Blin actually stray from the text or Genet's written instructions. The few points where he did so, such as having Saïd's wheelbarrow on stage from tableau three, arose out of

93   Ibid.

limitations inherent in the staging, or out of a desire to keep the dramatic momentum alive. The most radical change that Blin made was to have the controversial scene in which the corpse of the lieutenant receives the 'air de France' from each of his soldiers enacted on stage, and not in the wings as Genet had originally envisaged.[94] Another notable addition of Blin's was to have Saïd's mother laugh and dance at the end, as her son dies:

> In the final tableau, when Saïd is killed, to my great astonishment the mother, who, dead herself, witnesses it and gives no reaction. Genet said to me 'yes, it's true, it's true'. He wanted a noble ending. So I said to him, 'above all she mustn't cry, she mustn't mourn, and naturally she should dance.' 'OK, let her dance' Genet said.[95]

The cuts that Blin made in the text were not carried out in deference to the time of the last metro train and never in the name of delicacy, but calculated to reinforce the dramatic unity of the performance as a whole. He over-ruled cuts proposed by Barrault as, for the most part, they would have removed some of the play's provocative edge ('If I'd followed his instructions, his suggestions,' Blin remembered 'then there would have been no uproar in the house').[96] Played in its entirety, *Les Paravents* would have run to over five hours and Blin decided to trim it to around four, a length that he felt reasonable for an audience to sustain. He also inserted an intermission after the twelfth tableau. Tableau seven was cut altogether, being tangential in subject matter, to permit the scene in which La Mère asks the dead Si Slimane if she has the right to mourn him to follow directly and flow smoothly on from the scene in which she is rejected by the mourning village women. The passage involving the prisoner condemned to death in the eleventh tableau was also cut, at Genet's request. In the twelfth tableau Blin decided to omit a scene where a mannequin is decorated with medals while the signs of

---

94 'Genet, in rehearsal, accepted the idea of staging the 'hommage' to the lieutenant which, in the printed text, took place in the wings.' Blin in *Le Monde*, 4.5.66.

95 Blin to Jacques Bioules, Fonds Blin, IMEC, p.10.

96 Ibid., p.3.

revolution become apparent around the ceremony; having rehearsed this scene he found that it jarred against the growing build towards the explosion of revolution and, in order to maintain the appropriate rhythm, decided to run straight into Kadidja's death and her calling of the Arabs to revolt.[97] Some smaller entrances had to be cut owing to the complicated system of doubling necessary to perform the play with a limited number of actors: one such was the entrance of the drunken Sir Harold and the Banker, who should walk past the sleeping Saïd and Leïla in the thirteenth tableau, but the two actors concerned would have had no time to change for their following entrances as Salem and the Gendarme. Blin was quite content that the sequence should finish on Saïd's closing of a screen sporting the design of a dragon enveloping him and his wife. He also suppressed all mention of flatulence at the beginning of the fourteenth tableau so as not to take the wind out of the sails of the notorious 'scène des pets' that was to come at the close of that section of the play. Despite the beauty of the final tableau, Blin felt that it too needed cropping, not simply because the doubling of roles prevented so many characters from appearing at once but primarily to bring forward the re-entrance of Saïd, who otherwise would have been absent too long for his death to achieve its full impact. This cutting also helped to avoid a slackening of pace at the end of the play, allowing it instead to accelerate towards the glorification in Saïd's debasement.

The production opened at the Odéon-Théâtre de France on 16 April 1966 with five premières and had an initial run of less than a month, closing on 7 May until September, when it re-opened for a further twenty nights. Genet, who attended performances irregularly, often doing so in order to amuse himself at the disruptions and demonstrations against the play, was more than satisfied with the production and lauded Blin's work on it. No testimony could be more eloquent than the following letter of gratitude:

That you have understood my play as I desired is not surprising, for you are quick to understand and discriminating, but you have had the talent and tenacity to apply your understanding. [...] In *The Blacks*, the text of which was more carefully prepared as to its effects, your work amazed me less. In any case, it

97   In his revised edition of *Les Paravents*, Genet also applied this cut.

182

seems to me that I was as much responsible for its success as were you. In *The Screens*, the full credit goes to you. If I had thought that the play could be performed, I would have made it more beautiful – or a complete failure. Without touching it, you have taken it and made it light. It's very beautiful. You have my friendship, and my admiration.[98]

Despite the legendary 'scandal' of the first production of *Les Paravents* in France, the disturbances did not in fact begin until the twelfth performance, after which they occurred regularly every night. On the first occasion, objects were thrown on stage and an actor and a stage-hand were injured trying to defend themselves and other actors from some of the demonstrators who climbed onto the stage to take their objection to the play out on its performers. Blin's 1963 prediction of the difficulties of mounting the play in France ('The Arabs versus the French on stage. Why, we would all be bombed')[99] proved to be not far wrong. Verbal and physical assaults on the actors continued, French paratroopers would mount the stage to interrupt the action, noisy demonstrations took place outside the theatre and Blin, Barrault and Genet all received death threats. On 1 May the police ejected sixteen young men for throwing eggs, tomatoes, broken glass and fireworks. Dead rats and excrement are also reported to have been thrown on stage. The actors' union S.F.A. offered legal support to the cast and crew at the Odéon. One evening during the disruption 'It's the battle of *Hernani*' was heard whispered in the wings, invoking the infamous riot at the premiere of Victor Hugo's 1830 play. The main controversy involved the scene of the 'homage' to the dead lieutenant which Blin had brought on stage. He later recalled the controversy with characteristic humour:

> To start with it was the fart scene that automatically set off the outrage. They waited more or less in silence for this moment to cause havoc. We lowered the curtain, Barrault gave his little *spiel* and on we went. But quite soon they began to tire of waiting to be really offended in order to let loose and began to jeer from the outset. We all had a great time. I was particularly happy.[100]

98   Genet, *Letters to Roger Blin*, p.36.
99   Blin to Bettina Knapp, in *Tulane Drama Review*, 7.3 (1962), p.119.
100   Blin, *Souvenirs et propos*, p.181.

Even when the fire curtain was lowered, and Barrault came out in front of it to appeal for calm and tolerance in the name of freedom of speech, the fighting between cast and interlopers would continue behind it. The police were called if necessary and the stage was cleared for the play to continue. This became more or less the scenario each night as an organised group of protesters, consisting mostly of military school trainees and, Blin believed, police in civilian clothing, mounted their attack. Right-wing activists bought tickets on the black market or took up the more expensive seats. For a fortnight the play ran to full houses at 120 percent of the threshold capacity and with a closed box office, such was the scale of the 'succès de scandale' and the zeal of the would-be saboteurs. There were some 500 people involved in a demonstration of the 3 May, arranged for a half hour before the curtain was to rise, and therefore at a time most likely to disturb or threaten an arriving audience. The angry crowd was made up of members of the 'Comité de Liaison des Anciens Combattants 14-18, 39–45, d'Indochine et d'Algérie', who had previously called for the play to be banned, and who were supported by the 'l'Association française pour le soutien de la République du Vietnam du Sud', the extreme-right group 'Occident' and the 'Cercle du Panthéon', led by the outspoken right-wing politician Jean-Marie Le Pen. Genet looked down on the crowd from the window of Barrault's office as the mob repeated the homophobic chant 'Gen-et, Pé-dé'; he turned and mischievously smiled at Barrault and Blin, asking in mock innocence 'How do they know?'[101]

On 4 May there were as many as sixty arrests and on the same day, at the peak of the demonstrations, it was reported in the press that Blin had capitulated to the extent of relegating the offending 'fart scene' to the wings, as Genet had originally conceived it, following an incident when a chair was thrown and almost injured Germaine Kerjean. The words would still be uttered, but the scene would no longer be performed and it was reported in *Paris-Presse* the same day that Blin looked very unhappy about having to give in under threat of violence. A few days later, when the chief of police could no longer guarantee the safety of cast and crew, the show had to close pre-

101   André Acquart to Mark Batty, 23.5.93.

maturely. Barrault, who was at the eye of the public storm unleashed by *Les Paravents*, was called upon constantly to defend the production. In frequent television and radio broadcast and in print, he showed admirable fortitude, championing Genet's right to be heard, deploring the distorting effect which the demonstrations had had on the play and condemning the violence of a minority faction:

> The organised demonstrations which began from the twelfth performance of *Les Paravents* misrepresent the essence of the play and were met with the almost unanimous disapproval of the audience, who themselves demanded that the troublemakers be ejected.[102]

To add to the threats and acts of violence, many critics were less than kind to the production, seemingly far more concerned in a partisan way with the controversial nature of Genet's work than with the qualities and values of the theatrical event. Among the great deal of bad press it received, the bulk of critical response was directed at the 'scandal' of such a play being performed at a state-subsidised theatre ('In taking on this play', stated Jean-Jacques Gautier, 'The Odéon has committed a government-authorised impropriety')[103] or laid heavily into Genet's text and its indelicate language. The reviewer of *La Croix* described the play as 'insistent scatology'. Pierre Marcabru in *Le Nouveau Candide* added 'Four hours of shouting, violence and filth. It's a lot. It's too much. The nerves cave in from such an attack'.[104] Swallowing his admiration yet voicing his indignation, Gabriel Marcel in *Les Nouvelles Littéraires* stated that 'there is a lot to admire in it all, but this beauty, alas, yet again provokes outrage.'[105] Genet was defended in some papers, however – most significantly by Bertrand Poirot-Delpech (*Le Monde*) and Claude Olivier (*Les Lettres françaises*) – and some of the more sympathetic reviews disregarded the scandal that the production had provoked to devote their column space to commend the work of the actors and their director:

102   Jean-Louis Barrault in *Paris-Presse*, 3.5.66.
103   Jean-Jacques Gautier, *Le Figaro*, 23.4.66.
104   *La Croix*, 23.4.66 and Pierre Marcabru, *Le Nouveau Candide*, 25.4.66.
105   Gabriel Marcel, *Les Nouvelles Littéraires*, 21.4.66.

Roger Blin has directed *The Screens*. He has done so with an exceptional mastery of stage space: a variety of performance levels, the scrupulously regulated movement of a hundred or so actors and walk-ons, silently moving screens, hierarchical, segmenting the dramatic action with a golden razor's edge, opulence, dazzling beauty of the ensemble.

The merit for the success goes to Roger Blin. He had to both piece together an overlong text, less precisely structured than previous ones, inscribe its themes spatially, and distil within the performance the chaos of its violent ruptures. The success is complete. With one glance the most obscure of symbols come across as self-evident.[106]

This degree of success and recognition, supported by his history of similar artistic achievements, ensured that by the mid-sixties Blin had come to be regarded as one of the most significant and accomplished French directors of the last century.

106   Jean Paget, *Combat*, 23.4.66 and Bertrand Poirot-Delpech, *Le Monde*, 23.4.66.

Ethics and Aesthetics

Roger Blin's endeavours at the Gaîté-Montparnasse led to his receiving the script of *En attendant Godot* in 1949 and the recognition that its production brought him in 1953. By the end of the 1950s, with his production of Jean Genet's *Les Nègres*, he had come to be regarded as one of the leading exponents of the Parisian Left Bank avant-garde theatre. During the 1960s he consolidated his links with Beckett and Genet while working with other playwrights whose work interested him and his name became linked with the Théâtre Lutèce under the progressive Lucie Germain and the Odéon under the innovative Barrault. In the 1960s and 1970s he took a number of original pieces into production, playing a significant role in introducing the French public to authors such as Roland Dubillard, Athol Fugard, Eduardo Manet and Slawomir Mrozek. In the thirty-four years of his directing life he presented twenty-one French premières of new works, representing two thirds of his total output. In the majority of his productions he worked in tandem with the author. This emphasis on the playwright and his written material as the heart of the dramatic process is of the utmost importance in reaching an understanding of Blin's view of the role of the director. A survey of his aesthetic leanings might therefore start with a consideration of the type of play to which he was attracted.

At the onset of his directing career, Blin's stated intention was to present a diet of modern classics which were unjustly neglected:

> In 1948, my notion was to play homage to the great ancestors [such as] Strindberg. Not to the classical authors, but to those who has always been marginal. I wanted to work my way forward chronologically before dedicating myself to contemporary theatre [...] but I never wanted to mount a 'classic' [...] I wanted to make theatre precisely against that kind of thing.[1]

---

1   Blin, *Souvenirs et Propos*, p.54.

Uncontentious today, now that Strindberg's and Büchner's plays enjoy their place in the world dramatic canon, that Blin should have referred publicly to the programme of Strindberg's *Sonate des spectres* and Büchner's *Woyzeck* as 'classics of the theatre'[2] was a deliberately provocative statement given the then traditionally acknowledged notion of the French classic repertoire. An attitude reminiscent of Artaud's article 'No More Masterpieces', Blin's initial rejection of the traditional classics is scarcely surprising; such distaste would have been nurtured by his participation in Surrealist circles where artistic emphasis was firmly on the expression of an inner, subjective reality as opposed to the objective psychologising of traditional drama. His dismissal of the French classical repertoire was also on formalistic grounds. He considered Racine's work to be 'extremely naïve, crude even'[3] and though he reserved some respect for Corneille's early work he disapproved of the writer's later capitulation to the strict composition requirements of the seventeenth century, the rules of dramatic construction which he dismissed as 'Boileau and all that rubbish'.[4] This virulent rejection of the classics sets him apart from the majority of twentieth-century French theatre innovators, from Copeau, the Cartel to Jean Vilar, who built their public reputations in part on their bold annexation of dramatic territory previously considered the exclusive property of the Comédie-Française. This is not to say that Blin's dismissal of a traditional repertoire was a conditioned reflex: although he chose to devote most of his time and energy to new works, he was not automatically averse to some 'classics' of the traditional canon, if they might suit his tastes in formal terms. In 1968, for instance, he planned a production of Seneca's *Thyestes*, which had to be abandoned as a result of the student revolution of that year. He also held Molière in some esteem, and nursed an ambition to direct one day an interpretation of *Le Misanthrope*, which he planned to set in Ancient Greece. His great admiration for

2   Blin to Frédéric O'Brady, in *Combat*, 4.10.49.
3   Blin to Emmanuelle Klausner, in *La Croix*, 10.2.83. It is an interesting insight into Blin's nature that he freely and happily made such comments in an interview given while he was temporarily working for the Comédie-Française.
4   Ibid. A friend and colleague of Jean Racine, Nicholas Boileau introduced in his *Art poétique* (1674) a system for the regulation of French versification.

Shakespeare whose works he considered 'untranslatable, and yet must be translated' and 'cannot be performed, yet must be performed'[5] was gratified by an opportunity to mount *Macbeth* at the Théâtre National de Strasbourg in 1972, one of the few occasions when he accepted a commission to direct a play. What he found congenial in Shakespeare was the freedom of form that allowed humour to follow bleak scenes of horror and vernacular expression to occur alongside poetic discourse. He would cite Shakespeare's mastery of his language as illustrative, by contrast, of all that was wrong with French classical drama:

> It's a shame that a free spirit, or a man of the theatre wasn't able to journey from Paris to London in 1606 – with the spirit strong enough to take courage from what he saw and sweep aside Malherbe, Boileau and company [...] Victory remained with the Aristotle/Descartes/Malherbe conspiracy, whose goal was to stuff our consciences with all of nature, to have Rabelais overlooked, to restore a restrictive humanist conception from the Renaissance. And at what price to our language: the poverty of Racine's language! Twenty or so beautiful verses, blown out of proportion, where their equivalents constitute the very language of Shakespeare.[6]

Shakespeare's *Macbeth* was one of only four productions Blin mounted of non-living authors; all his other productions he directed within ten years of the play's composition. Of the three other non-contemporary plays he tackled, two were by Strindberg[7] whose highly subjective drama, unrelenting treatment of cruelty, and the freedom of composition of his post-*Inferno* work made his plays the subject of much avant-garde interest in France. In his study *Strindberg's Impact in France*, Anthony Swerling emphasises that Strindberg maintained something of a cult status in the 1930s and 1940s and illustrates the appeal he had 'to the demolishers of conventional morality, pretensions and the theatre' and 'to the men who wish to oppress and jolt

---

5   Blin to Colette Godard, in *Le Monde*, 6.4.72.
6   Blin, 'Les vers du nez', in William Shakespeare, *Macbeth*, trans. Pierrette Tison (Paris: Théâtre Ouvert/Stock, 1972), pp.163–71 (p.166).
7   *Ein Traumspiel* (A Dream Play) (1975) and *Sonate des spectres* (Ghost Sonata) (1949). The third was by Ramón del Valle-Inclán's – *Divines Paroles* (1963).

rather than to entertain and flatter their public'.[8] The description suits Blin well.

Blin chose plays that would make a powerful emotional impact on an audience and defined a text's capacity to do so as its 'affective density', a term which can be understood as the combined emotional vitality of various elements in a play's construction: the language in which it is written, the concrete stage pictures that it permits or requires, its ability to shock, and the generation of dramatic momentum through the use of humour and inference. A survey of the plays that he directed reveals two apparently disparate elements: there is a clear penchant for the 'poetic', for plays whose principal form of expression embraced the spatial and gestural capacities of the live event (exemplified by the works of Beckett, Genet and Strindberg) and at the same time a certain impulse to stage polemical works (such as *Les Paravents* and other anti-military plays, *Boesman and Lena* which depicted victims of Apartheid, and *Minimata and co.* which dealt with industrial pollution). He seems therefore to have adopted an artistic policy which combined ethical as well as aesthetic considerations. It is not possible, however, simply to divide Blin's theatrical activity into political militancy and poetic experimentation. He himself was at odds to find a middle route and to 'give performances that are significant in terms of the problems and events of the day, but without neglecting the text, without compromising the poetry'[9]

Poetry and the 'non-dit'

When first confronted with the script of Beckett's *En attendant Godot*, Blin was struck by the 'marvellous economy of the means of expression and a great poetic sense'[10] and was concerned during rehearsals

---

8   Swerling, *Strindberg's Impact in France*, p.25.
9   Blin, *Souvenirs et propos*, pp.59–60.
10   Blin to Peter Lennon, in *The Guardian*, 20.9.63.

of this and subsequent Beckett plays to respect faithfully the punctuation and what he referred to as the 'breathing' of the play. Furthermore, the 'zero degree' of drama in Beckett's world, where characters are simply present, beyond situation, and with no plot to propel them, appealed to Blin's vision of the theatre. In Genet's work he admired the way in which the playwright constructed through inventive, graphic poetry 'a veritable declaration against realism, and for truth of a different order.'[11] He considered Genet's lyricism unique and 'the opposite of what you hear in so-called poetic language'.[12] Blin found the offensive nature of Genet's language to be an integral part of this lyricism; for him 'the crudities and vulgar phrases are part of Genet's language, as are the most elegant constructions',[13] and he would dismiss the numerous complaints about Genet's use of vulgar sexual and scatological vocabulary by remarking: '[e]verything seems natural, beautiful, straightforward to me'.[14]

Jean-Louis Bauer, whose *M'appelle Isabelle Langrenier* (*Name's Isabelle Langrenier*) Blin mounted in 1979, defined his director's attitude towards dramatic writing, stating that 'for Roger Blin, I think that the theatre is first of all poetry, on the condition that it can be poured into the theatrical mould.'[15] From Pichette's 'lyrical tide',[16] as Blin described *Les Épiphanies* (1947), to plays such as *M'appelle Isabelle Langrenier,* Billetdoux's *Ai-je dit que je suis bossu* (*Did I say I was a hunchback*, 1981) and Semprun Maura's *Le Bleu de l'eau de vie* (*The Blue of Eau de Vie*, 1981), Blin enjoyed working with texts that employed a distinctive linguistic playfulness. Of the last of these, for instance, he said he admired the density of the construction of its dialogue, 'density served by gentle, fluid, cruel writing, without literature'[17] (the rejection of 'literature', of language that draws attention to itself, is there once more). Bauer's play, *M'appelle Isabelle Langrenier,* written as an extension of a monologue which Blin had read

11   Blin to Nicole Zand, in *Le Monde*, 16.4.66.
12   Blin to Claude Morand, in *Arts*, 6–12.4.66.
13   Blin to Bettina Knapp, in *Tulane Drama Review*, 11.4 (1967), p.109.
14   Blin to Nicole Zand, in *Le Monde*, 16.4.66.
15   Jean-Louis Bauer, *L'Aurore*, 22.1.79.
16   Blin in Anne Philipe and Claude Roy, *Gérard Philipe*, p.45.
17   Blin, 'La réalité entre chien et loup', *L'Avant-scène théâtre*, 703 (1982), p.3.

and advised the author to develop, weaves a web of words around its central character. As one reviewer commented:

> You can understand how the man who mounted Pichette's Les Épiphanies was attracted to this poem. Here too, language, coming apart at the seams, going from one play on words to another, from meanings reduced to loose syllables, ends up trapping the character, tied up by words. But instead of lyrical exuberance, this time it is tragic aphasia.[18]

Whether it was the poetry of the language that struck Blin or the manipulation of narrative through dialogue, it is clear that the writing, the raw material of the text, was of primary importance to him as a director. To provide another example, in a play by the Israeli Amos Kenan, Le Lion, which he staged at the Lutèce in 1960, he was excited by the manner in which individual lines would suddenly 'break away towards something else, but only just break away'.[19] He was attracted by the childish behaviour of the characters of Kenan and Dubillard, which reminded him to some extent of those of Beckett. Speaking of Robert Weingarten, a young American writer whose Les Charognards (The Carrion Eaters) he staged in 1968, and Roland Dubillard, whose ...Où boivent les vaches (...Where the Cows go to Drink) he staged in 1972, he referred specifically to this appealing quality of childlike innocence in their writing:

> Both of them have an astonishing sense of burlesque poetry. Dubillard is the harshest. They are the kinds of author, like Arrabal, who have not grown up. They haven't yet reached maturity. They place themselves in a sort of shelter of childhood, in the unconscious, in the irrational, and it is really very very good![20]

The language could be baroque and colourful, such as Genet's or Faye's, cleverly imaginative like Bauer's, plain yet demanding such as Adamov's, Beckett's or Bernhard's or even straightforwardly realistic, provided always that it was organic to the fabric of the drama, compelling actors to make discoveries. Le Bleu de l'eau de vie, by Carlos

18 Gilles Sandier, Le Matin, 31.1.79.
19 Blin in Les Lettres françaises, 20.10.60.
20 Blin in Acteurs, 5 (May 1982), p.65.

Semprun Maura was exemplary of this latter condition. The play presented a Pinteresque, 'huis-clos' situation in which two alienated friends are bound together by the same woman, who does not appear. Ex-wife to the one and lover to the second, she is the pivot of the intrigue:

> I'd been seduced by the subtlety, the quality of the writing in this text, which is totally devoid of lyricism, which operates around a constant return to the principal character's obsession, and within which the relationship between the two characters is revealed through that which remains unspoken.[21]

Blin was frequently enthusiastic about the use of the unspoken, the 'non-dit', as he called it, in a number of authors' work, and related Semprun Maura's play to some of his most admired authors: 'What appealed to me in this absolutely truthful writing was that between the lines there was that "between the lines" that great authors such as Strindberg and Beckett employ',[22] adding in a preface to the version printed in *L'Avant-Scène Théâtre* in 1982 that in this work 'Chekhov, Pinter, the Strindberg of *The Stronger* are in the air'[23] The ability of some playwrights to create a verbal texture of ambiguity was something that always intrigued him: 'The unspoken, the not quite spoken, not beneath banal conversations (so dear to adherents of light drama) but through what is spoken; through lies, paralipses, red herrings.'[24]

Militant acts

Confronted by a complex text, and with adequate production resources to support his interpretation, Blin's initial reaction could be one of overwhelmed apprehension which was transformed into inter-

21   Blin, *Souvenirs et propos*, p.292.
22   Blin to Emmanuelle Klausner, programme *Le Bleu de l'eau de vie*, Petit-Odéon, 17.11.81.
23   Blin, 'La réalité entre chien et loup', p.3.
24   Ibid.

pretative energy. He described this state of inspiration as a 'dizziness' ('vertige') which could in itself be motivation enough for him to take on a production. Speaking of Max Frisch's *Triptyque*, which he directed for the Comédie-Française in 1983 he explained:

> I saw a very beautiful subject there and felt a certain dizziness before the multiple aesthetic and technical problems. I'm no enemy of dizziness [...] of a political sort, which I felt with *The Screens* or with *Boesman and Lena*. I don't have any idealism or Christian view to motivate me either. Quite simply, it's a great work, and my motivation to do it is simply the politics of theatre.[25]

This 'politics of the theatre' was clearly not a question of pure aestheticism. Blin was keen to point out that '[m]aking art, that suits me fine, but to make art for art's sake; that doesn't do much for me.'[26] Nor was he interested in the promotion of spectacle and production effects unrelated to the requirements of the text. Persistently labelled a 'disciple' of Artaud, Blin was wary of being categorised as a director who was interested solely in experimentation, in theatrical art devoid of specific social commitment. When asked in 1961 why he had been so keen to mount *Les Nègres* he replied that, after having signed the 'Manifeste des 121' (in favour of the soldier's right to insubordination during the Algerian war), 'had I not done so I would be merely an aesthete'.[27] A recurrent feature of Blin's work was this commitment to political issues and the desire to portray images of oppression and of the manipulation of the individual.

> There's always been one thing that I've prioritised: the furious desire to disturb a certain type of person. I've always been tempted by political plays if the text is beautiful and if it is poetic. I'm always excited by the prospect of being able to piss people off. And so I put on *The Blacks* against whites, *The Screens* against the army, *Boesman and Lena* against apartheid. My motivations are about ninety per cent for the value of the play and ten per cent for its provocative power.[28]

25   Blin to Josanne Rousseau, in *Comédie-Française*, 116 (1983).
26   Blin in *Masques*, 12 (Winter 1981–82), p.37.
27   Blin to Nicholas Garnham, in *Varsity*, 20.5.61.
28   Blin, *Souvenir et propos*, p.87.

194

Here Blin puts the 'militant' side of his work into perspective. He derived great satisfaction from mounting plays of a controversial nature or with a manifest political significance but on condition that the statements they made were set within a structure of formal beauty. He spoke of experiencing 'an extraordinary elation' at stirring up the amount of explosive reaction that greeted his production of *Les Nègres* and more especially that of *Les Paravents*.[29] Indeed, Genet's work offers a paradigm of the kind of drama that could satisfy Blin on both poetic and political grounds: 'Genet's theatre satisfied my desire to revolt and, whilst carrying a certain beauty, was also able to maintain a certain ambiguity without which there can be no art [...] I entered Genet's world with both feet', he declared.[30]

Blin would often choose plays that, although they did not deal directly with a political issue, had been set by their authors against a background of political upheaval. Such choices were a function, perhaps, of Blin's humanism: he was more interested in the survival of human dignity in the face of overwhelming circumstances than in illustrating political arguments. His attitude is summed up succinctly by Jean Martin who described him as 'a constructive anarchist who demolished things in order to construct things',[31] someone for whom the theatre, by presenting the base elements of our nature, could act as a crucible for human social and interpersonal issues.

Robert Weingarten's *Les Charognards*, staged at the Théâtre de Carrouges in Switzerland in 1968, though set in the war-torn Vietnam of the late 1960s, did not address the subject of U.S. military intervention or of the political instability of Vietnamese society, but explored instead the dream/nightmare world of a young American paratrooper, Johnny (played by François Germond), who is stranded in a tree following a failed parachute jump into Vietcong territory. The drama unravels around the thoughts of this character as he awaits his inevitable capture, his enacted memories and fantasies serving to present a faint satire of the 'American dream'.

29 'Mounting *The Blacks* and, later on, *The Screens*, gave me an extraordinary elation'. Ibid., p.133.
30 Blin, *Masques*, 12 (Winter 1981–82), p.35.
31 Jean Martin to Mark Batty, 11.1.95.

Les Emigrés (*The Emigrants*), by the Polish writer Slawomir Mrozek, was suggested to Blin by his friend Laurent Terzieff in 1974. Terzieff, who had already done much to introduce Mrozek's work to Parisian audiences,[32] asked Blin to direct him in the part of the intellectual character AA opposite Gérard Darrieu as the opportunistic XX. Though the form of the play, with its naturalistic dialogue and psychological characterisation, did not immediately appeal to Blin,[33] he found the urgency of its situation intriguing. Mrozek's play concerns two emigrants sharing a stark, windowless basement apartment in a city of an unnamed Western democracy, one of them in self-imposed political exile from the Eastern bloc, the other trying to earn himself enough money to buy his family a large, comfortable house on his return. Political comment on the plight of the emigrant, however, is of only secondary importance as Mrozek uses the predicament in which he places his characters to build a psycho-drama in which the financially motivated emigrant is subject to the taunts and criticisms of his companion within a claustrophobic situation.

Minimata and Co. by Osamu Takahashi was a form of documentary play based upon a true incident in which Japanese industry and government sought to cover up the mercury poisoning of the inhabitants of the coastal village of Minimata, caused by industrial waste being dumped at sea. The play is episodic in form, constructed as a sort of documentary-drama and purposefully didactic in intention, it is written using plain, unpretentious dialogue. Despite its rigid structure, when offered the play by its translator/adaptor Catherine Cadou, Blin felt that such a horrific case of abuse and oppression of the individual needed to be articulated:

> Osamu Takahashi's play is a heart-wrenching cry, the cry of victims, not a lyrical and vague protest against destiny, but a ferocious, detailed, cry of accus-

---

32   He had been responsible for French première of Mrozek's *Tango* in 1967, directing and acting in the piece at the Théâtre Lutèce.

33   'He made it clear to me that it wasn't the kind of play that he himself would pick to put on.' Terzieff in Claude Mauriac, *Laurent Terzieff* (Paris: Stock, 1980), p.252.

ation, one which concerns us all, because if the tortured souls we show are Japanese, we know that the killers are amongst us too.[34]

Blin was keen to relate this specific Japanese incident to similar cases of industrial negligence and pollution in Europe: 'I wanted to put the play on as a militant work. I was strongly taken by wanting to speak of this terrible Japanese affair, but I wanted to relate these distant to serious matters that had occurred in France and this play gave me the opportunity.'[35] Ecological issues were among the most primary political causes for Blin, and abuses of power where financial concerns superseded human ones were for him one of the most insidious forms of oppression:

> Our body is all we have. It permits us to be united with those we love, nearby or far off. Industrial society, under the vestige of progress, pretends to operate for our well-being. In reality it causes, in pursuit of profit, the destruction of our bodies more stealthily than warfare.[36]

Perhaps possessed by an overwhelming repulsion at the facts behind the Minimata incident, Blin mobilised his artistic skills to enhance Takahashi's script and thereby add his outrage to those of the play's author and translator.

In 1971 Blin mounted José Triana's *La Nuit des assassins* (*Night of the Assassins*) at the Récamier. Having seen it performed by a Cuban company in Spanish at a Théâtre des Nations festival (held under Barrault's aegis at the Odéon in 1967), he was interested in the play and therefore pleased when Carlos Semprun Maura offered him an effective translation. Set in a basement where three adolescent characters, Lalo, Cuca and Beba (played respectively by Francis Huster, Michèle Moretti and Hermine Karagheuz) enact a secret ritual, the action becomes a cruel exposé of their parents and reveals their suffering under the rigid hierarchy of a bourgeois family. With its background of pre-revolutionary Cuba, in which the petty bourgeois imitated the colonial estate owners, Blin felt that the play's political

---

34   Blin, 'Le Crime de Minimata', in Takahashi, *Minimata and Co.*, p.3.
35   Blin, *Souvenirs et propos*, p.287.
36   Blin, 'Le Crime de Minimata', p.3.

thrust was universally applicable in that it represented a violent attack on the institution of the family. Blin was attracted strongly to this provocative element, constructed upon the ambiguous relationship between the different characters which created, as he saw it, a kind of strong incestuous relationship and he sought to emphasise it in his *mise en scène* by arranging tussles between the characters which incorporated intimidating physicality and a good deal of rolling around on the floor.

The work of another Cuban, Eduardo Manet (whom he had met in 1951 as a student on one of the courses he ran for the E.P.J.D.), provided Blin with further new material of interest. In 1969 he directed Manet's *Les Nonnes* (*The Nuns*) at the Théâtre de Poche-Montparnasse and staged the same author's *Lady Strass* there eight years later. In a programme note for the latter of these two plays, which Manet considered the opening and closing pieces of a triptych,[37] the playwright identified the common ground between his plays as the 'class struggle seen from a perspective of dark humour, and the impossibility of an authentic human relationship in a world in which money and social success are the only criteria for happiness.'[38] With *Les Nonnes*, in which he drew upon his personal experience of Castro's 'people's revolution', Manet sought to show aspects of a society in a state of revolt and perverse elements of human response to such an upheaval, remarking in a programme note to the play: 'When violence is brewing in the streets, primitive fears are triggered in a lot of people.'[39] Set in Haïti during the slave revolt of the nineteenth century, *Les Nonnes* is centred upon a rich aristocrat (played by Suzel Goffre in Blin's production) who accepts the protection of three nuns, played by men (Étienne Bierry, André Julien and Pierre Byland), who shelter her from the uprising but who plan only to rob her of her jewellery and escape by fleeing to a neighbouring island. The play offers a portrait of greed, opportunism and betrayal and is suffused by

37   *Les Nonnes, L'Autre Don Juan* and *Lady Strass*.
38   Manet to Jorge Amat, programme for *Lady Strass*, Théâtre de Poche-Montparnasse, 18.3.77.
39   Manet in the programme for *Les Nonnes*, Théâtre de Poche-Montparnasse, 5.5.69.

the atmosphere of panic which these generate. The revolution, and the divisions in society that brought it about, are not discussed. Instead, by focusing on the vagaries of human behaviour in response to social disorder, Manet aims to promote a socio-political awareness without recourse to overt didacticism. He constructed his play on the premise that 'latent anxiety and fear of revolution exposes a variety of re-actions in people' and hoped to demonstrate how '[p]eople's best as well as their worst emotions come to the fore whenever a revolution or any catastrophe occurs.[40] The background to *Lady Strass* is not dissimilar: an English widow (played by Éléonore Hirt) has chosen to remain in Bélize after the former colony has gained independence from Britain, having for company a young man who has previously acted as servant to an exiled Nazi. The play opens as two fugitive criminals (played by Étienne Bierry and Tony Gatlif) break into her boarded-up home, assuming it to be empty, only to find themselves held captive by the suspecting expatriate. Colette Godard's review of Blin's production noted how Manet's treatment of this situation veers distinctly away from the didactic towards the theatrical:

An English woman, a French man, an Indian and the phantom of a Nazi in an enclosed space. The situation could lend itself straightforwardly to a thesis play. Eduardo Manet had preferred to complicate matters, shaking the whole up to create a multi-coloured cocktail, an enigmatic knot with poetic, dreamlike, bar-oque, even burlesque tendencies.[41]

In both plays, then, Manet's views emerge through the develop-ment of the action and the relationships between characters rather than through direct comment. It was the humanity of such plays that commended them to Blin, and their theatricality lured him more than their ideological content as such: their power to make implicit social comment lay embedded in their emotional texture. Commenting in 1977 on his two most recent productions of *Lady Strass* and Athol Fugard's *Boesman et Léna*, Blin spoke specifically of his interest in the authenticity of the emotion in the plays and 'the essential problems

40   Manet to Simone Benmussa, in *L'Action théâtrale*, 2 (1969), p.16.
41   Colette Godard, *Le Monde*, 26.3.77.

they raise, in these cases racism and the pain of emigration'.[42] They did not confront racism or emigration directly, nor were they plaintive indictments of social conditions, but instead they examined human responses, both positive and negative, to such experiences. As he said of the characters in Fugard's play, 'They exist from a human perspective and not simply as mouthpieces for the Black cause'.[43]

Beyond its apparent critique of the system of apartheid in the playwright's native country, Fugard's play seems to be an attempt to express dramatically a much more fundamental contemplation of the human condition. As such, this play occupies the middle ground of Blin's directorial spectrum. Notwithstanding the palpable realism of the dialogue and the environment through which the characters roam, he found the humour of the play and the profound humanity of its three characters irresistible, as the dramatic interest is focused on their tragic plight rather than the socio-political situation which is its cause. Political comment is made indirectly, but with undeniable force as the play presents a view from inside the guts of apartheid.

Boesman and his wife Lena arrive on stage to the barking of dogs and the squealing of gulls. The scene is a neutral one, 'an empty stage' as Fugard specifies in the text, somewhere on a path out on the mudflats of the Swartzkopf river, seven miles from Port Elizabeth. Cast out of their shanty that morning, the couple are homeless but free, being 'coloureds' (as opposed to 'blacks' who, under the apartheid laws, could not venture outside their townships) to roam the countryside and make what living they can from scrounging chores and collecting bottles for the deposits. Settling for the night on the mudflats, the couple become aware of an old man in the shadows. Lena invites him to join them, much to Boesman's displeasure. Despite her not being able to speak the old man's Xhosa dialect Lena befriends him and, in a sadly absurd scene, attempts to confide her sorrows in him. The old man dies, after being struck by Boesman, and the couple depart, afraid of the implications of a murder charge.

Despite the vivid poverty which the play put on show for its audience, it offers no overt political statement: Fugard's characters are

42   Blin in *La Tribune de Genève*, 15.7.77.
43   Blin, *Souvenirs et propos*, p.283.

politically inarticulate and their primary concern is simply their daily survival. Their very ineloquence on the subject of the social order which keeps them 'in their place', and their desperate resignation to the material inadequacy of their existence makes the point all the more starkly. However, by concentrating so graphically on the human consequences of an unjust system, the play effectively frustrates any evasion of the blatant injustice presented. By depicting characters at each others' throats, Fugard shows how all three are victims of a dehumanising society and Blin was particularly struck by the way in which the social sickness of segregational policies is seen to have entered the blood of the 'coloured' characters themselves:

> What excited me in *Boesman and Léna* was the extremely vigorous criticism of Apartheid, but above all the fact that this denunciation of Apartheid could be read not just in the speeches the characters deliver on their experiences with the whites, but also in the kinds of segregation and racism between the black characters.[44]

That Blin, who had an active interest in the issue of apartheid long before he encountered *Boesman et Léna*,[45] should have seized on it as a powerful dramatic weapon is scarcely surprising, as his passion for the fundamental issues presented by the play was undeniable:

> The abasement, the crushing of the individual by society is very strong in South Africa... a hell that is unknown elsewhere. All the big problems are stirred up in the mud, and that's what interests me.[46]

When asked directly in interview whether he was attracted to the play by its political dimension or its poetic quality his answer was an evasive one, and he remarked instead that his primary interest in the play was 'its profound humanity'.[47] The socio-political environment of the work creates an uncertain world where there are no easy answers

---

44   Blin, *Souvenirs et propos*, p.281.
45   He had taken part, for example, in a protest and benefit concert at the Orsay Theatre in 1973 in favour of the South African poet and activist Breyten Breytenbach.
46   Blin to Françoise Hubscher, in *Jeune Afrique*, 801, 14.5.76.
47   Ibid.

to the questions posed, only a struggle for existence to continue. In this way, the play functions broadly as a metaphor for the human condition, and there is evidence to suggest that this was as much Fugard's intention as it was to write a political play. As the play was in its embryonic form Fugard puzzled over quite what it was he had to express, and tried to define the mood of a vivid memory that served as inspiration. He remembered a day when he had to turn away a Lena figure, having had no job to offer her:

> Last sight of her about two hours later... trudging up the hill... That hill, the sun, the walk! Possibly even a walk that my Lena has not yet made, but will one day in the course of the little time that lies ahead of her as she takes up her load and follows the frightened Boesman across the mudflats. A walk beyond the moment of rebellion – that possible past, even forgotten... a walk into the final ignominy of silence, burdened at the moment as never before by those unanswerable words... Why? How? Who? What?[48]

Critics at Blin's French première of the play were not oblivious to this. Jacques Poulet's review in *L'Humanité* likened it to a meeting of Beckett and Büchner in the Transvaal landscape[49] and Pierre Marcabru in *France-Soir* confessed his thoughts turned immediately to Beckett, and wrote of how Blin's '*mise en scène* is inscribed with a sort of tangible solitude, like that in *En attendant Godot.*'[50] Matthieu Galey spoke of the evocative effect of the play: 'It's no fun! You come out of it wounded. However far away, however foreign it seems, this misery is ours too.'[51] The comparison to Beckett, if overstated, is not without foundation. Two characters in search of employment, of a home, of an ultimate meaning to their lives, lost in a nondescript landscape, and locked in a volatile, dysfunctional relationship outside of which neither could survive; the parallel to *En attendant Godot* is self-evident. Lena's list-like repetition of the route she and her husband have taken since the morning in her futile attempt to distinguish the surroundings from places already seen, is a routine to be sure of,

---

48   Athol Fugard, *Boesman and Lena and other plays* (Oxford: Oxford University Press, 1978), p.xxii.

49   *L'Humanité*, 12.5.76.

50   Pierre Marcabru, *France-Soir*. 21–22.6.76.

51   Matthieu Galey, *Le Quotidien de Paris*, 4.5.76.

like Winnie's toothbrush and Hamm's pain-killer. Her attempt to locate herself, to assert some conscious control over the repetitious nature of her existence and work out how the past has brought her to the present, is ultimately absurd:

> Boesman – What difference does it make? To anything? You're here now. [...]
> Lena – Every time we come back here it feels like I've never left.[52]

'Here' is nowhere, a wasteland of dirt and industrial scrap. They carry their lives on their heads and in their arms, all their possessions bundled up and weighing them down with as powerful a metaphoric load as Lucky's suitcases. They drag their life around, heavy and tiresome, from place to place, each new place as infertile as the last. There is no progression, no hope for improvement in their unending search, only a slow deterioration and a reluctant acceptance of their lot. It is strongly tempting to conclude that Blin's enthusiasm for this play stemmed from a recognition within it of much of what we have established he cherished most in dramatic writing: 'What appeals to me above all else are human issues,' he said of his choice of plays, 'provided that they are filtered through an effective text and that gives way to a certain formal beauty.'[53] As can be expected, Blin's work consisted primarily of working with his actors to examine the human elements of the play and present the characters' plight by approaching each one's individual response to the condition of life rather than turn them into mouthpieces for the attack of apartheid. He spoke of how his *mise en scène* 'should attempt to suggest reality, not reproduce it. As it unravels, it should allow the words to express their force and poetic dimension' and emphatically added '[t]hat's better than just giving a lecture, is it not?[54]

Though it is clear that Blin was not interested in political statement at the expense of theatricality, it is also true that, conversely, to underestimate the importance he attached to political content would be a misrepresentation of his temperament. He did not so much avoid making statements as believe that their place was within the fabric of

52   Fugard, *Boesman and Lena and other plays*, p.246.
53   Blin, *Souvenirs et propos*, p.59.
54   Blin to Françoise Hubscher, in *Jeune Afrique*, 801, 14.5.76.

the drama, and of the manner in which an audience interacted with a performance. 'I don't seek out scandal,' he claimed, 'but if there is at the same time a sort of elation in provocation and if there is beauty too, that makes me very happy.'[55] An example of this desire to provoke can be found in a twist at the end of his 1972 production of *Macbeth*. Rather than a struggle of righteousness over inhuman ambition, he interpreted the play as a nightmarish account of petty gang warfare and Malcolm's accession in the final scene was presented not as a triumph of justice, but instead as the transfer of corrupt authority from one king to the next: 'Malcolm [...] states that he will "perform in measure", and only lay claim to what is his. Nothing is to say he won't be worse than the rest.'[56]

Dealing with a Shakespeare play, Blin presumably felt he could allow himself the indulgence of an interpretation of this order. With contemporary plays, on the other hand, he avoided any such personal input of a political nature, limiting himself to minor details which served to underline the author's intentions. In his 1967 Rotterdam production of Genet's *Het Balkon*, for instance, he introduced a small cloth, the colours of the Dutch (and, consequently, the French) tricolour flag, into the opening scene, and later in the play Irma entered dressed as the Queen of the Netherlands. Similarly, his costuming of the colonial whites in *Les Paravents* was intentionally non-specific while at the same time offering a suggestion of British, Dutch and French colonials. For the second half of his production of Weingarten's *Les Charognards* Blin added a huge backdrop of a map of Vietnam as a permanent reminder of the relationship between the action of the play and the war which was its background.

Such insidious or oblique handling of political and social reference was in keeping with Blin's instinctive distrust of plays that set out to lecture an audience. Although he considered the theatre a valid forum for addressing political issues, he did not believe that it was a function of drama to provide solutions. Whether or not he agreed with their point of view he fought shy of plays that sought to force it upon an audience:

55   Blin to Emmanuelle Klausner, *La Croix*, 10.2.83.
56   Blin, 'Les vers du nez', p.169.

I very much like Sartre the polemicist, and the philosopher. But as a playwright, I'm nowhere near, given that for him it was the dialectic that counted above everything else, having a concept to prove, putting it into play with characters and so on. It's the opposite approach to that of Genet, Beckett and Artaud.[57]

The essence of Martin Esslin's definition of a 'Theatre of the Absurd' is to posit this distinction between the theatre of Camus and Sartre (and to some extent that of Anouilh and Giraudoux) on the one hand and, on the other, that of Beckett, Adamov and Genet, whose work, he says, 'renounced arguing *about* the absurdity of the human condition; it merely *presents* it in being – that is, in terms of concrete stage images'.[58] He described Blin, who was orientated to the new drama, as 'one of the most important directors of the Theatre of the Absurd',[59] in other words, of plays of a revolutionary but non-cathartic type of drama. Blin's preference for the avant-garde drama of the 1940s and 1950s to the works of the Existential philosophers, or to Anouilh whose use of the play within a play bored him, or to Giraudoux whose work he considered to be 'the most abominable of all'[60] is clear evidence of a taste for plays that functioned specifically in a theatrical context, the scripts of which would be lacking as simple literary artefacts, were inventive in structure or innovative in form and which, most importantly, conveyed an ambivalent reflection on human issues without making overt political comment. He never compromised his love of stage poetry:

> To me, avant-garde theatre is the opposite of political lecturing. I don't like plays that spring from a preconceived idea. With Beckett, I was straight away taken by each phrase in which both comic and tragic were mixed. Humour explodes through a very, very everyday language.[61]

His affiliation with the writers of the avant-garde and with the 'nouveau théâtre' awkwardly labelled 'absurd' in his early directing

57   Blin to Joan Stevens, from an unpublished interview, 2.3.75, Fonds Blin, IMEC, Paris, p.19.
58   Martin Esslin, *The Theatre of the Absurd* (London: Penguin, 1980), p.25.
59   Ibid., p.385.
60   Blin to Bettina Knapp, in *Tulane Drama Review*, 7.3 (1962), p.116.
61   Blin to Nella Bielski, in *Le Matin*, 1.4.77.

career can also be viewed in this light. Blin found great humanity in the plays of Adamov and Beckett and, more particularly, delighted in the opportunity such works gave him to disconcert an audience. 'When I read Beckett there was no question of politics,' he said, but considered staging *En attendant Godot* in 1953 as much a 'militant act' as he did his production of *Les Nègres* six years later, knowing the play 'was going to raze to the earth three quarters of the theatre.' In 1963 he maintained that these new authors, despite the distancing from specific social reference in their works, could not 'remain disinterested in fascism, anarchy, capitalism, in man's exploitation of man,' and that '[i]t is impossible to have a theatre today which does not reflect these problems, which is not tinged with blood.'[62] His initial response to the master/servant relationship of Pozzo and Lucky (see pp.104–5), his view of Hamm as a vain bourgeois clutching to some devalued vestige of power, or his emphasis on the persecution of characters in Adamov's plays testify in part to a 'political' view of the new drama, 'political', that is, in the sense that he was moved by the 'desperate tenderness',[63] with which characters were portrayed in situations that were beyond their control and comprehension and which they had little hope of overcoming. In a sense, then, he saw the avant-garde of the 1950s and 1960s as a fulcrum balancing the axis between poetry and politics; the contingency of the human condition, the essence of the struggle of existence and its implications in man's need for company are implicitly political notions, however divorced the presentation of these notions may be from actual worldly events or specific questions of political persuasion and political activity.

Blin's defence of the 'nouveau théâtre', and the personal aesthetic that this defence evinces, might also be contextualised in the intellectual climate of post-war theatre making in France. 'Is it possible for us to imagine today the importance that the theatre had in those years?' asked sociologist Jean Duvignaud of this period, pointing out that the 'theatre had held onto the literary and intellectual significance that it commanded in Europe and above all in France

---

62   Blin to Bettina Knapp, in *Tulane Drama Review*, 7.3 (1962), p.123.
63   Blin in *Combat*, 4.6.52.

since the seventeenth century'.[64] Between Blin's receipt of *En atten-dant Godot* in 1949 and its première in 1953, Paris had seen the opening of a revived Théâtre National Populaire (rebranded the T.N.P.) by Jean Vilar in 1951. This event initiated widespread debate over the ambitions and objectives of a truly 'public' theatre; issues of reper-toire, staging and audience were deliberated alongside questions of the responsibility of the theatre to address issues of social class and the relationship of the individual to society and the state. In 1953, the newly established journal *Théâtre populaire*, founded by Roland Barthes and associates, became the principle organ of such discussion, and the prime supporter of a politically engaged theatre. When Brecht's Ber-liner Ensemble brought their production of *Mother Courage* to Paris the following year, Barthes found his model for a theatre that might usefully invite an audience to deconstruct the processes of meaning that cause and control social attachments.

1953–5 had been a busy period for Blin, rehearsing and touring his French and a German *mises en scène* of Beckett's play, and conse-quently marking himself out as distinctly, notoriously even, set apart from the new social theatre. His first post-*Godot* production was of *Marée basse*, a play by the *Théâtre populaire* critic Jean Duvignaud, whom he had known from various political meetings. Duvignaud had wanted to write an anti-military play and on Jean-Marie Serreau's ad-vice had made his principle character an Arab, effecting a contentious nod at the Algerian War that had broken out in 1954. Blin had recent-ly signed the 'Manifeste des 121' (see pp.160–1) and as such, the play represented Blin's first militant production, and perhaps also an effort to engage with the 'popular' theatre structures of the times, including Duvignaud's attempted assimilation of Brecht's theories. Set in a penal colony, where Gédeon (played by a young Laurent Terzieff) is im-prisoned on suspicion of killing his benefactor, a retired army officer, the play worked in two halves, the second offering a 'play within a play' scenario where the protagonist is made to re-enact the night of the alleged murder.

---

64   Jean Duvignaud, '"Théâtre populaire": Histoire d'une revue.' *Magazine Lit-téraire*, 314 (October 1993), pp.63–64 (p.63).

Performed at the Noctambules in January 1956, the production received a poor press but did gain considerable coverage in the March edition of *Théâtre populaire*, with articles by the play's author, by Michel Zéraffa and by Barthes, whose criticism of the production reveal much of Blin's attitude to political theatre, most notably his desire to provoke an audience, but also of Barthes's own adherence to Brecht's theories. 'To provoke the bourgeois by means of foul language or the brutality of the show, without giving that provocation any foundation in historical clarification, seems to me to carry great formalistic risks,' Barthes complained, describing the production as 'more a theatre of personal liberation that of collective persuasion'[65] and considered this in terms of Artaud's ambitions, something that must have rankled the director considerably.

Barthes dissatisfaction with *Marée basse* nevertheless accurately captures Blin's approach to the place of political debate in theatrical spectacle, and the 'formalistic risks' Barthes warned against would lead to the kinds of audience engagement that Blin sought. Blin's interest in Genet's plays gives us the best insight into this aspect of his working attitude. It has been shown that his desire to mount *Les Paravents* can be ascribed at least as much to the beauty of its construction and its powerful theatricality as to its militancy and audacity. Genet himself declared that he did not wish to communicate any form of political message beyond a satirical portrayal of the colonials and an impertinent side-taking amongst those whom he considered were morally stronger, and urged Blin not to politicise the play. Blin, argued that Genet 'does not try to correct the society he denounces. He does not try to substitute one order for another'.[66] Similarly, in *Les Nègres*, Genet can hardly be said to have presented the exponents of the black cause in a wholly positive light. These plays are undoubtedly political, but assuredly politically ambiguous. Indeed, Adamov criticised Blin's 1959 production of *Les Nègres* precisely because it did not make any directly applicable comment about racism.[67] Even

65   Roland Barthes, 'Sur "Marée basse", de Jean Duvignaud', *Théâtre populaire,* 17 (March 1956), pp.88–90.
66   Blin to Bettina Knapp, in *Tulane Drama Review*, 7.3 (1962), p.112.
67   Blin, *Souvenirs et propos*, p.137.

Fugard's *Boesman et Léna*, which appears to be more overtly concerned with the extreme implications of racism, had been passed for performance by the South African government's censors. As such, these plays are exemplary of the type of 'social' drama that Blin advocated; they could rattle cages without providing a clear argumentative target to which critics could respond, as any 'comment' was embedded in the emotional force of the plays in performance. Speaking, once again, of his approach to the *mise en scène* of *Les Paravents*, Blin clarified his attitude towards the political flavour of the play:

> There is no deliberate provocation, neither on the part of the author nor from me. An aggressive stance is not the goal. Beauty is the goal. It's the actors' job, the designers' job, my job to reproduce the maximum beauty in the work as we have read it, as far as our means permit. If there is no beauty, we have failed.[68]

There is, of course, no doubt that Blin had strong, extreme even, political views and he knew precisely against whom or what he stood. He was simply not convinced that theatre was a medium through which one could change the world. He felt rather that it could function to initiate a slow osmosis of new concepts and bring about an adjustment in the consensus of thought:

> I don't personally believe that Brecht brought one new communist into being nor that Beckett ever persuaded a single spectator to give up his daily struggle; that's not how it works, its reach is much further away, it can enter into an irrational part in each of us which might actually make a difference.[69]

At the time of his involvement with the Groupe Octobre, Blin and his comrades were ignorant of Brecht's *Lehrstücke*. Later, while greatly admiring Brecht's dramas for their lyricism Blin was left cold by their political charge, stating that 'the works of Brecht offer much more than what he wanted theoretically.'[70] If he admired the achievements of the German playwright he was nevertheless appalled by the ripples that radiated from the splash that his published theories made,

68   Blin to Nicole Zand, *Le Monde*, 16.4.66.
69   Blin in *Libération*, 15.6.77.
70   Blin in *De Groene Amsterdammer*, 21.11.59. Trans. Terence Raghunath.

and by the new artists and critics he referred to as 'Brechtian police',[71] who sought to have influence extended beyond the works of their master. The cold application of theory dismayed Blin: 'Just look at what some of his disciples have done with his theories beyond Brecht's texts' he once exclaimed, dismissing the dull theatrical work this may have produced.[72] Despite his pronounced political views he had a passionate distaste for the didactic, for the doctrinaire political engagement which spread through the new dramatic writing of the post-war period.

It was this distrust of the efficacy of drama as a tool for political argument that was the cause of his disenchantment with Adamov's later work. In fact, his reaction to Adamov's complete *œuvre* provides an accurate measure of the qualities Blin sought in a dramatic text. After welcoming the first plays with such enthusiasm, Blin dismissed pieces such as *Paolo-Paoli* (1957) and *Le Printemps 71* (*Spring '71, 1960*). Though he understood and sympathised with the motives behind their composition, he nevertheless felt these later plays lacked the qualities of humour and anguish and the lively dialogue that had characterised *La Parodie* and *La Grande et la Petite Manœuvre*. He was naturally disappointed when the inventive playwright turned towards composing 'thesis plays in which Adamov, the individualist, the man riddled with anxieties, has disappeared'.[73] With the latter's conversion to Communism, Blin felt that his friend had developed into a professionally engaged writer as opposed to the innocent for whom writing was a form of therapy, and who, through exorcising the demons that troubled him, had produced works of curious, haunting beauty. His later writing evinced a move away from Strindberg's influence towards that of Brecht which, for Blin, had served to deaden it:

> To me, they [the later plays] represent a kind of abandonment of what he was. The fear of a rootless person in a hostile city, exposed to the police, the conversation of a kind of child, were the themes of Adamov's plays. I became aware all of a sudden of a voluntary engagement with politics and the loss of an

---

71   Blin, *Souvenirs et propos*, p.59.
72   Blin in *De Groene Amsterdammer*, 21.11.59.
73   Blin to Bettina Knapp, in *Tulane Drama Review*, 7.3 (1962), p.124.

aspect that was what made him rare, his sense of humour. That distinctive sense of humour that allowed him to reproduce admirably well a certain petit-bourgeois language. There's an author who's pulled the rug from beneath his own feet.[74]

This attitude of striving to balance the poetic with the polemic was also reflected in the increasing difficulty that Blin experienced later in his life to find plays that satisfied his individual brand of theatrical provocation. As the differentiation between the political left and right shifted to become less conspicuous than it had been in the 1930s, so the targets became less clear, and in the late 1970s and early 1980s Blin felt politically disillusioned. 'There are no more models,' he complained. 'We were excited by the USSR, later by Mao, Castro. We were let down. Today, to be honest, you have to look for the least bad. I don't know where to look.'[75] In *Minimata and Co.*, a scene in which a union official accepts a bribe had a distinct and symptomatic force for him. Discouragement with the weakening of the left deprived him of suitable material: 'When I staged *The Screens*, *The Blacks*, *Boesman and Lena*, or even *Minimata and Co.*, it was clear. I knew who I was fighting against. Today, it's all become more confusing.'[76] The manifest failure of independence in some African countries to produce democratic states undermined the possibility of any consideration of a revival of *Les Nègres* (the original actors were unwilling to entertain a proposed revival in the 1970s).[77] When asked in 1983 if a subversive theatre was still possible, his answer was guarded:

> One is still possible. But it isn't so straightforward, like it used to be possible when I started out, or when I mounted *The Blacks*: I was very happy then to be able to strike out at the whites! Obviously, things are more complex these days.

74 Blin in Gaudy, *Arthur Adamov*, p.53.
75 Blin in *Libération*, 12.2.83.
76 Blin, *Souvenirs et propos*, p.295.
77 'In 1959, the time before the independence of Africa, it was easier to be [...] completely in favour of the blacks or against the whites. Nowadays [this is] no longer possible, since Amin Dada, Bocassa and people like that. It's for this reason that actors no longer want to revive the play.' Blin to J. Savona, *Entrevue de Roger Blin sur Jean Genet*, 14.10.80, Fonds Blin, IMEC, Paris, p.3.

What is certain is that you can't agitate in the name of a global aspiration any more.[78]

In retrospect, however, this lack of unifying aspiration serves to vindicate Blin's lifelong avoidance of didactic theatre and his determination to balance the interests of poetry and politics. In his *Souvenirs et propos* he claims to have enjoyed *Boesman et Léna* and *M'appelle Isabelle Langrenier* above all the productions of his later years,[79] precisely because they possessed this balance and confirmed his belief that 'a good text complies with all requirements simultaneously'.[80] His whole career was characterised by attempts to satisfy these competing demands and to fit the square peg of his anger into the round hole of his aesthetic tastes:

Stage directors of my generation and those of the generation that followed us have sought to resolve the squaring of the circle, that of a free theatre, one that maintains human values and holds political significance. But for us, especially those of us on the left, the themes were quite straightforward. It's far more complicated today. None of us, to tell the truth, has global aspirations. You can always say that you're making art, but that isn't enough. I don't want to make escapist theatre.[81]

78   Blin to Emmanuelle Klausner, in *La Croix*, 10.2.83.
79   Blin, *Souvenirs et propos*, p.299.
80   Blin in *De Groene Amsterdammer*, 21.11.59.
81   Blin to Vincent Phillipe, in *Télé-soirs*, 21/21.8.82.

A Methodology

In the obituaries that appeared following his death, Roger Blin's legacy was appraised not simply by the listing of his many achievements, but principally by evoking the nature of his working character. He was depicted as 'an artist who never broke faith'[1] and as a director who was 'clear, precise, warm'.[2] His temperament was summed up as his being 'an eternal student, a distant dreamer'[3] and an 'imperturbable apprentice';[4] someone who was always prepared to adopt fresh approaches and consider new perspectives. Odette Aslan concludes her study of Roger Blin by describing his legacy as a seamark that might act as to steer less vigilant practitioners on course.[5] It is the aim of this final chapter to offer an analysis of this guiding light, to examine the techniques Blin employed to achieve the remarkable results of which he was capable, and go some way towards defining the methodology of a director who sought to leave no trace.

When Blin directed his first production at the age of forty-two, his reputation as an actor was already firmly established. For many, his work up to that point represented all that was exemplary about the experimental drama and non-commercial theatres of the Parisian Left Bank and he was considered '"the purest of the pure" of the avant-garde theatre.'[6] Boris Vian described him at this time as an artist of integrity, as 'too much an enemy of compromise to have totally

1   René Saurel, 'Cendres fertiles de Roger Blin', *Les Temps Modernes*, 40 (1984), p.2347.
2   Jean Martin in *Parcours de Roger Blin*, programme to the 'Exposition Roger Blin' at the Théâtre du Rond-Point, 24.1.85 to 17.2.85.
3   Irène Sadowska-Guillon, 'La partie n'est pas finie', *L'Avant-Scène Théâtre*, 764, 15.2.85, pp.66–7 (p.66).
4   Bernard Dort, 'Blin: l'imperturbable débutant', *Théâtre en Europe*, 2 (April 1984), pp.18–19 (p.19).
5   'Like a lighthouse', Aslan, *Roger Blin*, pp.159–60.
6   Henry Magnan, *Le Monde*, 4.6.52.

succeeded so far.'[7] Once in charge of a theatre, he was to some degree expected to carry the torch of those innovators before him who had striven to bring quality and dignity to the profession. Journalist Jean le Forêt, summing up the expectations held of Blin early in his career as director, declared that, in the artistic direction of the Gaîté-Mont-parnasse, a theatre of integrity was still very much alive:

> Since Pitoëff's disappearance, Dullin semi-retirement, the retirement, alas, of Baty and Jouvet's now solely commercial work, we were beginning to worry whether we would ever again see the reappearance of true theatre enthusiasts. We already knew that Roger Blin belonged to such a group of people, but until now he had no theatre. With the help of Christine Tsingos, he has found one and the three shows he has put on there in a few months demonstrate a quality that predestines him to play a significant role at a time when money, above all else, sets the tone and determines the quality and length of all artistic efforts![8]

In a letter that Blin wrote at this time, during his production of *La Sonate des spectres*, he explained how he set about creating the necessary atmosphere for the piece, and discussed a little the way in which he approached the role of director:

> I have fewer and fewer theories about theatre. What's more, I've preferred to work my friends [the actors] as though we were dealing with a contemporary crime drama, to maintain a human grounding, and then to lift the tone, rather than going straight away for disorientation. The play has anyway demonstrated itself in practice to be much more robustly constructed than one would have thought.[9]

It is interesting that in 1949, just as Blin was embarking on a career as director in the theatre that would continue for the rest of his life, he should express the opinion that he had come to hold 'fewer and fewer theories about theatre'. It is revealing that he should have digested the numerous and varied sources of influence to which he had been exposed in his acting career and come to the practical conclusion that the best approach is one of flexibility, and of

7   Boris Vian, *Manuel de Saint Germain des Près* (Paris: Le Chêne, 1974), p.164.
8   Jean le Forêt, *Heure médicale*, December 1949.
9   Letter from Blin to Henri Membré, dated 11.10.49, quoted in Swerling, *Strind-berg's Impact in France*, p.180.

214

sensitivity to the text. In this first, and rare example of Blin's thoughts on how he has achieved an effect he gave away only a vague suggestion of any working method. The result with Strindberg's play was to arrive at a performance which did not attempt to be anything more, nor to say anything more, than the director believed its author had set down in ink. Jacques Lemarchand summed up Blin's accomplishment then as 'the work of someone who knows Strindberg, who knows the mass of things that his head was stuffed with',[10] implying the director's intuitive response to the author's creative ambitions. If this was Blin's ethos, then it was barely to change in the following thirty-five years of his career. Here, at this earliest stage of his work as director, we can already see an inkling of the way in which Blin worked his actors, his non-intellectual approach and the manner in which he discovered a text in rehearsal. Most significantly, as an accomplished actor taking on the role of director he was concerned primarily with what an author that he admired had to say, and wanted simply to let this be heard as clearly as possible. In any attempt to know something of the director, we are deflected and brought back to the playwrights whose work he sought to mount.

Roger Blin's relationship with his work might be considered more that of a craftsman than of a practitioner. He never thought of himself as a theatre professional, and only undertook productions when he felt driven to do so: 'I have to be kicked in the arse by my pride, by the given poetry, or by the desire to piss people off,'[11] he once claimed, later adding 'I couldn't make theatre eleven months out of twelve. I want to draw too, and read... I can make do with dole money, my needs are few.'[12] This attitude explains in part why he never felt compelled to write about his work, would refuse to or felt unable to indulge in theorising, and declined to be drawn into any analysis of the dramatic processes he exercised. For example, reluctantly drawn once into a theoretical discussion, and asked whether he saw his friend Adamov's work in terms of the 'Absurd', as delineated by Martin Esslin, he replied: 'I am completely incapable of making

10   Jacques Lemarchand, *Combat*, 25.10.49.
11   Blin to Maria Crapeau, *France Observateur*, 17.10.63.
12   Blin to Fabienne Pascavel, *Télérama*, 11–17.11.78.

classifications,' and added, 'I can only speak of what I have experienced, of a direct attachment I have had with the theatre.'[13] This strict view of himself as an artisan goes some way towards explaining why, after his ill-fated period as manager of the Gaîté-Montparnasse, he never became attached to one theatre, nor would he accept any appointment which was anything more than nominal (such as his being named co-director of the Théâtre Récamier by Madeleine Renaud and Jean-Louis Barrault in 1971). His freedom to choose what to produce, and when to do so, was of paramount importance to him.

Not only did Blin refrain from writing and publishing his thoughts on the theatre, neither did he keep notes during the process of putting plays onto the stage. He did not believe in preparing material before rehearsals and he rarely noted down comments during or after them. Only four examples of Blin's note-taking are extant and the paucity of such material is straightforwardly demonstrative of how little reliance he placed upon it. Of these four, two are concerned solely with lighting (the notes for *La Parodie* [see pp.86–7] and *M'appelle Isabelle Langrenier*), another consists simply of two pages of annotations detailing plans for the prologue and first scene of *Ein Traumspiel* (see pp.220–2) while the fourth, and most significant, is a collection of eight pages of notes taken during run-throughs of *Oh les beaux jours* (see pp.125–7). In the rehearsal room he worked off the top of his head, as it were, discovering the texture of the pieces he was working on in collaboration with his actors as they progressed towards performance, sketching scenes, discovering movements. He rarely discussed his directing in interviews and chose instead, on such occasions, to laud the creativity of the authors whose work he was producing, promoting their achievements and not his own. Only in later interviews, in which he himself was the sole subject of the journalist's interest, can he be found more freely discussing his own work. This scarceness of primary sources is the first stumbling block in any detailed assessment of Roger Blin's *oeuvre*.

13   Blin to Emmanuel C. Jacquart, 'Adamov etait le roi des trois points: Interview avec Roger Blin', *French Review*, 48.6 (May 1975), pp.996–1004 (p.1003).

A Blin production

Often, a director's work can be noted by certain characteristic traits or 'signature' techniques left consciously or accidentally in a *mise en scène*, which visibly marks it as their work. Blin, however, voiced the ambition to create productions that stood independent of his input and that would speak as strongly and characteristically as possible with the voice of their author. He recognised the crucial significance of the director's contribution to a performance, but disapproved of the practice of stamping an author's work with the brand of a director. 'I don't give a damn about the signature,' he once declared, 'the signature is that of the ensemble or of the author. And I'm wary of ensemble work because there is always a leader.'[14] When once asked directly if he chooses simply to 'serve the text' he replied that he'd much rather discover things in that way: 'I get a greater pleasure from discovery than from saying "This will be a Blin production, it'll be great. It's not quite as it should be but who cares about the author?"'[15] Yet, without such a 'signature', the distinctive colour or imprint that would create the 'Blin production', there is no obvious way of identifying a working method or any characteristic stance.

Blin evolved certain abstract notions of what might constitute his ideal theatre. With these in mind, one might speculate what shape a 'Blin production' might have had. It is certain, for example, that for Blin the theatre was a place for both magic and confrontation, for both the poetry and the politics that appealed to him in newly discovered texts. When recalling his production of Shakespeare's *Macbeth*, for example, he stated that he had worked from the premises of 'the baroque and ambiguity', which he believed constituted 'the theatre's lifeblood'.[16] By the word 'baroque' he meant the absorbing, illusionistic potential of a detailed, crafted stage image. In other interviews he explained, for example, how he liked dealing with large casts and

14 Blin in *Libération*, 14.6.77.
15 Blin in Tom Bishop and Raymond Federman (eds.), *Samuel Beckett* (Paris: L'Herne, 1976), p.146.
16 Blin, *Souvenirs et propos*, p.258.

large sets, and how he was fascinated by the scenic potential of multiple levels.[17] Interestingly, he once offered a vision of an imaginary production, describing it as 'a tragedy on a bare stage with only nets, suspended from which the actors could deliver their speeches'.[18]

Blin once commented that a production of his own would resemble the type of expression he achieved in his drawings. Much of the body of work he produced consisted of frantically etched images in wiry, thick black lines of Indian ink, representing tortured characters or abstract forms. These, which he self-mockingly referred to as his 'electrocardiograms',[19] offered a highly personal vision of the world. This body of work is Blin's fullest, freest form of expression and was for him as much a kind of therapy as it was an outlet for artistic creation: 'If you know how to scream, you know how to draw',[20] he once explained. Applying this sentiment to the theatre has powerful consequences, seen best perhaps in the outrage he sought to communicate in productions such as *Les Paravents*, *Minimata and Co.* and *Les Charognards*. The implied expressionism in his statement might also allow us to infer a rejection of straightforward realism in favour of a more symbolic approach, and he did frequently advocate a rediscovery of a purely theatrical language or space and gesture: 'Certain conventions need to be re-established, returning to ideograms,' he once said, offering by way of example: 'if a black screen crosses the stage, let that mean that night has fallen.'[21] In this respect he often spoke of his high regard for the simplicity of Oriental theatre techniques, as he understood them, and bemoaned the lack of such conventions in European theatre: he admired, for instance, how 'In Japan you can go up a few steps and people will accept that you are on Mount Fujiyama.'[22] Blin's ideal theatre art, therefore, would make use

17 'Personally I like great masses and movement, a big cast.' Blin to Peter Lennon, *Guardian*, 20.9.63.
18 Blin to Nicholas Garnham, in *Varsity*, 20.5.61.
19 Blin in a note in the programme to an exhibition of his drawings, later used as the preface to the posthumously published collection of his drawings: *Dessins – Festival d'Avignon*.
20 Ibid.
21 Blin in *Combat*, 3.5.66.
22 Blin to Peter Lennon, in *Guardian*, 20.9.63.

of such conventions, where simple movements and gestures might hold metaphorical force and could efficiently convey mood, intent and experience to an audience. Perhaps he even envied periods in the history of the theatre, such as in ancient Athens or Elizabethan London, when theatrical entertainment was integral to how a society considered and debated its achievements and values:

> I think the theatre will come into its own only when it returns to its origin: the open air. There should be only a platform, a place raised above the audience as in the ancient theatres. The proscenium theatre is outmoded, particularly in the way it segregates the audience according to money. I like amphitheatres, where everyone can see. Lighting should return to the sun.[23]

The elements of Blin's philosophy identified here define a theatre where audience and actor consciously occupy the same space and collaborate in the cathartic act, one where signs and conventions participate in creating in each performance a unique, spontaneous cultural event, experienced and invested in by the spectator both emotionally and intellectually, one where the consuming illusionism of the theatre could capture an audience's imagination, shock and surprise them and provide moments of self-revelation. Perhaps the closest he got to achieving these ideals was in his production of *Les Paravents*, which was certainly one of his most personally satisfying. When he was given the opportunity to direct Strindberg's *Ein Traumspiel* (*A Dream Play*) at the Zurich Schauspielhaus in 1975, he found that it accommodated his vision quite straightforwardly. Speaking of his admiration of Strindberg, Blin again summarised his attitude to the theatre:

> I have a quite magical vision of this play, and of theatre in general. However much Strindberg's texts are packed with symbols, the effects I seek in the theatre are not sophisticated, but of a magical, fairy-tale order, when the text permits, of course.[24]

It is this quality of 'magic', of deploying theatrical illusionism, that Blin enjoyed and he was most free to experiment when working either on plays that required a specific theatrical environment to be

---

23   Blin to Paul Gray, in *Tulane Drama Review*, 11.1 (1967), p.112.
24   Blin, *Souvenirs et propos*, p.69.

created for them in order to function dramatically (such as with *Minimata and Co.*, *Les Nègres* or *Les Paravents*) or for plays that were written with such density and which made such exacting demands of a director that a certain ingenuity was required to stage them. Strindberg's *A Dream Play* was just such an enigma to Blin, with its call for a rapidly metamorphosing acting space and an associated disjointed reality. Similarly, Shakespeare's *Macbeth* gave him an opportunity to indulge his fondness for illusionism:

> For *Macbeth*, I tried with the means at my disposal, which were all too few, to push the show towards a kind of magic. For example, I used ultra-violet lighting, which is a music-hall thing. So, in certain scenes, only light colours are seen; white, light blue – all other colours disappear. I was pleased to be able to make certain objects appear out of the dark, notably the murderer's knife which was painted on a piece of wood and which suddenly came out of no-where.[25]

Both these plays, and the interpretative opportunities mounting them offered, fitted the kinds of tastes outlined above and provided a legitimate opportunity for Blin to give free rein to his imagination in the elaboration of an otherwise restrained personal style. Significantly in this regard, these plays are two of only four texts by non-living authors that Blin ever directed. As such, these productions are likely to be of some use in establishing his working method and they both represent, arguably, some of the closest approximations to a 'Blin production' that he ever achieved. Here we see him at work in total independence from the author – or at least from his physical presence – but inspired by an enthusiasm for a favourite text, aspiring to do it the utmost justice by the application of a creative imagination.

Conspicuously, *Ein Traumspiel* was the only production for which Blin is known to have made preparatory notes in advance of rehearsals, an approach which he never otherwise advocated. Though it was not uncommon for him to note down his ideas before departing to work on a foreign language production abroad, in order better to facilitate working through an interpreting assistant director, Blin only felt this practice was necessary when transferring an already achieved

25   Ibid., p.251.

mise en scène, such as those of *En attendant Godot*, *Les Nègres* and *Les Paravents*, all of which he revived in foreign productions. The notes for *Ein Traumspiel* at Zurich are unique in that they seem to be prepared ahead of any rehearsals. What survives of these, however, is scant, amounting to no more than two pages in a large red notebook. These were apparently abandoned after the first scene of the play, leaving only that and the play's prologue 'prepared'. The notebook appears not to have any pages removed, which suggests that Blin may have started to put down his ideas in an inspired moment of enthusiasm but soon tired of the procedure. The notes are concerned with the whole stage picture and deal with all elements of the performance of these first scenes, including lighting, sound and other effects. They therefore give us a brief, rare insight into Blin's creative processes as he prepared himself for the production of a play which had previously been out of his financial league but which he nevertheless had long wanted to direct.[26] Within them, for instance, can be found a description of the manner in which Agnes was to descend from the heavens during the prologue, and this signals the slow, fluid style that Blin had in mind for the production:

> Gauze, lit low from front. Below, in the pit, downstage centre, the head of the sleeping poet. Gentle sleeping movements. Behind the tableau everything is still dark. Indra's voice in the dark. Agnes's 1st line, in the dark. Then the stars light up [...] then Agnes's face for the second line. Agnes still immobile – just before Indra's voice 'you have just left the 2nd universe' [...] Agnes begins to descend – a very slow movement [...] other lights: the constellation Libra. Other lights come up. 'I can see how beautiful it is' [...] in the centre sounds begin, plants can be made out – Agnes descends further and the cloud descends – on the descent 'it is pulling me down to earth.' Movement from the poet (perhaps his arms hide his face) when the light flashes on him [...] All of Indra and Agnes's recorded lines echo except the last word 'I'm falling' spoken live [...] actors get up in time to meet and hide her – cross-fade of lights to dark to remove Agnes's machinery.[27]

---

26 He had been disappointed when, in 1970, the Comédie-Française had arranged a production of *Le Songe* but had approached Raymond Rouleau, instead of himself, to provide the *mise en scène*.

27 Blin's notes are kept in the Archives Roger Blin at the Bibliothèque Nationale, département des arts du spectacle (Arsenal), Paris.

In performance, this outlined idea was fully realised. Renate Schroeter, in the role of Agnes, was placed upon a large pedestal, concealed from view beneath her long dress. As this platform lowered her towards the stage floor, clusters of oriental lamps representing the stars rose up to the flies to create a more intense illusion of her rapid descent to earth. As she reached the ground a group of extras, disguised and camouflaged as earth or flowers, rose gently to meet and engulf her, thereby permitting the actress to rid herself of the oversized dress and the harness which had brought her down and for these to be removed from the stage. In this way, Blin also succeeded in effecting the first smooth change of décor from the opening scene of stars and clouds to the forest of blooming hollyhocks designated by Strindberg. The fluidity of this first chain of orchestrated stage events, occupying perhaps no more than a minute or two of performance time, was to set the tone for the rest of the play which, under Blin's direction, would flow with dream-like smoothness from scene to scene. Another fine example of such nuances was his introduction of the Officer into the first stage-door scene. Wolfgang Stendaar in the role appeared with his bouquet of flowers from beneath a long shawl being knitted by the stage-door keeper, using a trapdoor to give the impression of his emerging out of the ground.

Blin contrived to realise all of Strindberg's fantastical directions within a theatrical milieu conceived to allow fully for the oneiric shifts of the written text, without awkward interruptions for scene changes. Blin wanted a décor that would transform itself before the eyes of the audience, with the use of only a few short blackouts, his underlying concept being that the stage was to appear to have a life of its own:

> There was a continuous movement of objects. Scenic elements moved around and from one scene to the next changed position. I was looking for a kind of fluidity with all scene changes made in full view. We'd put scenic elements on stage that were only used two or three scenes later. The appearance of objects or characters created permanent surprise. Everything was completely connected, as Strindberg had prescribed.[28]

---

28   Blin, *Souvenirs et propos*, p.272.

Not only did the decorative elements evolve and adapt from one appearance or usage to another in a later scene, but the numerous trap-doors of the Schauspielhaus stage floor were brought into use to facilitate sudden exits and entrances for actors and properties. Parts of the set would serve a multitude of purposes: Fingal's Cave, for example, was evoked by a manipulation of the church organ structure from the preceding scene, in the spirit of Strindberg's instructions. Blin extended another of the author's stipulations by having the gate, which had first appeared in the early scene with the officer, mutate into the counter in the advocate's office, and later the desk for the handing out of degrees, then to feature again in a different guise in the opera scene. For the ending of the advocate's scene, the actor playing the advocate was engulfed by the dismantled interior set within which the scene had been played, and disappeared from the stage with it.

Blin had applied this type of free-flowing movement three years earlier in his *mise en scène* of *Macbeth*. A good example of similar manipulation of time and space on stage in this production is provided by the attack on Dunsinane castle. For this actors came rushing down-stage in a dim green light, screaming and brandishing the branches that so troubled Macbeth (played by Jean-Pierre Kalfon). Birnam Wood had all the time been simply suggested upstage by having goboed green lights illuminating a gauze with the outline of forestry, but during this downstage charge a subtle change of lighting transformed the backcloth into a representation of the castle walls and the actors simply rounded their assault to return upstage towards it. In this way, having overcome the technical problem of conveying the rapid shift in location and the focus of attack in one swift movement, Blin also managed to intensify the rising climax to the play, thereby minimising the jarring nature of the short successive final scenes of Act five (often heavily cut in performance) and maintain the fluidity of the action from scene to scene without pause. Earlier, in the banquet scene during which Banquo's ghost appears to Macbeth, Blin orchestrated a whole sequence of movements between actors and extras to create the effect of hysteria. He had Banquo's ghost played by one of the many servants who entered with food and drink for the seated guests. A mask of the actor playing Banquo (Benoist Brione) was attached to the back of this servant's head and his costume was that of Banquo when seen from the rear. At the appropriate moments this servant would slowly walk backwards into the darkened upstage area, turn around and torment Macbeth with the sudden apparition of Banquo. As with *Ein Traumspiel*, all scene changes in *Macbeth* took place in full view of the audience, and some pieces of staging were manipulated by the actors themselves. An accomplished example of this occurred in the sleepwalking scene. Catherine Cadet as Lady Macbeth entered at an upper door in the set, from which the stage floor could not be safely reached. Timed to match her pace, a group of actors placed a staircase at her feet for her to complete her descent to the stage. This compares directly to the Zurich production of Strindberg's play, in which whenever an interior scene was to be evoked, actors walked on with pieces of stage wall and held them in place throughout the scene.

'Poetry is the only way of expressing reality'

Whilst preparing the revival of *En attendant Godot* at the Théâtre de l'Odéon in 1978, Blin and his designer Matias came to the conclusion that to create the least realistic impression of a tree on stage they should in fact use a real tree. This, they reasoned, when placed in the vacuous environment Vladimir and Estragon inhabited on the broad, deep stage of the Odéon, would assume the necessary aura of strangeness they both desired. Their intuition proved judicious and the fragile looking lemon tree that Matias acquired for the décor looked suitably out of place, standing in lonely isolation on the large stage. Part of Blin's specific talent was this keen intuition as regards what might work visually on stage and how, through a diversity of means, it is possible to conjure the appropriate static and fluid stage images for a play. This perspective then plays a role in forming the scenic environment within which a play may operate:

> I am not aesthetically in favour of Vilar's black drapes and have no prejudices, not even against realist decor. I'm not in favour of absolute fantasy and fantasy

can be very well understood in a single, straightforwardly realistic, element of decor. I am on the side of the real and could use a completely realistic decor if, at some point, a disruption comes about. I'm not interested in putting on a play in a bourgeois decor with a white telephone, but what would interest me is that at one moment the telephone gets eaten by one of the actors.[29]

By breaking with picture book realism, even in the context of a naturalistic set or situation, Blin aimed to provide the audience with the kind of mild shock that makes them apprehend a different level of reality. The tearing up of the paper sun to represent nightfall in *Les Paravents* is precisely such an effect (see p.179). The procedure is rooted in the Surrealist promotion of subjective reality. For Blin such a state of mind is the key to true realism:

> Take a telephone, for example; place it on a table on stage. That's all right. But I want that telephone to be able to eat, to talk, to have a life of its own. It must be an animate object. The prop must be a composite of what you see and what you have seen. The décor must be alive, move and breathe. It must be human. Take a street. The street most frequently placed on stage today is the street you see every day. If you reproduce it on the boards as such... well, I call this stupid realism. But the street you see at night when you are drunk – you see it in a different way. You are wobbly. The street turns, it assumes weird shapes, it's alive. What do you see in the street now? How do you see the street? This is true discovery. You are perceiving reality; for the first time all the bonds and restrictions have been broken. Objective reality has been dislocated. You now perceive a far deeper reality. That street has become flesh and blood for you.[30]

This observation is revealing in that it acknowledges the intoxicating power of the theatrical experience and thereby places Blin firmly in the Expressionistic European dramatic tradition, distanced from that group of political dramatists and practitioners of the twentieth century who distrusted and sought to disrupt the mesmeric effect of live drama. Blin made his political, moral and emotional impact by means of a subtle fabric of highly theatrical reality; a reality composed of poetic imagery and vocal constructions and the distinctive resources of the stage, one that offered the audience a world of tantalising uncertainty and beautiful coincidence:

29   Blin, *Souvenirs et propos*, p.61.
30   Blin to Bettina Knapp, *Tulane Drama Review*, 7.3 (1962), p.118.

In fact, poetry is the only way of expressing reality. Realism arises from this surrealistic fact. It should give the impression of 'never been seen', of the thing appearing for the first time, at every instant, all the time. A Louis XV salon would never be truly realistic except in a landscape of desert dunes.[31]

To achieve the ambition locked in such abstract conceptualisation, Blin would cultivate a state of mind vis-à-vis the production in hand. He would absorb himself totally in the world of a play and keep it in mind, almost obsessively, outside rehearsals. Once in the rehearsal room, he would try out ideas that had struck him in dreams or which had spontaneously come to mind, pursuing what might be an unconscious chain of associations. During the preparatory stages of his production of *Triptyque*, for example, he awoke one morning after having dreamt of the second act of the play taking place in a kind of subterranean aquarium.[32] He communicated this vision to his designer, Acquart, who then set about integrating the idea into his design. The second tableau of the play was in fact staged against a backdrop of large, convex, folds of white gauze. On another occasion, the isolation of two apes holding each other tight in a cage at the zoo gave him inspiration for physicalising the character dependency of Vladimir and Estragon in *En attendant Godot*. In 1957, during his stay in London for the première of *Fin de partie*, he saw a curious chair with legs and arm rests carved in the shape of human legs and arms in an antique shop on the King's Road and this, twenty years later, inspired him to visualise the grandmother in Jean-Louis Bauer's poem *M'appelle Isabelle Langrenier* as a large, rooted, totem-like character upon which her granddaughter would be able to sit. Again the designer, Chantal Petit, executed this scenic idea from his descriptions. Bauer's play held a specific attraction to Blin, who related directly to the character Isabelle Langrenier's inability to express herself clearly and eloquently. He instructed Petit to construct a carriage in the shape of a swan for the entrance of the character of the Cantatrice and this invocation of the plastic swan that was remembered as the cause of his stutter (see p.21) is a rare example of Blin allowing himself a personal indulgence in one of his *mises en scène*. His constant aim all the time,

31   Blin in *Combat*, 3.5.66.
32   Blin to Vincent Phillipe, in *Télé-soirs*, 21–22.8.82.

utilising such spontaneously generated images, was to attain the most direct form of communication with an audience:

> Don't neglect the text, don't deny the poetry, that's what has guided me. So, for a long time, I've had a saying which I often repeat, perhaps too often. I'm looking for density, and now I add the 'maximum affective density by honest means'. For without density there is no theatre, but everything in the theatre is a lie, so you have to know how to cheat honestly. It's simple.[33]

This search for 'affective density', of which he indeed spoke often, was Blin's way of identifying the essential truths he believed a play to carry and the means to communicate them as vividly and faithfully as possible ('I look for things that might be the object of a communication with the audience.')[34] This acquired state of mind during production was the source of the vigour that Blin was able to bring to each new production. A number of his *mises en scène* were marked by strokes of inspiration connected with this search for affective density, the search for beautiful means of communicating the layered tones of a piece of written drama. Blin, a 'visual glutton'[35] by his own admission, was able to appropriate images and incidents from everyday life and transfer them cleverly onto the stage, enhancing the dramatic texture of the text he was serving. This process was in no way calculated or analytical, but relied on intuition and instinct, and a keen eye for detail. Still less were ideas like the humanoid chair or the deathly aquarium incorporated gratuitously, but rather as a way of communicating the tones of a piece, of furthering its development in rehearsal or establishing a precise environment for it.

When searching for a way of presenting the dead in *Triptyque* he wanted to create an impression of non-living characters without resorting to hackneyed images of pale walking corpses or decomposing zombies. Perhaps remembering how he had marked the dead in his production of *Les Paravents* by circling their faces with a thin line of make-up he chose a similar symbolic approach for Frisch's characters by making up their faces in a strongly unpleasant pink colour,

---

33   Blin, *Souvenirs et propos*, p.60.
34   Blin in *Libération*, 15.6.77.
35   Hermine Karagheuz to Mark Batty, 5.1.95.

'the colour of lung tissue'.[36] In addition, he encouraged his actors to invent a particular walk and voice for these denizens of Frisch's limbo zone. A further good example of Blin's intuitive appreciation of the dramatic needs of a text in performance is provided in his *mise en scène* of *La Sonate des spectres* in 1949:

> For that production I made up something of which I'm quite proud. Towards the end of the play, the old company director Hummel goes into the closet to atone for his sins. Behind the screen, which represented death, he became a parrot, as had the old mummy before him. But at the end of that terrible scene, dealing with the balancing of accounts, and up to the moment when the old man is in the closet, I'd asked the mummy to bang on the floor with her crutch to count out time and all the actors, the guests at the ceremony, to suddenly perform in slow motion.[37]

There is a necessary restraint in the use of such applied ideas; and it is through the use of such effects that Blin demonstrated how finely tuned he could be to the rhythms of a playwright's work.

When a text required a great deal of imaginative input to give it visual interest, such as the journalistic *Minimata and Co.*, Blin's imagination was capable of providing the necessary flesh. A beautiful example of how stage reality can be manipulated to suggest a great deal about the characters to an audience is the blocking of the scene in this play where a union leader is 'bought out' by the company manager. The Japanese industrialists in Blin's production all wore glasses and western clothes. In this scene the manager removed his glasses and placed them on the table; the union official toyed with them during their conversation and when he finally accepted the deal offered to him, the scene ended with his putting them on. The detail was subtle and patently unrealistic, but made its point effectively in a visual, symbolic manner. Such precise but allusive ways of conveying a mood, atmosphere or subtext detected in a play, is typical of what Blin meant by his search for affective density. One particular device of which he was fond reappeared in a number of his productions. In his blocking of *Divines Paroles*, Valle-Inclán's drama of a violent,

---

36   Blin, *Souvenirs et propos*, p.294.
37   Ibid., p.69.

claustrophobic Spanish community, the dwarf who features in the play was drawn around on a small cart. At one point in the performance Blin arranged for this cart to disappear behind a wall and for the actor to get off and enter downstage on an identical cart for his lines in the following scene. Meanwhile, the original cart simultaneously re-appeared upstage from behind the wall, with another actor doubling for the dwarf, visually creating an impossible route for the character between scenes. This same conceit re-emerged in Blin's production of *Les Paravents* when, in the thirteenth tableau, the mother was drag-ging the corpse of the dead soldier Pierre into the wings only to reappear, incarnated by another actress further upstage on a higher piece of rostrum, dragging on the head and shoulders of the corpse whose legs were still being shifted downstage. The trick was used once again in the first scene of *Ein Traumspiel*, where Agnes and the glazier were replaced by doubles to facilitate their entrance into the following scene, and later, a similar ruse proved effective in the second act of *Triptyque*, where the character of Proll began upstage in a rocking chair smoking a pipe with his back to the audience, only to have the real actor playing Proll walk on downstage of him.

These and other such effects were all devised to be accomplished on a human scale, without recourse to sophisticated machinery, perhaps a legacy of Blin's long schooling in low-budget performances in the pocket theatres of the Left Bank. He maintained a preference for effects created by actors on stage and within the parameters of the performance itself. Sound effects, for example, would be provided as much as possible by the actors themselves rather than through the technology of sound generating and amplifying equipment. In *Les Paravents*, certainly, noises were created as far as possible and if appropriate, as part of the action: Blin had one actor, playing an Arab, produce the whinnying of Sir Harold's horse in the fourth tableau and later in the fifteenth tableau when the village women came on to gloat around the corpse of the prostitute Warda, the sound of their knitting needles was enhanced by other actors manipulating scissors. Similarly, where music was called for, Blin preferred live perform-ance to recorded material. For Any Diguet's *Rue noire* in 1984, he enlisted the talents of the Théâtre du Soleil's Jean-Jacques Lemètre, and for *Macbeth* he hired a curious beast of a musical instrument, la

229

Bronte (an invention of the percussion composer Geminiani) which produced odd, deep reverberating sounds.

Clearly, Blin's concern for the texture of live performance, constrained only by his need to feel he was dealing honestly with the requirements of the written text, formed the basis of his approach to every play he directed. Only by extending this examination to his relationship with playwrights and his work with actors, can acquire an understanding of Blin's personal agenda and a rounded appreciation of his methodology. For this we need to enter the rehearsal room.

Actors and text

> If there is anything consistent about my various *mises en scène*, I haven't tried to put it there. For me, the pleasure of serving a text is more than enough for that pleasure to remain a secret. Within the work, in a certain manner of expressing, in the movements of a human body or different human bodies, I look to have everything arrived at through necessity, from the structure, from the respiratory rhythm of the words.[38]

Clearly, a play cannot direct itself, and yet Blin's professed subservience to the text was absolute. 'To even speak of the paternity of a *mise en scène* seems highly debatable to me' Blin insisted. 'Without even taking into consideration the indications noted in the script by the author, there are gestures that are self-evident.'[39] The apparent simplicity of this statement belies the complexity that it implies for the rehearsal process. What, precisely, did Blin mean by gestures and movements that are 'self-evident'? How can they be identified within a text and in what manner are they determined by the nature of the play? To begin to understand the implications of such a statement it is necessary to examine the approach he took when first considering the staging of some of his productions.

38   Ibid., p.98.
39   Blin in Mignon, *Théâtre d'aujourd'hui A-Z*, p.57.

Slawomir Mrozek's *Les Émigrés* deals with two emigrants, both exiled from their common, unnamed country, one on political grounds, and the other voluntarily on economic grounds. The action is confined to their shared home, in the basement of an apartment block. 'You could imagine that as an exchange of words between two men seated face to face, in profile for the whole play,' Blin recalled, but insisted that 'the text contains a whole group of movements that was necessary to realise.'[40] The play's script, however, is mostly devoid of stage directions and Blin here is referring to the kind 'self-evident' movements implied above. Whereas some directors will often map out the blocking for a particular scene in advance of rehearsals in order to concentrate on other aspects of the *mise en scène*, or even order his or her actors about to discover the blocking haphazardly, Blin was intent on discovering it within rehearsal time in concert with the actors. Laurent Terzieff, a close friend of Blin's, recalled an example from a rehearsal of how during a twenty-minute piece of dialogue 'Roger would have liked us to move around a little, but waited for me to feel the necessity to move and decide to get up'.[41] Thus Blin would arrive at his blocking by allowing the text to take its interpreters where it would, even if this meant starting again from scratch if a particular avenue of enquiry led nowhere: 'It's better to underestimate the efficiency of a text than to avoid all research',[42] he justified. This extemporary, instinctive approach was characteristic of Blin's directing. He held the view that if an author had enough vision to create a play that responded to performance in a vital way, what need was there for precise stage directions? 'No play is difficult to produce if its dramatic substance is rich, if the "theatricality" is strong', he reasoned.[43]

In a sense then, Blin relied on the text to create its own blocking through the way in which it might provoke the actors, and was content to allow the movements to evolve naturally from the 'structure' of the

40   Blin, *Souvenirs et propos*, p.261.
41   Laurent Terzieff to Odette Aslan, 12.3.84, in Aslan, *Roger Blin – Qui êtes-vous?*, p.332.
42   Blin in *L'Aube*, 6.4.50.
43   Blin to Robert Marrast, in 'Pièce espagnole sans guitares', *Les Lettres françaises*, 20.3.63.

script. Recollecting the rehearsals for *En attendant Godot*, Blin offered a good illustration of this approach to blocking:

> They've been saying for a long time in drama schools that you mustn't walk when speaking. It's not true, I like it very much. In *Godot* in particular, Vladimir gave rhythm to his words on his feet. He walked up to the edge of the playing area and turned back suddenly on a significant word. Vladimir and Estragon from time to time take one other in arm to walk about, and stop still when they have nothing else to say to one another. They walk, they're happy:
> '– I'm curious to hear what he has to offer. Then we'll take it or leave it.
> – What exactly did we ask him for?
> – Were you not there?
> – I can't have been listening', etc.
> All this to a rhythmic pace
> '– Before taking a decision.'
> They suddenly separate.
> '– It's the normal thing
> – Is it not?
> – I think it is.' Estragon continues walking on his own.
> '– I think so too.' Estragon stops suddenly and turns around.
> '– And we?'[44]

This casual demonstration of how the blocking of the two tramps' moves might be found simply within the way they speak to one another reveals much about Blin's distinctive approach to preparing a play for performance. He would take a sequence of dialogue covering a page or two and, by repeatedly reading it aloud with actors and hearing them do the same, he would seek to achieve a receptiveness to the rhythms and oscillations of the written words which would inspire research into appropriate accompanying movement, developing what Jean Duvignaud described as a 'veritable architecture of words and gestures.'[45] In this way the poetry of stage motion would be allowed to grow organically out of the verbal poetry of the written text. The rehearsal room, therefore, was the only place where all the work on a play was accomplished and finalised. Unlike many dir-

---

44 Blin, *Souvenirs et propos*, pp.99–100. For the text, see Beckett, *En attendant Godot*, pp.23–4 and *The Complete Damatic Works*, pp.19–20.

45 Jean Duvignaud, *Le Théâtre contemporain – culture et contre culture* (Paris: Larousse, 1974), p.125.

ectors who might undertake independent research and plot blocking ahead of scheduled rehearsals, Blin would read through the text, be struck by images that it inspired in him, come into rehearsals without notes but with a head full with images and ideas, and simply suggest a certain way of moving or talking for certain characters at certain points in a scene. He would then continue in that manner, trying out ideas and encouraging experiment, attempting to determine precisely what the text demanded in terms of movement and delivery at any particular moment.

> The manner in which space is occupied derives directly from the action as described, but even more so from the breathing of the phrases, the words. The musical scanning suggested by a lot of full stops is of crucial importance in a text that resists all metaphoric poetry.[46]

By literally discovering the blocking in this way, rather than dictating it from premeditated plans, Blin fostered an organic development from page to stage and consequently a greater fluency and 'naturalness' in performance.

After this spontaneously generated blocking process Blin would set to work on shaping his and the actors' discoveries, channelling their energies in the right direction towards an embryonic performance. He would act as overseer to a collaborative enterprise, ensuring that all fruitless experimentation was dropped and leaving only what was apt and significant:

> I try to integrate the verb, the thought, the sentiment into a choreography which I don't know in advance but which I discover in rehearsal with the actors. As much as is possible, I absolutely believe in making use of all the red herrings in a text. I try to avoid, to get a good spread, a powerful spread, that an actor be led through his own excesses towards the centre of the stage. I make use of the centre for particular moments. These are tricks of the trade, these are things I feel at the tips of my fingers [...] My work therefore consists of regulating matters within a continuity like a film director thinking of how his film is structured, and tell which scene he wants to insist does not extend beyond a certain number of seconds, for the sake of equilibrium. With a *mise en scène*, I'm concerned, in each scene, to be able to imagine the next. So, when two actors need to confront one another, I choose to place them the furthest apart so

---

46   Blin in Le Nouvel Observateur, 26.9.81.

that the scene remains open for the audience and because the further apart the actors are, the more central their confrontation is.[47]

Blin's input, as described above, is analogous to that of a manual craftsman. Just as a sculptor may be inspired by his material to mould certain shapes or certain juxtapositions of form, so Blin was inspired to build the shape of a performance from the material of the play itself and the plasticity of the actors' presence. The process was slow and required great concentration and commitment from actors to be successful. More importantly, however, Blin felt that this process of discovery ought to be a relaxed and enjoyable one and, though it might often have taken more time compared to more 'traditional' methods, it had the advantage of relaxing actors into their roles: 'There is a rehearsal technique by which it's better to enjoy yourself than not to enjoy yourself,' he contended, 'I don't like shouting, I'm not a barrister. I prefer to persuade through jokes, through images.'[48] Having spent the first decade and a half of his career as an actor, and having continued to act in parallel with his work as a director, Blin had too great a respect for his company to want to assume a dictatorial role and he eschewed any hierarchy in theatrical. Rather than impose his ideas upon them, he encouraged actors to discover not just the blocking but their own characterisations as well. Indeed, he considered the two creative activities to be interdependent: blocking arose from within the nature of the characters themselves and from their interaction, as an integral part of the development of the play in rehearsal. Amidou, speaking in 1967 of his experience in the cast of *Les Paravents*, described Blin's style in the following terms:

> Blin's directing is quite special, and disconcerting. He doesn't give much direction, yet at the end of a day's work we seem to know everything. He lets the actors do what they feel in the character. But he lets us improvise only if it is in the spirit of the sentence. Then he erases everything that is peripheral to the character. He explains what has to be explained: then he works within that frame.[49]

47   Blin, *Souvenirs et propos*, pp.98–9.
48   Blin in *Libération*, 14.6.77.
49   Amidou to Bettina Knapp, in *Tulane Drama Review*, 11.4 (1967), p.105.

234

This recollection indicates a subtle, gradualist approach, with Blin steadily inducing a performance from within his actors, while retaining firm overall control and a clear objective. Robert Liensol, who worked with Blin in both *Les Nègres* and *Boesman et Léna*, provides corroboration:

> He makes corrections little by little, he allows you to express yourself, things take shape bit by bit. He is patient, and an extraordinarily good listener. He accepted our individual suggestions, and encouraged our spontaneity a great deal, whilst all the time imposing a certain rigour upon us. It might happen that a whole rehearsal would pass without him saying anything, but he was the one who regulated everyone's movements.[50]

Blin's contribution was applied in small touches, shifting the tone of an individual's performance to suit his whole vision of a piece, or gently coaching them to reach the expression they themselves were striving for with helpful suggestions and insights. He required them to repeat passages over and over, however small the detail in question, in order to establish the most efficient and most effective performance. Often rehearsals would unfold 'without much being spoken, without complications and with a certain nonchalance' and actors who enjoyed his steady method 'thrived on those silences, those hesitations, those uncertainties which led eventually to an assurance'.[51] His respect for and fastidious attention to the actors' input was appreciated by many of those with whom he worked. Éléonore Hirt summarised working with him as being able to benefit from 'the overwhelming possibility of giving yourself over to the trust of an observer whose great qualities obviated all resistance.'[52] He himself would compare his work to that of a milliner, who would slowly add detail upon detail to accumulate toward an accomplished whole. Jean-Pierre Faye summed up this careful and considered approach well when describing the director's work on his play, *Hommes et pierres*, produced in 1965:

---

50   Robert Liensol to Odette Aslan, in Aslan, *Roger Blin – Qui êtes-vous*, pp.199–200.

51   From the programme to the 'Exposition Roger Blin', an exhibition of his drawings, Théâtre du Rond-Point, 24.1.85 to 17.2.85.

52   Letter from Éléonore Hirt to Mark Batty, dated 23.2.95.

Roger Blin works like the conductor of an orchestra. His terseness is the evidence for how straightforward his suggestions are. He works by little touches, without anger, he 'moulds', so that in some way the actor and he come to the same decisions. He systematically keeps experimenting right through to the end of rehearsals. He adjusts, has things adjusted. Unlike Barrault who writes out his *mises en scène*, Blin remembers everything, tries out new movements on the back of spontaneous movements.[53]

Blin's own testimony provides further elaboration. Never the distanced regulator, he worked with the actors as another actor but always attentive to their efforts and difficulties:

I do sometimes get up on stage to try stuff out. When it doesn't work, if the actor doesn't get it, or when there's a problem of moving around on stage, then the actor tries again. If he doesn't succeed, I question myself. I never think that an instruction has to be obeyed at all costs, and it is quite possible that the actor is right and I'm wrong. It doesn't bother me. Some day's rehearsals just don't work, you stop, or you go over certain details.[54]

Even if he were to demonstrate exactly what he had in mind he never wished simply to be copied, and Robert Liensol remembered how Blin would 'indicate gestures, offer the intonation, but he sketched these – he never wanted to be imitated.'[55] This overwhelming humility towards, and respect for, the work of his actors meant that creativity from all sources was free to flow into a production. Blin was always prepared to consider suggestions from his actors and would allow them freedom to try out their ideas to convince him of their worth. On one occasion, for example, he permitted an actor to adapt the script of *En attendant Godot* during the rehearsals for a production in Toulouse: 'One [of the actors] suggested that instead of the "Do do do do..." given by Beckett,' John Fletcher recounts, 'Vladimir should sing a lullaby of Languedoc in dialect, "Soun soun soun Veni veni doun" ('Come then, sleep'), in order to send Estragon to sleep in Act II.'[56]

53   Jean-Pierre Faye, *Le Nouvel Observateur*, 28.1.65.
54   Blin, *Souvenirs et propos*, pp.100–1.
55   Robert Liensol to Maria Craipeau, in *France observateur*, 22.10.59.
56   John Fletcher, 'Roger Blin at work', in *Modern Drama*, 8 (1965–66), p.408.

Since Blin preferred to consider himself as one of a group of many collaborating artists in each production, he tended to cast actors possessing a sense of vision that matched his own and who held a passion for performance. 'Blin detested "brilliant" actors, emotive actors,' his friend Jean Martin recalled, 'he considered that showing everything was a way of hiding everything, and keeping it inside.'[57] This may explain to some degree why he never attempted to become part of the theatre establishment and often preferred to work with enthusiasts and dedicated young performers rather than salaried thespians. This predilection, besides the administrative conveniences which motivated its being set up, may also have been behind his consenting to found the 'Compagnie Roger Blin' in the late 1970s.

When working in Essen in 1968 with a troupe of German actors on *The Screens*, a transfer of his recent Paris production to Germany, Blin completely despaired of the passive and obedient stance they assumed toward him, waiting upon his every indication and lacking any personal initiative. He also found cause to bemoan the approach of the established French actors he had occasion to work with. In 1983, rehearsing Max Frisch's *Triptyque* at the Comédie-Française, he found the company's approach too instinctively realistic and sought to confuse and discourage it with non-naturalistic staging (including rotating discs integrated into the stage floor) and make-up. 'My job is to get in the way of it becoming natural, boulevard, all the things I hate'[58] he said of that production. At Barrault's Odéon in 1966, the lengthy and exhausting work on *Les Paravents* resulted in the actors naturally dividing into two camps: those of Barrault's regular group and the small group of lead role actors, most of whom Blin had cast from outside the permanent company. Although intended as a criticism, the distinction that actress Michèle Oppenot drew between the two camps, when looking back on the production in 1983, serves to illustrate the attitude of Blin and those with whom he enjoyed working. She explained how the 'Blin family found it difficult to separate their social lives from their stage lives, whilst the Barrault family was made up of people whose career was divorced from their private

---

57   Jean Martin to Mark Batty, 11.1.95
58   Blin in *Libération*, 21.2.83.

lives.'[59] It was precisely the engaged, creative work of this small group that had excited Blin in rehearsals; 'I realised how certain actors were acting with their own fantasies, so violent was their dramatic intensity,' he later recalled, 'whereas it seemed to me the others had no idea of the gravity of the poetic theme they were in the middle of defending.'[60]

In rehearsal, Blin would act as a go-between for the author's text and the actor's efforts and spoke in terms the actors could understand. He preferred to avoid any systematic analysis of the play and did not allow rehearsals to become contaminated with cerebral discussion or psychological inquiry. Speaking of his preparatory work on Beckett's *En attendant Godot*, for example, he maintained that he had not been interested in deconstructing the play for the actors:

> I didn't want to press the symbolic side – I know that at the end of the day the audience must get the play at the second level but to arrive there, it's necessary to achieve the first level. I didn't bother the actors by saying, 'look, careful, this is very important, it means something other than it seems'. I wanted them to discover it for themselves; through the rehearsals they should give something surpassing the everyday realism of tramps – who finally are not tramps but you and me.[61]

Throughout his career he retained a healthy scepticism for all theorists and intellectual ideologies:

> I work with my eyes and fingertips, as we've been for too long the victims of dramaturges, the Brechtian police. I find things on the underground, or in dreams. In a certain dreamlike brooding rather than in dialectic intellectual-isation. I can feel at the tips of my fingers what has to be done. A play is a paste and, at the centre, there are actors, noises, sounds, general movement [...] And I believe in all that before intelligence, because I want to forget the time I spent at the Sorbonne. There has to be an almost manual pleasure in creating stuff.[62]

59   Michèle Oppenot to Anne Laurent, in *Libération*, 10.6.83.
60   Blin to Jacques Bioules, unpublished interview, Fonds Blin, IMEC, Paris, p.4.
61   Blin to Mary Benson, in 'Roger Blin and Beckett', *London Magazine*, 18.7 (October 1978), p.52.
62   Blin to Josanne Rousseau, in *Comédie-Française*, 116 (1983).

This devotedly artisan-like stance kept faith with an instinctive, almost visceral response to a play text and he always declined to be drawn too far into thinking about scripts in abstract analytical terms. This is clearly evidenced in his refusal to make preparatory notes before embarking on a production and his reliance on spontaneous creation in rehearsal. He would purposely preserve a distance from the 'messages' a work might carry and concentrate on its living tissue, its vital pulse:

> I try to keep my initial impression fresh and to put that across. If I have any qualities, it's a matter of vision. That's why I'm against the so-called dramaturges who explain the how and why of it all. I discover in the work. By trial and error. I give indications to have them [the actors] do less. I never write anything down in advance. But one gets obsessed by images, the direction comes out of that, it all goes through the fingers.[63]

This obsessive technique of slowly sculpting a dramatic form out of a text with the aid of his actors meant that the greatest emphasis of Blin's work as the director was placed upon the day-to-day work in the rehearsal room rather than contemplation and conceptualisation outside it. This ensured the very human dimension to his contribution to the theatre. He was often at his happiest and most productive when he could work at the simplest, most immediate level, unravelling the human structure of each drama, as he perceived it. 'Within the various things I've done', he recalled, 'I'm much happier about what I've been able to make up in character relationships than with scenic solutions.'[64]

63   Blin in *Libération*, 21.2.83.
64   Blin, *Souvenirs et propos*, p.61.

Design and structure

Blin's attitude to set-design was in keeping with the rest of his approach: décor should be simple and functional and not too overbearing in its ingenuity of design or operation. He disliked cluttering the stage with unnecessarily elaborate sets or entangling a performance with excessive decorative or spectacular fuss. This policy was integral to the making of his reputation during his lifetime and has helped to define his legacy:

> Audiences may be momentarily excited by fire and water on stage, but they come and go without experiencing theatre as a need, seeing it as more or less competitive entertainment. And the actors and French playwrights must wait in the café théâtres, the Bouffes du nord, or the Théâtre de l'Est Parisien until the magicians take a holiday. All of which makes a Roger Blin production all the more worthwhile.[65]

To Blin, the pursuit of spectacle was a waste of money that might be better spent supporting the work of new writers. As a matter of principle, he would never devote more than half a production's budget to the set. For his production of José Triana's *La Nuit des assassins* at the Récamier in 1971 he was satisfied to raid Barrault's stock of old props and scenic material rather than have things made anew. This is not to say that Blin underestimated the role of décor in realising a text on stage – set-designs for the works that he directed had an integral part to play in the visions he was attempting to conjure up – he was simply adamant that they should facilitate the actors' work and not be features in themselves.

His taste was for the kind of stylisation in décor that he demanded from his actors in their approach to the written word, as long as such stylisation was appropriate (a realistic set being acceptable where the play demanded it). Above all he preferred that a set could act as part of the dramatic fibre of a play, that its structure should reflect the workings of the drama in a similar way to that in

---

65 Neil Boyd, 'Planchon and Blin in Paris', in *Plays and Players*, 26.6 (March 1979), p.34.

which the blocking he had evolved reflected the rhythms of the text, both working together to achieve a 'spatial poetry'.[66] Ideally he thought that a set should 'take on a life of its own'[67] and participate in the play it served to frame by allowing the actors to manipulate and further define it, thus creating an environment that was specifically theatrical. 'I always avoid purely decorative décor,' he stated, 'and am keen for it to be utilitarian, accessible for the actors.'[68] Examples of this sort of palpable, structured staging abound in Blin's *oeuvre*. During the sleepwalking scene in *Macbeth*, for example, he arranged for Lady Macbeth to appear to carry a candle whilst simultaneously rubbing at her imagined bloodstained hands. This was arranged by having the actor descend a staircase while the hands of supernumeries emerged from holes in the wall to pass the candle downwards in a disembodied relay ahead of the actress. In the second act of *Triptyque* he contrived a strange non-voluntary walk for the dead characters by having large revolving circular discs, cut into the stage floor, which carried the actors slowly from one wing to the other, or onto the stage to deliver their lines. The eerie effect created was described as a 'funereal ballet' by one critic.[69] In *Les Nègres* all the props necessary for the performance were on stage from the beginning, with handker-chiefs, masks, wigs and dolls tied to the scaffolding set as if part of its structure, only to be peeled off and used at each appropriate moment. For his Dutch production of *Het Balkon*, in the short fourth tableau between the old man and the girl, he imagined a means by which the mirror could easily and quickly be pushed and pulled around the stage by a simple effortless tug of the index finger and the thumb.

Many of the plays that Blin chose to present lent themselves to this kind of set design, the décor for *Les Paravents* perhaps being the most obvious example of a set which slowly evolved with the plot, the movement of characters and the growing atmosphere of the play. As such this production represents the centrepiece of Blin's collaborative

---

66   This is how Éléonore Hirt described Blin's touch. Letter to Mark Batty, dated 23.2.95.
67   Blin to Bettina Knapp, in *Tulane Drama Review*, 7.3 (1962), p.120.
68   Blin, *Souvenirs et propos*, p.136.
69   Guy Dumur, *Le Nouvel Observateur*, 25.2.83.

relationship with the designer André Acquart, with whom he had first worked on *Les Nègres*. Acquart's design for *Les Paravents* had been adumbrated three years earlier in the way in which they had jointly conceived the set for Valle-Inclán's *Divines Paroles*, produced at Barrault's Théâtre de l'Odéon in 1963. This production was perhaps Blin's first attempt consciously to apply his particular vision of theatrical environment, endeavouring, with Acquart, to devise a set that would both capture the essence and locale of the play whilst also permitting a functionally fluid movement from one scene to the next in a manner that was entirely theatrical and non-realistic:

> I was interested in finding a kind of continuity for the performance, a rhythm that wouldn't be cut up by blackouts for changes between scenes. I wanted scene changes to be done in full view and as much as possible by the actors themselves, for scenes to interweave and for the characters and scenery for the following scene to be already on stage in the preceding scene. It's an old idea that I'm keen on.[70]

Anxious to avoid the visual clichés of Spanish rural life so commonly used in contemporary presentation of Spanish plays, Blin took advantage of the funds at Barrault's disposal to make a research trip with Acquart and his wife to Galicia. He was determined to construct on stage the distinctive atmosphere of this corner of Spain, which reminded him of his favourite holiday spots in Brittany. Acquart came up with an ingenious way of representing the granite townscapes that they saw in Galicia. By covering material with sheets of newspaper print, he discovered he could recreate the sense of that cold stone without resorting to realism and used this for the construction of walls and doorways, whilst also littering the stage with giant flagstones that could be moved about to represent the different locations required by the action of the play. Other elements of décor, such as the edifice of the village church, glided visibly into position on rails. Blin was pleased with the design, as he was specifically concerned not to lose any of the theatricality of Valle-Inclán's play by having to worry too much about the limitations of realistic staging:

70   Blin, *Souvenirs et propos*, p.158.

242

My concern for the production was to both avoid all cinematic temptations and reject painted backdrops and projections, however convenient. Simple, palpable elements, almost realistic, went together to build a system inspired by that ever-present granite which had so tempted André Acquart and me in Galicia.[71]

Unfortunately, it was the lack of a recognisable Spain that displeased many Parisian critics, who compared the production unfavourably not only with the play's première, which had been given during the war at the Théâtre des Mathurins, directed by Marcel Herrand (ironically, at Blin's suggestion) but also with Georges Wilson's production of Valle-Inclán's *Lumières de Bohême* (*Bohemian Lights*) which was playing concurrently at the T.N.P., both of which had corresponded to a more conventional, if less authentic (i.e. Andalusian) notion of life south-west of the Pyrenees. In response, a group of Spanish artists (including Fernando Arrabal, José-Luis Mayoral, Luis Arnaiz and Antonio Fernandez Molina) wrote a short note of thanks to Blin and Acquart dated 8 April 1963, intended for publication as an open letter:

The *mise en scène* of *Divines Paroles* by Roger Blin seemed to us to adapt exactly to the world of Valle-Inclán. This fidelity to a writer's work deserves the highest praise. Roger Blin knew to avoid all 'spanishness' and has given us an authentic vision of a region of Spain, Galicia, which serves as the frame for *Divines Paroles*. As Spaniards and Hispanisists, we take joy in a foreign director having demonstrated an awareness of the diversity of the Spanish peoples, and kept himself away from a commonplace aesthetic. To represent Galicia as a country of light, sun and guitars would be as inaccurate as a Scottish landscape in Sicily. We thank Roger Blin for his precise and scrupulous *mise en scène*.[72]

Blin maintained a good professional relationship with Acquart, subsequently soliciting his creative insight whenever he thought that a play could be well served by a set of architectural dimensions, for which the designer's capacity to create 'an absence of décor, a mechanism in which the scenography and the actors would have their place [...] a means of circulation'[73] would be the most apt. The set for

71   Blin to Robert Marrast, in 'Pièce espagnole sans guitares', *Les Lettres françaises*, 20.3.63.
72   Unpublished. From Blin's collection, Fonds Blin IMEC, Paris.
73   André Acquart to Mark Batty, 23.5.93.

Minimata and Co. offers perhaps the perfect example of just such an environment. In contrast to the realistic sets used by Takahashi for his original touring production in Japan, Blin opted for a clearly theatrical space which, through its beauty and visual simplicity, supplied a suitable platform for the emotive text, believing that in the play 'the multiplicity of locations the action took place in offered the possibility of a certain schematisation'.[74] Perhaps inspired by traditional Japanese theatre, Blin requested a non-realistic locale that could be made to represent the numerous places where the action took place. He subsequently reckoned the design for this Japanese play to be amongst Acquart's best and 'of an incredible simplicity and effectiveness.'[75] The designer had devised a system of wooden platforms which slid in grooves along a structure of rails, raised two feet off the ground, to form bridges over the stage floor. Actors and stage hands dressed in dark shirts manipulated the slatted platforms, to create different permutations of stage space. Below this construction a coloured plastic sheet was spread to represent polluted water:

> I made a kind of decking from planks of wood at a certain level off the ground, and beneath it I put [...] shining material, on the stage floor. Like you find in port; at the water's edge you see stuff floating, corks, leaves gathered together like that... so there was a feeling of there being water but then there was this kind of mass of stuff, dark, slightly unpleasant.[76]

Here was a suitable background atmosphere for the action, a constant on-stage reminder of the physical and moral contamination which permeates the Minimata story. The stage sky was a backdrop of striped cloth which, when lit from different angles and with different shades of colour and levels of intensity, could effectively alter the dramatic tenor of the action.

According to Takahashi's script, the illnesses and mutilations of the victims of mercury poisoning are to be recreated by actors and exhibited to the audience vividly by projecting slides onto a screen. Following images of dead cats in the first tableau and the introduction

74   Blin, *Souvenirs et propos*, p.287.
75   Ibid.
76   André Acquart to Mark Batty, 23.5.93.

in the second of Sato, a disabled woman wishing she might have her health restored, the third tableau is set aside specifically for such photographs to be displayed. Blin, however, did not want to allow any recourse to the sentimentality which such photographs might induce. In place of their documentary realism he chose theatrical puppetry, asking Claude Acquart (André Acquart's son) to construct a small, wretched, furless cat and human figurines to represent the sick and the disfigured. These large leather mannequins, crude and unpleasant to behold, were manipulated by actors trained in puppetry by a marionettist of Phillipe Genty's company. Rather than use the puppets straightforwardly to display the illnesses and deformities caused by the mercury poisoning, Blin decided that their appearance was to be used in a grotesque way, to bring about a deep discomfort in an audience. A single actor was deputed to evoke illness physically; with this exception, Blin elected to communicate the reality of the villagers' suffering through a conscious poetry of the stage, arguing that '[t]he beauty of the show can also provoke that emotion. I put puppets into *Minimata and Co* simply because I found them to be beautiful.[77] Acquart, too, was convinced that this policy had been the most effective dramatically, stating that he believed that 'no actor could give that impression of sickness, of deformity.'[78]

Once an environment had been designed for a production, Blin would continue exploratory research with the actors within it, and this final coming together of all the creative energies of his team permitted the refining of the performance. He saw all the varied elements of production as parts of an organic whole, the cultivation and compilation of which was ultimately his responsibility:

> I arrange groups, characters, heads with my fingers, and only afterwards do I arrange the lighting accordingly. Moments in darkness don't bother me too much. I never work out the lighting states in advance.[79]

77   Blin to Fabienne Pascavel, in *Télérama*, 11–17.11.78.
78   André Acquart to Mark Batty, 23.4.93.
79   Blin, *Souvenirs et Propos*, p.98.

Active humility

A hallmark of Blin's working attitude was his belief in the need to respect an author and their text, and his attempts to discover modes of achieving that objective, made clear in remarks such as: 'you should always adapt to the writing of a text, respect its syntax. You have to commune with an author in the manner in which he has breathed his text.'[80] One might expect a director who advocated such complete deference to the text to respect to the letter the author's own stage directions, but this was not necessarily the case. When he pointed out that the text always dictates the *mise en scène* he did not mean simply that a director's job consisted in religiously structuring a performance according to the italicised instructions provided by the playwright. Commenting, for example, on Beckett's *La Dernière Bande* he expressed some frustration at the precision with which Beckett had pre-empted his own interpretative work: 'I'd prefer the bare text. The *mise en scène* dislikes the inventive processes being blocked by the author.'[81] Later, discussing Genet's *Les Paravents*, and the letters he received from the author, he made the point even more bluntly: 'As much as possible, I was vigilant in respecting all of his instructions,' he remembered, 'but occasionally I ignored them because I couldn't take all his suggestions seriously.'[82] Examining the discrepancy between these sentiments and his often-repeated maxim '[w]hen I direct a play, the text dictates my decisions, always'[83] takes us a final step closer to Blin's thinking on the role of the director. To resolve this apparent contradiction requires directly addressing the interface between director and playwright, which, in Blin's case, is fundamental to defining his achievement. Above all, it was the manner in which he perceived the synapse between himself and the living authors that constituted a measure of his distinctiveness as a director.

80   Ibid., p.63.
81   Blin to Guy Verdot, in 'Recherche de Beckett chez eux qui l'ont découvert les premiers', *Paris-théâtre*, 206 (1964), p.15.
82   Blin, *Souvenirs et propos*, pp.202–3.
83   Ibid., p.64.

Blin did not consider that the playwright's authorship of a play was dormant, or complete once a manuscript was finished. He expected or inferred a continued authorial investment in the development of any *mise en scène*, not simply by an author's physical presence or correspondence during rehearsals, but more latently, by virtue of the authorial intentions inscribed in the body of the text, however he chose to 'read' these. To achieve these intentions, Blin sought to get under the skin of the text, immersing himself in the world of the play in hand and connecting, as far as he believed he could, with the state of mind of the author as he wrote it. He admitted that the creative process for him began with a period of total obsession with a script, carrying it around in his head for days. 'I throw myself in like an idiot,' he claimed, 'I try to understand what's happening in the text, between the lines, and to find the technical means to realise that.'[84] He was driven, in other words, by a consuming enthusiasm that arose from having discovered a great and inspiring work and a subsequent overriding desire to communicate that discovery to others with precise force:

> What I try to do when directing a play is to translate the author's ideas, his aesthetic that is, both visually and emotionally. I want the audience to feel the immense elation Genet felt when he wrote *The Blacks* and *The Screens* [...] He is showing humanity with all its passions, its hatreds, jealousies, and vices. He is trying to penetrate the inner core of man, to understand it [...] My role as a director is to make this clear to the spectator.[85]

Assuming that so total an emotional and intellectual fusion with a text via production is attainable, it is possible to imagine that, in certain circumstances, the director may legitimately disagree with a playwright who may perhaps have become distanced from the unique period of creativity that gave rise to their work. Blin firmly believed that by 'communing' with a play he could help it to reach its full dramatic potential, even if this meant fraught negotiations with the playwright:

---

84   Blin to Collette Godard, in *Artaud, Beckett, Genet*, unpublished interview, Fonds Blin, IMEC, Paris, p.3.
85   Blin to Bettina Knapp, in *Tulane Drama Review*, 7.3 (1962), p.114.

I've never been concerned with stamping my work with any kind of Blin hallmark. [...] The 'Blin' in it is a certain energy that I place at the disposition of the author. Not in any humble or submissive way, because it isn't unusual for an author to have ideas to which they are strongly fixed but which have no dramatic value. I call these *vues de l'esprit* and I've had to struggle with Genet, Beckett or others to impose what I believe. But, in a general way, I believe in being completely faithful to authors, because that's what interests me. To understand, and fit perfectly in with an author when I'm putting on one of his plays. To work out his thoughts or his being when he wrote it. And perhaps to help him realise theatrically the spirit of his text. To always be in what I call a state of active humility. I sometimes fall short or overreach that which the author had in mind, but I think I'm always going in his direction.[86]

Here Blin offers a concise definition of the seeming oxymoron ('active humility') that he was often to use when describing his own approach. To be humble towards an author's creativity and yet to struggle actively with him in order to do a text full justice, to stubbornly argue an author out of a *vue de l'esprit* which is seen to act against the interests of the play in question, this is behaviour typical of Blin. Such conflicts are not merely a question of a director's interpretation clashing with an author's original intentions – none of the playwrights with whom he worked ever complained of anything of the sort – but represent, rather, a kind of theatrical midwifery, in which Blin sometimes had to fight to coerce the parent of a work to allow its healthy delivery on the stage. They presuppose a deep theatrical knowledge being lent to the creative vision of a writer: 'I only go up against an author in the case of a *vue de l'esprit* which turns out to be sterile in practice with the actors.'[87]

One such dispute can be found in the rehearsal process for *Les Paravents*. In a note to Blin, later published in his *Letters to Roger Blin*, Genet explained how he wanted every scene of his play to be performed under a full wash of lights and the end of each scene to be punctuated by a blackout, arguing that within these blackouts the audience would come to understand his play. For Blin this was a typical *vue de l'esprit*:

---

86   Blin, *Souvenirs et propos*, p.58.
87   Blin to Josanne Rousseau, in *Comédie-Française*, 116 (1983).

248

Authors always think that what they've written, what has just been said, is so precious that it needs to be sustained, and I understand that. They think that the audience want to be impregnated by what they've just heard and a blackout is necessary to facilitate that, like silences in certain pieces of music.[88]

He realised that to resort to repeated blackouts would risk exhausting the patience of an audience with what was already a lengthy production. He fought against Genet's explicit wishes to maintain the play's momentum and to apply a more supple way of passing from one scene to the next:

I had no blackouts whatsoever. So he went even further, didn't he? After having wanted blackouts and complicated lighting, he told me: 'everything should be done in bright light.' 'Be careful', I told him, 'you have to keep the interest evenly distributed'; light changes flow with a rhythm. But no blackouts, no frantic scene changes in the dark. It has to flow; certain objects have to be on stage already.[89]

Alternatively, Blin's stubborn insistence would sometimes be employed to force an author to follow their own characteristic mode to the limit, to realise the inherent logic of his own text, without any of the limitations or constraints he may himself have imposed upon its theatricality in the course of writing or tried to impose in the course of the rehearsal of the piece. Blin would do this with the sole aim of maximising the potential of the work within its stage incarnation:

As regards living authors, I adopt a position of active humility, that is to say I want to push them as far as they can go. I don't give a damn about Blin! There will always be too much of me in my productions. What's interesting is putting on a Beckett, a Genet, going perhaps further in their direction than they themselves imagined; making them remove passages which they want to hold onto but which, in practice, turn out to be *vues de l'esprit*, or, on the contrary, force them to overcome any manner of timidity [...] If I get a kick out of seeing a performance taking shape, what I want to bring to that is my dynamic. Not my own dynamic, but the dynamic of someone who had bent over backwards to become Beckett or Genet within my own personal aesthetic.[90]

88   Blin, *Souvenirs et propos*, p.204.
89   Blin to Jacques Bioules, unpublished interview, Fonds Blin, IMEC, Paris, p.6.
90   Blin to Collette Godard, in *Artaud, Beckett, Genet*, unpublished interview, Fonds Blin, IMEC, Paris, p.4.

This is the very essence of Blin's methodology. It is as though he considered the role of the director as a kind of surrogate playwright, temporarily effacing his own personality and mind-set in favour of that which created the work in question. This is how the relationship between author and director should operate in Blin's view. It could never be an excuse for self-expression: 'I've never used a text to make it say anything other than what the author wanted,' he claimed, 'A text is never for me a pretext for expressing my own fantasies.'[91]

Blin aimed to efface himself from the final product and often defined his work as 'invisible directing'. On the other hand, he did quite plainly believe that in certain cases, with certain plays, a directorial contribution should be explicitly visible:

> For certain plays, for certain projects, I concede, when you want to work on a long text you could try to find a visible *mise en scène*. You have to find a balance between the various elements of the play. For example, with *Les Paravents*, it was a matter of balancing the appearance of the screens, all the movements of the play and even the text.[92]

For such projects Blin needed to have access to a whole armoury of theatrical knowledge and to activate his individual imagination in order to create an appropriate structure. Among these projects were plays which required a purposefully designed stage milieu in which they could function at all, as with Jean-Pierre Faye's wordy *Hommes et pierres*, Takahashi's episodic *Minimata and Co.* or *A Dream Play* for which Strindberg demanded such ambitious scenic images. Indeed, Blin's work on the latter and on *Macbeth* provides good examples of 'visible directing' in the service of a text. Nevertheless, his capacity to tune into an author's mode of expression and render it in apt and forthright theatrical terms was ultimately the supreme mark of his peculiar talent. Of the many eulogies made to his prowess as a director this comment by Jacques Lemarchand, in his review of *Les Nègres*, is the most succinct:

91   Blin, *Souvenirs et propos*, p.58.
92   Blin in *Libération*, 15.6.77.

One of Roger Blin's greatest powers is to translate secret reveries into immediately receivable images and gestures – I'm thinking, amongst other productions, of *The Ghost Sonata*, *Waiting for Godot* and this *The Blacks* – poets inhabited by a very personal vision of human relationships; Roger Blin's *mises en scène* are those of a perfect conductor; they establish, quite precisely, a relationship between the author and us.[93]

'Active humility', then, was the strategy that Blin developed to create productions which he deemed to be either invisibly directed, where his own input is no longer apparent in the ultimate performance, or, conversely, predicated on the most appropriate *mise en scène* for the work to achieve its maximum potential. It was the fruit of a highly developed methodology, requiring, as has been seen, a close acculturation with the mind of the playwright and a complete submission to the demands of the individual text in the pursuit of a suitable theatrical language. In performance, this implied a manipulation of stage reality and an exploitation of simple illusionistic effects, the ultimate aim of which was to produce an 'affective density' capable of evoking strong responses from an audience. To achieve as much, preferably without blatantly showing his hands, was for Blin a source of great satisfaction: 'At the end of one show I'd put on,' he contentedly recalled, 'this bloke said "It's good, interesting, the actors were tremendous, we were gripped from start to finish but... the *mise en scène*?..." I was very happy. That's what *mise en scène* is about, more or less'.[94]

It is such overwhelming modesty in the face of significant personal achievement that is perhaps the most inspiring trait of Blin's legacy. It is the modesty of a craftsman who regarded his role as an intermediary one between the true artist and his public. It is these qualities of modesty, of respect and of self-effacement that coloured all he achieved in the theatre within a career that spanned almost half a century. The interest does not lie so much in his innovations, or in the broad body of dramatic literature that he served, but in the fact that he recognised the theatre as a place where humanity faces itself and where a society can be asked to examine its failings. For these

93   Jacques Lemarchand, *Le Figaro Littéraire*, 7.11.59.
94   Blin in *Libération*, 15.6.77.

objectives to succeed he felt all aspects of theatrical work had to be approached with honesty, humility and integrity; it is for this that he was considered by many as 'the reference point for rigour':[95]

95 In 1976 Roger Blin was given the director's award of 'les prix nationaux des arts et des lettres'. The journalist for *Le Monde*, reporting the event, described him thus: 'Roger Blin is arrogantly modest and has sharp words to offer about the excesses of theatrical spectacle. He is the reference point for rigour.' (*Le Monde*, 16.12.76.)

Bibliography

i.) Books and articles

Adamov, Arthur, *L'Homme et l'Enfant* (Paris: Gallimard, 1968)

—— *La Grande et la Petite Manœuvre, La Parodie* (Paris: Gallimard, 1953)

—— *La Parodie, L'Invasion* (Paris: Charlot, 1950)

—— 'La Parodie est la première...', in *Arts*, 29.5.52, p.4.

—— *La Parodie*, in Programme note, Théâtre de Lancry, June 1952

—— 'Deux classiques de théâtre: Strindberg et Büchner' (programme) *La Sonate de spectres* and *Woyceck*, Gaîté-Montparnasse, October 1949

Anon., 'Une odieuse mascarade communiste', in *L'Echo de Paris*, 21.6.35.

—— 'Le groupe "Octobre"', in *L'Humanité*, 1.7.36

—— 'Manifestations au Théâtre de Babylone', in *Le Monde*, 1–2.2.53

—— 'Controverse autour de Godot', Letters to the editor, in *Arts*, 27.2.53.

—— 'Ecole Critique des Arts et des Spectacles', in *Combat*, 8.10.68.

—— 'Les Renaud-Barrault prennent Roger Blin comme directeur...', in *France-Soir*, 21.1.70.

—— 'Roger Blin, dessinateur', *Le Figaro*, 8.8.75.

—— 'Roger Blin cinquante ans au service du théâtre', in *L'Aurore*, 15.12.76.

—— 'Les grand prix nationaux des arts et des lettres', in *Le Monde*, 16.12.76.

—— Atelier de la Création Radiophonique, programme no. 621, 27.1.85.

—— Atelier de la Création Radiophonique, programme no. 622, 3.2.85.

Artaud, Antonin, *Œuvres Complètes* (Paris: Gallimard, 1956–94)

—— *Pour en finir avec le jugement de dieu* (Paris: Gallimard, 2003)

—— *The Theatre and its Double* (London: Calder and Boyars, 1970)

—— *Le Théâtre et son double* (Paris: Gallimard, 1964)

—— 'Un mot à propos de quelque chose', in *Théâtre en Europe*, April 1984, no.2, pp.17–18.

Aslan, Odette, '*Les Paravents* de Jean Genet' in *Les Voies de la création théâtrale*, vol.III, C.N.R.S., Paris, 1972, pp.11–107.

—— *Roger Blin and Twentieth Century Playwrights*, trans. Ruby Cohn (Cambridge: Cambridge University Press, 1988)

—— *Roger Blin – Qui Êtes-Vous?* (Paris: La Manufacture, 1990)

Auclaire-Tamaroff, Élisabeth ed., *Jean-Marie Serreau – Découvreur de théâtres*, (Paris: L'Arbre Verdoyant, 1986)

Bair, Deirdre, *Samuel Beckett: A Biography* (London: Routledge and Kegan Paul, 1976)

Baratier, Jacques, *Le Désordre à vingt ans*, in *L'Avant-Scène Cinéma*, no.75, November 1967, p.36–52.

Barber, Stephen, *Antonin Artaud: Blows and Bombs* (London: Faber and Faber, 1993)

Barrault, Jean-Louis, *Memories for Tomorrow*, trans. Jonathan Griffin (London: Thames and Hudson, 1974)

—— 'Retours à Numance', *Entretiens sur le theatre*, 18 (September/October 1966), p.2.

—— *Saisir le présent* (Paris: Robert Laffont, 1984)

—— *Souvenirs pour demain* (Paris: Seuil, 1972)

Barthes, Roland, 'Sur "Marée basse", de Jean Duvignaud', *Théâtre populaire,* 17 (March 1956), pp.88–90.

Beckett, Samuel, *The Complete Dramatic Works* (London, Faber and Faber, 1986)

—— *En attendant Godot* (Paris: Éditions de Minuit, 1952)

—— *La Dernière Bande, Cendres* (Paris: Éditions de Minuit, 1959)

—— *Eleutheria*, trans. Barbara Wright (London, Faber and Faber, 1996)

—— *Éleuthéria* (Paris: Éditions de Minuit, 1995)

—— *Fin de partie* (Paris: Éditions de Minuit, 1957)

—— *Oh les beaux jours* (Paris: Éditions de Minuit, 1963)

Ben-Zvi, Linda, *Samuel Beckett* (New York: Twayne publishers, 1986)

Bernold, André, *L'Amitié de Beckett* (Paris: Hermann, 1992)

Bishop, Tom, in Bishop/Federman (eds.), *Samuel Beckett* (Paris: Cahiers de L'Herne, 1976)

Blau, Herbert, 'Meanwhile, Follow the Bright Angels', in *Tulane Drama Review*, September 1960, vol.5, no.1, pp.89–101.

—— 'The Popular, The Absurd, and the Entente Cordiale', in *Tulane Drama Review*, March 1961, vol.5, no.3, pp.119–25.

Blin, Roger, 'L'Argent', in *La revue du cinéma*, January 1929, no.2, pp.68–9.

—— 'Atlantis', in *La revue du cinéma*, August 1930, no.13, p.71.

—— 'Aussi loin du réalisme possible...', in Programme to *M'appelle Isabelle Langrenier*, Petit T.E.P., January 1979.

—— 'Le Crime de Minimata', in Osamu Takahashi, *Minimata and Co.* Trans. Catherine Cadou (Paris: Imprimerie IPCC, 1977) p.3.

—— 'Dans les déclarations publique...', in *Le Monde*, 2–3.11.69

—— 'Le défenseur', in *La revue du cinéma*, August 1930, no.13, p.68.

—— *Dessins (Festival D'Avignon)* (Paris: A+A, 1985)

—— 'Une extraordinaire jubilation', in *Les Nègres au port de la lune: Genet et les différences*, Jean-Bernard Moraly (ed.) (Bordeaux: Éditions de la Différence, 1988)

—— 'F.W.Murnau', in *La revue du cinéma*, August 1931 no.25, p.24.

—— 'King Vidor', in *La revue du cinéma*, June 1930, no.11, pp.9–18.

—— 'L'homme qui a vendu son appétit', in *La revue du cinéma*, April 1930, no.9, pp.59–60.

—— 'Nuit des princes', in *La revue du cinéma*, May 1930, no.10, p.65.

—— 'L'œuvre de Thomas Berhard...' in Programme to *Le Président*, Théâtre de la Michodière, March 1981.

—— 'Les Paravents de Jean Genet présenté par Roger Blin', in *Entretiens sur le théâtre*, September/October 1966, no.18, p.17.

—— 'Le premier contact...' in Programme to *Triptyque*, Odéon-Théâtre de France, February 1983.

—— 'Qui était Sylvain Itkine', in *Revue d'histoire du théâtre*, 1964, vol.16, pp.231–4.

—— 'La réalité entre chien et loup', in *L'Avant-Scène Théâtre*, 1.2.82, no.703, p.3.

—— 'Roger Blin et les "gougnaffiers"', in *Nouvel Observateur*, 16–22.9.68.

—— 'Un solidarité entre maigres', in *Arts-Spectacles*, 3–9.7.53, no.418, p.5.

—— *Souvenirs et propos, recueillis par Lynda Bellity Peskine*, Lynda Bellity Peskine (ed.) (Paris: Gallimard, 1986)

—— 'Témoignage Roger Blin', in Pierre Mélèse, *Adamov* (Paris: Seghers, 1972) pp.156–8.

—— 'Témoignage', in Arthur Adamov, *La Parodie, L'Invasion* (Paris: Charlot, 1950), p.18.

—— 'Terre sans femmes', in *La revue du cinéma*, April 1930, no.9, p.67.

—— 'Les travaux, les ouvrage et les inventions de Marey', in *La revue du cinéma*, August 1930, no.13, pp.65–6.

—— 'Trente-trois ans après', in *Le Nouvel Observateur*, 26.9.81. p.60.

—— 'Les vers du nez' in William Shakeseare, *Macbeth*, Trans. Pierrette Tison (Paris: Stock/Théâtre ouvert, 1972) pp.163–71.

Boyd, Neil, 'Planchon and Blin in Paris', in *Plays and Players*, March 1979, vol.26, no.6, p.34.

Bradby, David, *Beckett: Waiting for Godot (Plays in Production)* (Cambridge: Cambridge University Press, 2001)

—— *Modern French Drama* (Cambridge: Cambridge University Press, 1984)

—— and Maria M. Delgado, *The Paris Jigsaw: Internationalism and the City's Stages* (Manchester: Manchester University Press, 2002)

Brater, Enoch, *Beyond Minimalism – Beckett's Later Style in the Theater* (New York: Oxford University Press, 1987)

Cadou, Catherine, 'Plus jamais d'autre Minimata', in *Lutte Santé Sécurité*, November 1977, no.7, p.21.

Caracalla, Jean-Paul, *Lever de rideau: histoire des théâtres privés de Paris* (Paris: Denoël, 1994)

Casarès, Maria, *Résidente privilégiée* (Pairs: Fayard, 1980)

Cohn, Ruby, *From Desire to Godot: Pocket Theaters of Postwar Paris* (Berkeley and Los Angeles: University of California Press, 1987)

—— 'Godot par Beckett à Berlin', in *Travail Théâtral*, 1975, no.20, pp.124–8.

—— *Just Play: Beckett's Theater* (Princeton: Princeton University Press, 1980)

Courrière, Yves, *Jacques Prévert* (Paris: Gallimard, 2000)

Delgado, Maria M., *'Other' Spanish Theatres* (Manchester: Manchester University Press, 2003)

Dichy, Albert (ed.), *The Declared Enemy*, trans. Jeff Fort (Stanford: Stanford University Press, 2004)

Dort, Bernard, 'Blin: l'imperturbable débutant', in *Théâtre en Europe*, April 1984, no.2, pp.18–19.

Dubillard, Roland, *...Où boivent les vaches* (Paris: Gallimard, 1973)

Duvignaud, Jean, *Marée basse* (Paris: Gallimard, 1971)

—— and Jean Lagoutte, *Le Théâtre contemporain – culture et contre culture* (Paris: Larousse, 1974)

——_ '"Théâtre populaire": Histoire d'une revue.' *Magazine Littéraire*, 314 (October 1993), pp.63–64 (p.63).

Ehrlich, Evelyn, *Cinema of Paradox, French Film-making under the German Occupation* (Irvington, New York: Columbia University Press, 1985)

Fauré, Michel, *Le Groupe Octobre* (Paris: Christian Bourgois, 1977)

Faye, Jean-Pierre, 'Artaud vu par Blin', in *Le Récit hunique* (Paris: Seuil, 1967), pp.305–18.

Fletcher, John, 'Roger Blin at work', in *Modern Drama*, 1965/1966, vol.8, pp.403–8.

Fehsenfeld, Martha and Douglas McMillan, *Beckett at Work* (London: Calder, 1986)

Frisch, Max, *Triptyque*, trans. Henri Bergerot (Paris: Gallimard, 1980)

Fugard, Athol, *Boesman and Lena and other plays* (Oxford: Oxford University Press, 1978)

Garel, Lisane, 'Ceux de chez Chéramy', in *Marianne*, 28.6.39, no.249, p.18.

Gaudy, René, *Arthur Adamov* (Paris: Stock, 1971)

Genet, Jean, 'à Pauvert', *Obliques*, 2 (1972), pp.2–4.

—— *Le Balcon, précédé de 'Comment jouer Le Balcon'* (Paris: L'Arbalète, 1956)

—— *The Blacks: A Clownshow*, Bernard Frechtman, trans. (New York: Grove Press, 1960)

—— *Les Bonnes, précédé de 'Comment jouer Les Bonnes'* (Paris: L'Arbalète, 1947)

—— *Dialogues* (Paris: Cent pages, 1990)

—— *Lettres à Olga et Marc Barbezat* (Paris: L'Arbalète, 1988)

—— *Lettres à Roger Blin* (Paris: Gallimard, 1966)

—— *Les Nègres précédé de 'Pour jouer Les Nègres'* (Paris: L'Arbalète, 1958)

—— *Les Paravents* (Paris: L'Arbalète, 1961)

—— *Reflections on the Theatre*, trans. Richard Seaver (London: Faber and Faber, 1972)

—— *The Screens* (London: Faber and Faber, 1963)

—— 'To a would-be producer', in *Tulane Drama Review*, 1963, vol.7, no.3, pp.80–1.

Gontarski, S.E., *The Theatrical Notebooks of Samuel Beckett, Vol.2, Endgame* (London: Faber and Faber, 1992)

Goodall, Jane, *Artaud and the Gnostic Drama* (Oxford: Clarendon Press, 1994)

Hanoteau, Guillaume, *L'Age d'or de Saint-Germain-des-Prés* (Paris: Denoël, 1965)

—— *Ces nuits qui ont fait Paris* (Paris: Fayard, 1971)

Harmon, Maurice (ed.), *No Author Better Served: The Correspondence of Samuel Beckett & Alan Schneider* (London: Harvard University Press, 1998)

Heed, Sven, *Roger Blin: Metteur en scène de l'avant-garde (1949–1959)* (Paris: Circé, 1996)

Hobson, Harold, 'Samuel Beckett – Dramatist of the Year', *International Theatre Annual,* 1956, no.1, pp.153–5.

Innes, Christopher, *Avant-Garde Theatre* (London: Routledge, 1993)

Itkine, Silvain, 'Théâtre et philosophie 1929', in *Revue théâtrale*, 1953, vol.8, no.23.

Kalb, Jonathan, *Beckett in Performance* (Cambridge: Cambridge University Press, 1989)

Karagheuz, Hermine, *Roger Blin: Une dette d'amour* (Paris: Séguier, 2002)

Knowlson, James, *Damned to Fame: The Life of Samuel Beckett* (London: Bloomsbury, 1996)

—— (ed.), *Happy Days: Samuel Beckett's Production Notebook* (London: Faber and Faber, 1985)

—— and Dougland McMillan (eds.), *The Theatrical Notebooks of Samuel Beckett, Vol.1, Waiting for Godot* (London: Faber and Faber, 1993)

—— (ed.), *Samuel Beckett: Krapp's Last Tape – A Theatre Workbook* (London: Brutus books Ltd., 1980)

—— 'States of Play: performance changes and Beckett scholarship', in *Journal of Beckett studies*, 1985, no.10, pp.108–20.

Kott, Jan, *Shakespeare Our Contemporary* (London: W.W.Norton & Co., 1964)

Lennon, Peter, 'Heroes and Villains', *The Guardian*, 1.12.90.

Latour, Geneviève, *Histoire du 'nouveau théâtre'* (Paris: Gallimard, 1966)

—— *Petites Scènes, Grand Théâtre: le théâtre de création de 1944 à 1960* (Paris: Délégation à l'action artistique de la Ville de Paris, 1986)

—— and Florence Caval, *Les Théâtres de Paris* (Paris: Délégation à l'action artistique de la Ville de Paris, 1991)

Louzon, Myriam, '*Fin de partie* de Samuel Beckett', in *Les Voies de la creation théâtrale*, vol.V, C.N.R.S., Paris, 1972, pp.377–445.

Manet, Eduardo, *Les Nonnes* (Paris: Gallimard, 1969)

—— *Les Nonnes*, programme note, Poche-Montparnasse, May 1969.

—— *Lady Strass*, in *L'Avant-Scène Théâtre*, 1977, no.613, pp.9–30.

—— *Lady Strass*, programme note, Poche-Montparnasse, May 1977.

Marowitz, Charles, *Artaud at Rodez* (London: Marion Boyars, 1977)

Martin, Jean, *Parcours de Roger Blin*, programme to the 'Exposition Roger Blin', Théâtre du Rond-Point, 24.1.85 to 17.2.85.

Martin, Marcel, 'Roger Blin', *La Revue du cinéma*, 392 (March 1984), p.19.

Mauriac, Claude, *Laurent Terzieff* (Paris: Stock, 1980)

McMillan, Dougald, and Martha Fehsenfeld, *Beckett in the theatre* (London: Calder, 1988)

Mélèse, Pierre, *Arthur Adamov* (Paris: Seghers, 1972)

—— *Samuel Beckett* (Paris: Seghers, 1966)

Mercier, Maurice, 'Divines Paroles', in *L'Avant-scène Théâtre*, 15.7.63, no.292, p.36–7.

Mignon, Paul-Louis, *Le Théâtre d'aujourd'hui A-Z* (Paris: L'Avant-Scène/Michel Brieunt, 1966)

Moraly, Jean-Bernard, *Jean Genet: La Vie écrite* (Paris: Éditions de la différence, 1988)

Mrozek, Slawomir, *Les Émigrés*, trans. Gabriel Meretik (Paris: Albin Michel, 1975)

de Nussae, Patrice, 'Un chahuteur s'explique', in *France-Soir*, 3.5.66.

O'Brady, Frédéric, *All told* (London: The Bodley Head, 1964)

Peskine, Lynda Bellity, and Albert Dichy, eds., *La Bataille des Paravents* (Paris: IMEC, 1991)

Philipe, Anne and Claude Roy, *Gérard Philipe* (Paris: Gallimard, , 1960)

Pichette, Henri, 'Peu avant votre défaillance...', in *Combat*, 22.11.47.

Plunka, Gene A., *The Rites of Passage of Jean Genet* (Cranbury, NJ: Associated University Presses. 1992)

Poirot-Delpech, Bertrand, 'Bilan de la saison théâtrale', in *Le Monde*, 21.7.66.

Prevel, Jacques, *En compagnie d'Antonin Artaud* (Paris: Flamarion, 1974)

Rougeuil, Jean, 'Les nouveaux talents', in *Paris Cinéma*, July 1947.

Roy, Claude, 'Prix nobel', *Le Nouvel Observateur*, 3.11.69.

Sadowska-Guillon, Irène, 'La partie n'est pas finie', in *L'Avant-Scène Théâtre*, no.764, 15.2.85. p.66.

Saillet, Maurice, 'Genet l'ortie', in *Quinzaine littéraire*, 15.5.66.

Saurel, René, 'Cendres fertiles de Roger Blin', *Les temps modernes*, 1984, vol.40, pp.2347–66.

—— 'Cendres fertiles de Roger Blin', *Les temps modernes*, 1984, vol.41, pp.810–31.

Sadowska-Guillon, Irène, 'La partie n'est pas finie', *L'Avant-Scène Théâtre*, 764, 15.2.85, pp.66–7.

Savona, Jeanette L., *Jean Genet* (London: Macmillan, 1983)

Schneider, Alan, 'Waiting for Beckett', in *The Chelsea Review*, Autumn 1958, no.2, pp.1–20.

—— 'Correspondance from Beckett', in *Village Voice*, 19.3.58.

Schumaker, Claude and Brian Singleton (eds.), *Artaud on Theatre* (London: Methuen, 1989)

Semprun Maura, Carlos, *Le Bleu de l'eau de vie*, in *L'Avant-Scène Théâtre*, 1982, no.703, pp.7–20.

Shakespeare, William, *Macbeth*, trans. Pierrette Tison (Paris: Théâtre Ouvert/Stock, 1977)

Simon, Alfred, 'Dans la légende de la mise en scène...' in *Esprit*, April 1984, no.88, pp.142–3.

Signoret, Simone, *La Nostalgie n'est plus ce qu'elle était* (Paris: Seuil, 1975)

Strebel, Elizabeth Grottle, *French Social Cinema of the Nineteen-Thirties* (New York: Arno Press, 1980)

Swerling, Anthony, *Strindberg's Impact in France 1920–1960* (Cambridge: Trinity Lane Press, 1971)

Takahashi, Osamu, *Minimata and Co.*, trans. Catherine Cadou (Paris: IPCC, 1977)

Thévenin, Paule, *Antonin Artaud, ce Désespéré qui vous parle* (Paris: Seuil, 1993)
—— 'Jean Genet', *Magazine littéraire*, 313 (September 1993), p.36.
Triana, José, *La Nuit des assassins*, trans. Carlos Semprun Maura (Paris: Gallimard, 1969)
Vian, Boris, *Manuel de St. Germain des prés* (Paris: Le Chêne, 1974)
Virmaux, Alain and Odette, *André Breton – Qui Êtes-Vous?* (Paris: La Manufacture, 1987)
—— *Antonin Artaud* (Paris: La Manufacture, 1991)
White, Edmund, *Genet* (London: Chatto and Windus, 1993)
Whitton, David, *Stage Directors in Modern France* (Manchester: Manchester University Press, 1987)

ii.) Interviews (with Roger Blin, unless indicated)

Anon., *Acteurs*, March 1982
—— *Algérien en Europe*, 1–15.5.66, no.14, pp.19–20. (Jean Genet and members of the cast of *Les Paravents*)
—— *Arts*, 6.3.57 (Arthur Adamov)
—— *Arts*, 8.1.58
—— *L'Aurore*, 22.1.79 (Jean-Louis Bauer)
—— *Le Bleu de l'eau de vie* (programme), Petit-Odéon, November 1981. (Roger Blin and Carlos Semprun Maura)
—— *CFJ information*, 24.4.66 (Jean-Louis Barrault)
—— *Combat*, 19. 3.50 (Arthur Adamov)
—— *Combat*, 10.11.50 (Arthur Adamov)
—— *Combat*, 4.6.52
—— *Combat*, 26.4.57
—— *Combat*, 3.5.66
—— *Combat*, 30.4.68
—— *Droit et liberté*, November 1959. (Roger Blin and Robert Liensol)
—— *De Groene Amsterdammer*, 21.11.59
—— *Le Figaro*, 8.8.75
—— *Le Figaro*, 15.3.77
—— *Le Matin*, 25.1.78 (Bernard Le Saché)
—— *Le Monde*, 4.5.66
—— *Le Nouvel Observateur*, 28.1.65. (Roger Blin and Jean-Pierre Faye)
—— *Le Nouvel Observateur*, 30.3.66
—— *Les Lettres françaises*, 7–13.5.69 (Eduardo Manet)
—— *Libération*, 25.1.61 (Jean Martin)
—— *Libération*, 14.6.77

—— *Libération*, 15.6.77

—— *Masques*, Winter 1981/1982, no.12, pp.30–7. (Roger Blin and Maria Casarès)

—— *Le Monde*, 10.2.70

—— *Les Nouvelles littéraires*, 24.2.65 (Madeleine Renaud)

—— *Les Nouvelles littéraires*, 31.3.77

—— *Paris-Match*, February 1981

—— Paris-Presse, 17–18.11.63 (Madeleine Renaud)

—— *Le Quotidien de Paris*, 17.3.77

—— *Le Quotidien de Paris*, 19.5.81

—— *De Telegraaf*, 1.4.67

—— *La Tribune de Genève*, 15.7.77

—— *T.V. À Propos*, 4.5.66 (Jean-Louis Barrault)

Autrusseau, Jacqueline, *Les Lettres françaises*, 20.10.60

Benmussa, Simone, *L'Action théâtrale*, 1969, no.2, pp.10–16. (Roger Blin and Eduardo Manet)

Benson, Mary, *London Magazine*, October 1978, vol.18, no.7, pp.52–7.

Bielski, Nella, *Le Matin*, 1.4.77

Bishop, Tom, in Bishop/Federman, eds., *Samuel Beckett* (Paris: Cahiers de L'Herne, 1976), pp.141–6.

Boursier, Guido, *Sipario*, June 1965 vol.20, no.230, p.28.

Chabert, Pierre, in Chabert, ed., *Revue d'Esthétique*, 1986, Numéro spécial Samuel Beckett hors série, Privat, Toulouse, 1986, pp.174–8. (Jean-Louis Barrault)

Costaz, Gilles, *Le Matin*, 19.3.83 (Max Frisch)

Craipeau, Maria, *France observateur*, 22.10.59. (Roger Blin and Robert Liensol)

—— *France observateur*, 17.10.63

Delay, Jean-François, *Combat*, 23.5.49

—— *Combat*, 1.11.50 (Arthur Adamov)

Duras, Marguerite, *France observateur*, 20.2.58 (Sarah Maldorer)

Duvignaud, Jean, *Les Lettres nouvelles*, 28.10.59

Fady, Stéphan, *Le Safa*, 15.8.73

—— *Le Safa*, 18.8.73

Garnham, Nicholas, *Varsity*, 20.5.61

Garrel, Maurice, *Libération*, 21.2.83

Gray, Paul, *Tulane Drama Review*, 1967 vol.11, no.1, pp.115–16.

—— *Tulane Drama Review*, 1967, vol.11, no.4, pp.110–11.

Greffe, Noëlle, *Combat*, 7.8.59

Hahn, Pierre, *Paris Théâtre*, 1963 no.201, p.22.

Hehn, Roland, *Frankfurter Rundschau*, 20.11.67

Hubscher, Françoise, *Jeune Afrique*, 14.5.76

Jacquart, Emmanuel C., *The French Review*, May 1975, vol.48, no.6, pp.996–1004.

Klausner, E., *La Croix*, 10.2.83

Knapp, Bettina, *Tulane Drama Review*, 1967, vol.7, pp.111–25.

—— *Tulane Drama Review*, 1967, vol.11, no.4, pp.105–8. (Amidou)

—— *Tulane Drama Review*, 1967, vol.11, no.4, pp.109–10.

Knowlson, James, in Knowlson, ed. *Samuel Beckett: Krapp's Last Tape*, Brutus, London, 1980, pp.65–6.

Laurent, Anne, *Libération*, 10.6.83 (Michèle Oppenot)

Lennon, Peter, *The Guardian*, 20.9.63

Lindholm, Karl Axel, *Studiekamraten: Tidskrift för det Fria Bildningsarbetet* 1984, vol.66, pp.30–1.

Louzoun, Myriam, *Les voies de la création théâtrale*, vol.5, C.N.R.S., Paris, 1977, pp.443–5.

Manceau, Michèle, *L'Express*, 5.11.59

Marowitz, Charles, in Marowitz, *Artaud at Rodez*, Boyars, London, 1977, pp.101–12.

Marrast, Robert, *Les Lettres françaises*, 20.3.63.

Morand, Claude, *Arts*, 6–12.4.66

—— *ATAC Informations*, November 1978, no.97.

Moyal, Edith, *Télé 7 jours*, 12.2.66

O'Brady, Frédéric, *Combat*, 4.10.49

Pascaud, Fabienne, *Télérama*, 11–17.11.78

Rapin, Maurice, *Le Figaro*, 14.11.50 (Arthur Adamov)

Roberts, Peter, *Plays and Players*, July 1961, no.18, pp.5 and 34.

Rousseau, Josanne, *Comédie Française*, February/March 1983, no.116, pp.17–9.

Sarraute, Claude, *Le Monde*, 27.4.57.

Savona, Jeanette Laillou, *Modern Drama*, 1981, vol.24, pp.127–34.

Terrasse, Marc, *Comédie Française*, September 1980

Thevenet, Réné, *Enfin-film*, no.12, 19.7.47

Thibaudat, Jean-Pierre, *Libération*, 10.6.83

Tillier, Maurice, *Le Figaro littéraire*, 14.11.63. (Roger Blin and Madeleine Renaud)

—— *Le Figaro littéraire*, 7.4.66 (Jean-Louis Barrault)

Unger, Catherine, *La Tribune de Genève*, 11.7.75

Valogne, Catherine, *La Tribune de Lausanne*, 15.5.66 (Maria Casarès)

Verdot, Guy, *Le Figaro littéraire*, 12.3.60

Verdot, Guy, *Paris-Théâtre*, 1964 no.206. (Roger Blin and Madeleine Renaud.)

Valogne, Catherine, *La Tribune de Lausanne*, 21.4.57

—— *La Tribune de Lausanne*, 27.10.63

—— *La Tribune de Lausanne*, 17.5.66

Van Gasteren, Josephine, *De Telegraaf*, 27.11.59

Phillipe, Vincent, *24 Heures*, 21–22.8.82

Zand, Nicole, *Le Monde*, 2.2.65 (Jean-Pierre Faye)

—— *Le Monde*, 16.4.66

—— *Le Monde*, 4.5.68

Zbinden, L.A., *La Gazette de Lausanne*, 28–29.5.66 (Paule Annen)

iii.) Cited reviews (Chronologically by production. Directed by Roger Blin, unless indicated)

Percy Shelley's *Les Cenci*, 1935, adapt., dir. Antonin Artaud
    Armory, *Comoedia*, 8.3.35.

Miguel de Cervantes' *Numance*, 1937, adapt., dir. Jean-Louis Barrault
    Itkine, Sylvain, *L'Intransigeant*, 13.4.37.
    Kemp, Robert, *Feuilleton du Temps*, 26.4.37.

Jean-Louis Barrault's *La Faim*, dir. Jean-Louis Barrault, 1939
    Anon, *La Lumière*, 5.5.39.
    Bidou, Henri, *Marianne*, No.340, 26.3.39, p.16.

Antonin Artaud's *Pour en finir avec le jugement de dieu*, dir. Antonin Artaud, 1948
    Anon, *Radio-Revue*, 1–7.2.48.

Henri Pichette's *Les Épiphanies*, dir. Georges Vitaly, 1948
    Monnier, Adrienne, *Mercure de France*, 9.12.48.

Gunnar Heiberg's *La Tragédie de l'amour*, dir. Fernand Ledoux, 1943
    Bauer, F.Charles, *L'Echo de la France*, 13.12.43.
    Pelorson, Georges, *La Révolution Matérielle*, 8.1.44.

Denis Johnston's *La Lune dans le fleuve Jaune*, 1949
    Ambrière, Francis, *Opéra*, 8.6.49.

August Strindberg's *La Sonate des spectres*, 1949
    Ahlström, Stellan, *Samtid och Framtid*, January 1950, pp.117–18.
    Anon, *Le Parisien libéré*, 25.10.49.
    —— *Ce Matin- Le Pays*, 27.10.49.
    Déon, Michel, *Aspects de la France et du Monde*, 24.11.49.
    le Forêt, Jean, *Heure médicale*, December 1949.
    Jacques Lemarchand, *Combat*, 25.10.49.
    —— *Combat*, 8.11.49.

Jean Silvant's *Le bourreau s'impatiente*, 1950
    Déon, Michel, *Aspects de la France et du monde*, 9.3.50.
    Marcel, Gabriel, *Les Nouvelles Littéraires*, 30.3.50.
    Saurel, Renée, *Combat*, 27.3.50.

Arthur Adamov's *La Grande et la Petite Manœuvre*, dir. Jean-Marie Serreau/Roger Blin, 1950
  Beigbeder, Marc, *Parisien Libéré*, 17.11.50.
  Lemarchand, Jacques, *Le Figaro Littéraire*, 18.11.50.

Arthur Adamov's *La Parodie*, 1952
  Beigbeder, Marc, *Le Parisien libéré*, 7–8.6.52.
  Lemarchand, Jacques, *Le Figaro Littéraire*, 14.6.52.
  Magnan, Henry, *Le Monde*, 4.6.52.

Samuel Beckett's *En attendant Godot*, 1953
  Anon, 'Manifestations au Théâtre de Babylone', *Le Monde*, 2.2.53.
  Kemp, Robert, *Le Monde*, 14.1.53.
  Lemarchand, Jacques, *Le Figaro littéraire*, 17.1.53.
  Sachs, Gustav and 'D.M.-C', 'Controverse autour de "Godot"', *Arts*, 27.2.53.
  Saurel, René, *Les Lettres françaises*, 15.1.53.

Jean Duvignaud's *Marée basse*, 1956
  Barthes, Roland, 'Sur "Marée basse", de Jean Duvignaud', *Théâtre populaire*, 17 (March 1956), pp.88–90.

Samuel Beckett's *Fin de partie*, 1957
  Adamov, Arthur and Eugène Ionesco, *Arts*, 6.3.57.
  Anon, *The Times*, 4.4.57.
  —— *The Times*, 29.10.58.
  Marcabru, Pierre, *Arts*, 8.5.57.

Jean Genet's *Les Nègres*, 1959
  Kanters, Robert, *L'Epress*, 5.11.59.
  Lemarchand, Jacques, *Le Figaro littéraire*, 7.11.59.
  Marcabru, Pierre, *Arts*, 11.11.59

Harold Pinter's *Le Gardien*, 1961
  Poirot-Delpech, Bertrand, *Le Monde*, 28.1.61

Samuel Beckett's *Oh les beaux jours*, 1963
  Morelle, Paul, *Libération*, 2.3.63.

Jean Genet's *Les Paravents*, 1966
  Anon, *La Croix*, 23.4.66.
  Gautier, Jean-Jacques, *Le Figaro*, 23.4.66.
  Marcabru, Pierre, *Le Nouveau Candide*, 25.4.66.
  Marcel, Gabriel, *Les Nouvelles Littéraires*, 21.4.66.

Paget, Jean, *Combat*, 23.4.66.
Poirot-Delpech, Bertrand, *Le Monde*, 23.4.66.
Tillier, Maurice, *Figaro Littéraire*, 7.4.66.

Athol Fugard's *Boesman et Léna*, 1976
Galey, Matthieu, *Le Quotidien de Paris*, 4.5.76.
Marcabru, Pierre, *France-Soir*. 21–22.6.76.
Poulet, Jacques, *L'Humanité*, 12.5.76.

Eduardo Manet's *Lady Strass*, 1978
Godard, Colette, *Le Monde*, 26.3.77.

Jean-Louis Bauer's *M'appelle Isabelle Langrenier*, 1979
Boyd, Neil, 'Planchon and Blin in Paris', in *Plays and Players*, 26.6 (March 1979), p.34.
Sandier, Gilles, *Le Matin*, 31.1.79.

Max Frisch's *Triptyque*, 1983
Dumur, Guy, *Le Nouvel Observateur*, 25.2.83.

Index

269

S T S S
S T A G E a n d S C R E E N S T U D I E S

This series of monographs is concerned with drama and allied entertainment in a wide variety of kinds in the theatre and on film, television and video screens. The emphasis is on the history and interpretation of dramatic entertainment, performance and production in regular and musical theatre, including music hall and variety stages, in para-theatrical activities, like fairground performance and festivals, and in the silent and sound cinema and on television and video.

The series engages particularly with the social, political and economic contexts of drama on past and present stages and screens, considering the work of dramatists, performers, directors, designers, technicians and administrators, and will aim to be very wide-ranging in scope, its subjects spanning Classical, Medieval and Renaissance European drama and theatre, Eastern theatre forms, and international modern drama in its various performance kinds. Within this broad remit, the series hopes to publish historical, critical and theoretical studies, annotated anthologies of critical, theoretical and dramatic texts, and collections of interviews and screenplays.